THE RENT OF FORM

Buell Center Books
in the History and Theory of
American Architecture
Reinhold Martin, Series Editor

The Temple Hoyne Buell Center for the Study of American
Architecture at Columbia University was founded in 1982.
Its mission is to advance the interdisciplinary study of American
architecture, urbanism, and landscape.

The Temple Hoyne
Buell Center
for the Study of
American Architecture

THE RENT OF FORM

Architecture and Labor in the Digital Age

PEDRO FIORI ARANTES

Translated by Adriana Kauffmann
Foreword by Reinhold Martin

University of Minnesota Press | Minneapolis | London

FUNDAÇÃO   MINISTÉRIO DA
BIBLIOTECA NACIONAL   CIDADANIA

This work is published with the support of the Brazilian Ministry of Citizenship / National Library Foundation. Obra publicada com o apoio da Fundação Biblioteca Nacional | Ministério da Cidadania.

The University of Minnesota Press gratefully acknowledges the editorial and translation assistance on this project provided by Timothy Frye.

The Rent of Form: Architecture and Labor in the Digital Age was first published in a different form in the original Portuguese as *Arquitetura na era digital-financeira: desenho, canteiro e renda da forma* (São Paolo, Brazil: Editora 34 Ltda., 2012).

Every effort was made to obtain permission to reproduce material in this book. If any proper acknowledgment has not been included here, we encourage copyright holders to notify the publisher.

Published by the University of Minnesota Press
111 Third Avenue South, Suite 290
Minneapolis, MN 55401-2520
http://www.upress.umn.edu

Printed in the United States of America on acid-free paper

The University of Minnesota is an equal-opportunity educator and employer.

25 24 23 22 21 20 19   10 9 8 7 6 5 4 3 2 1

Library of Congress Cataloging-in-Publication Data

Arantes, Pedro Fiori, author. | Kauffmann, Adriana, translator. | Martin, Reinhold, foreword. |
    Translation of: Arantes, Pedro Fiori. Arquitetura na era digital-financeira.
The rent of form : architecture and labor in the digital age / Pedro Fiori Arantes ; translated by
    Adriana Kauffmann ; foreword by Reinhold Martin.
Arquitetura na era digital-financeira. English
Minneapolis : University of Minnesota Press, 2019. | Series: Buell center books in the history
    and theory of American architecture | Includes bibliographical references and index. |
Identifiers: LCCN 2018045491 (print) | ISBN 978-0-8166-9928-5 (hc) |
    ISBN 978-0-8166-9929-2 (pb)
Subjects: LCSH: Architecture and technology. | Design—Technological innovations. |
    Architecture—Economic aspects.
Classification: LCC NA2543.T43 A7313 2018 (print) | DDC 721—dc23
LC record available at https://lccn.loc.gov/2018045491

To Professor JORGE HAJIME OSEKI, in memoriam

To my uncle ROQUE G. FIORI, who taught me to love
architecture and distrust architects

CONTENTS

FOREWORD
Reinhold Martin   ix

Introduction: Stars of Exception   1

1. The Forms of Rent: The Image of Architecture and
   Architecture as Image   5

2. Programmed Design   79

3. One to One: Full-Scale Construction Site   127

Conclusion: The Next Frontiers   201

NOTES   235

BIBLIOGRAPHY   267

INDEX   285

FOREWORD

Reinhold Martin

THIS REVISION AND TRANSLATION of *Arquitetura na era digital-financeira: desenho, canteiro e renda da forma* by the Brazilian architectural theorist Pedro Fiori Arantes is twice timely. First, although its trenchant critique of contemporary architecture's "digital turn," which originally appeared in 2012 in Portuguese under the colophon of Editora 34, was written largely in the present tense, little has changed since then. For some, the novelty—we could even say, the aura—of the digitally generated and fabricated architecture that its author targets may appear to have worn off. Accordingly, the contemporary architectural spectacle may seem to have shifted attention away from flamboyant displays of formal virtuosity and onto earnest encomiums to social and environmental "responsibility."

But, as Arantes suggests in his updated conclusion, such vicissitudes mask a long-term, systemic inversion. Now more than ever, life on the construction site is lived on finance capital's front lines. Slightly modifying the terminology of one of Arantes's theoretical sources, Henri Lefebvre, we might even say that a much-proclaimed revolution in the means of production, the digitalization of architectural design and construction, has, in fact, contributed to bedrock changes in the political economy of space.

Second, this critique is timely in the sense that to some it may seem impolite, even uncalled for, in its apparent belatedness, especially coming from outside its subject matter's inner circle. Again, to some, the ever-awkward neologism *starchitect* may now seem dated, almost anachronistic, especially in the present tense, which has been modified in this edition to minimize the dissonance. Canny observers tend today to look askance at the term's mention, and assorted captains of the culture industry originally responsible for propagating its mystique issue oblique mea culpas. Opportunistically, less critical forms of architectural theory seem also to have moved on, from the enchantments of formal play to the earnest fetishization of "generative" design and fabrication procedures. Few if any, however, have paid as close attention as Arantes does to the material particulars, not necessarily of "scripting" or otherwise writing architecture in silica, but of making it with—or without—one's hands.

Arantes is a careful reader of the dissident, exiled Marxist Sérgio Ferro, a protagonist in the group Arquitetura Nova formed at the Faculty of Architecture and Urbanism at the University of São Paulo (FAU-USP) around, but also against the imposing figure cut by Paulista architect João Batista Vilanova Artigas. Ferro and his colleagues argued for a transvaluation of modernist values, from the art-into-life formula favored by Artigas and his generation, to a worker-centric model of life-into-art built around the construction site. Architecture, they suggested, begins with physical labor, and the professional drawing is among many alienating instruments through which capital abstracts and commodifies the work of construction.

Arantes elaborates on an inconvenient truth that follows from this: that drawing lines is, in architecture, ultimately equivalent to issuing instructions. As command, the drawing, especially the construction drawing, orchestrates a division of labor that distances architect and client from builder, within a managerial hierarchy to which those on the job site remain subordinate, whether "documented" or "undocumented" in any of several senses. Addressing today's screen dwellers, Arantes elicits this fact's most refined, and only apparently postindustrial, implications. For where there are computers there is industry, labor, and sweat; and so, far from doing away with these, "digital" architecture and the easy circulation of featherweight renderings presuppose physical labor and its inequities.

When Arantes says "rent" he therefore means it in the Marxian idiom, as profit from labor and its derivatives, but not always in a direct sense. Instead, rent, as economic value or as "branding," can also be extracted from the images and forms extracted from the labor. We must therefore read the concept—"the rent of form"—through the many mediating layers covered by the analysis, from the professionally staged "architectural" photograph to the millimetric tolerances and intolerances of mass-customized stone.

In this story, all is extraction, and the construction site is like a mine for the primary accumulation of symbolic capital. Form becomes function not in any useful way, but as a locus of value, forcing signifier and signified together through the raw power of the command: measure this and make this, in this way. As in other factories, automation is its telos, where alienation becomes precarity and ultimately, disposability.

If this last point does not already make it clear enough, this story is also a story from the South. Not because it is riddled with favelas (it is not). But because Arantes shows the reader how the Northern (but also increasingly Southern) theaters of capital serviced by "global" (but also increasingly "local") architects are built on a system of expropriation that presupposes, and leads back to, what Mike Davis has poignantly called a "planet of slums."

At the Temple Hoyne Buell Center for the Study of American Architecture, we are therefore pleased to offer this translation in collaboration with our colleagues at the University of Minnesota Press, as a timely, worldly antidote to the air-conditioned claustrophobia of all things "digital." If, over the past several decades, a significant portion of that claustrophobia has been "made in America," there may still be time for a little fresh air to blow across its shimmering shapes, bearing just the slightest odor of the sweat, and blood, that built them.

It also takes a multitude to make a book. Among the many dedicated persons responsible for seeing this edition to print, I acknowledge Marta Caldeira's thoughtful early reading of the Portuguese original and, especially, the tireless efforts of Jacob Moore and Jordan Steingard at the Buell Center to make it real and make it happen.

INTRODUCTION
STARS OF EXCEPTION

OVER THE PAST TWO DECADES, architecture has unquestionably set off for the media universe of logos, having done so to the point that works are created to generate a new kind of revenue rather than traditional land rent. The new buildings are designed to circulate—as though they were *logotectures*.[1] Ostentatious technical sophistication, surface differentiations, and formal exuberance became requirements for building exclusive architectural images that are capable of bringing value to an investment, and subsequently, to the cities vying for them.

With the migration from the historical prevalence of industrial capital to the hegemony of global finance—the realm of fictitious capital, according to Marx—the new urban landscape is home to amazing figurations produced by cutting-edge architecture, an approach that explores technical and material restrictions with almost no limits, including budgetary ones. Seen everywhere are shapes that appear the exact opposite of the tectonic and spatial sobriety subjected, as a general rule, to the rigors of Euclidean geometry that dominated modern architecture for so long. In their inventive "freedom," the forms of this new phase of capitalism nurture themselves through a formal-technical paradox: the more polymorphic, twisted, deconstructed, or "liquefied," and ultimately reduced to "quasi immateriality," a building (which ought to be the built, the material, and stable object par excellence) is, the more successful it will be, and therefore, the higher its value as an image for publicity.

The new condition of architecture—the fetishizing of form, new digital design techniques and styles of construction-site organization—will be interpreted as being guided by design projects from award-winning architects, the recipients of the highest honors in the field. These are the star-architects (starchitects), the superheroes of our profession and diffusers of the ideology of the "great architecture" as an exceptional urban fact—or an artifact of exception. Their studios are increasingly run like businesses, and they participate in media contests, shift the cultural debate, write, prompt advertising campaigns, and are published in architectural magazines worldwide, taking root in the minds of other professionals, and especially of students, as role models to follow. They hold the promises that the discipline is still able to make, as "faculty" that encourage the constructed fantasy of the dominant classes. In this sense, to study them is to question both their power and the manner in which they have conducted this discipline, defining hegemonic criteria for evaluating projects, works, and careers.

From the standpoint of capitalist accumulation, their works are the exception, not the rule, in the social production of space. They are exceptions in many respects. Although accounting for less than 0.1 percent of the world's architectural production, they take up almost all of the space in specialized magazines, exhibitions, and award ceremonies, and have become the parameters of professional success. The type of valuation they promote is of a different nature than the real-estate market, *stricto sensu*. These works are generally not directly for sale, despite often being a part of "cities for sale" strategies or of brand valuation. Their use value is that of representation and distinction. They do not make up the everyday urban fabric and, in general, are not required to obey the laws of land use. They are exceptions intended to constitute the city's "primary facts" and to be acknowledged as monuments, even when built through private commissions. The income they generate is similar to, but different from, land rent. It is a monopolistic income intrinsic to their unique and spectacular architectural form.

As such, this type of architecture receives more dividends through its circulation than through its production, or rather, its production is driven by the gains from media distribution and its ability to attract wealth (through investors, tourists, public funds, etc.). It is an architecture that circulates as image, and is therefore born as a figuration of itself, in a tautological circle that reduces the architectural experience to pure visuality, which is the result of a ceaseless quest for uniqueness and for the "rent of form."[2]

In these projects, the most advanced software is employed, including programmable machines and even robots, but the old craftsman and unfettered exploitation of precarious and migrant labor are still at their base. These works mobilize productive forces, such as the pioneering application of new materials and techniques (or the revitalization of craft skills and other productive fields) that are not available to ordinary real-estate production. They are thus agents of a restricted innovation that you do not want to democratize because the secret to their profitability lies in maintaining the monopoly, that is, their status as the exception.

The changes we will analyze in the techniques of representation and production, and patterns of architectural forms indicate a greater rupture than critics of postmodernism have generally implied. We may in fact be entering a new phase of perception, production, and consumption of the architectural artifact, one that seems to modify some of the core foundations of previous phases. Some of these date back to the Renaissance, which, after having remained for centuries, are now being transformed and even turned upside down. It is not unlikely that we are living an inflection of grand proportions similar to the revolution provoked by Brunelleschi, arising from the conjunction of financial dominance and digital technologies. The ideology of the almighty master builder is revived, but is now at the discretion of the digital era and supported by new multidimensional models of project management, like architectural "ideation" turned total programming.

The dissolution of the architectural artifact is recurrent in many of the examples we will cover: buildings that disappear into the clouds or become ethereal like balloons, movable walls, towers that exist only through lighting effects, architects who automate morphogenesis through computing, and robots that replace bricklayers, all until the completion of a self-referencing circle in which architecture is born only to become an image of itself. The type of value that is associated with this architecture will end up leading it to an increasingly paradoxical, immaterial experience. It is this, the zero degree of architecture, reduced to mere signifier, a game of forms, seemingly without rules and limitations of any kind, seeking the highest level of income.

The answer to this terminal stage in architecture does not necessarily need to be restricted to resuming functionalist assumptions and stern moral lectures on building—though a bit of constructive honesty would do no harm. Surely schools, hospitals, public housing, sanitation systems, and transportation are part of an agenda of antispectacular architecture, a program of needs that has not yet been fully met—in the city center, they gradually degrade; on the outskirts, they have barely been addressed. The dismantling of welfare and illusory compensatory policies of "cultural entertainment," and now, of "stimulus of the senses," is part of the broad political defeat the working class has been suffering since the late 1970s. An answer to this is, of course, outside the realm of exclusively architectural intervention, but that does not mean it should not choose on which side its loyalties lie.

1

THE FORMS OF RENT
THE IMAGE OF ARCHITECTURE
AND ARCHITECTURE AS IMAGE

NELSON KON, who for decades has been the main photographer of architecture in Brazil, set up his tripod in front of the newly opened Iberê Camargo Museum, in the city of Porto Alegre, and was shocked. There he found, clicking at the same time, on that same sidewalk, three other representatives of the global star system of architectural photography: Japanese photographer Yoshio Futagawa, Italian photographer Duccio Malagamba, and the Portuguese Fernando Guerra. "It was a shock," recounts Nelson.[1] Four photographers of international importance shooting at the same time, in order to supply the media with spectacular images of the most anticipated recent work by Alvaro Siza while still in the model phase, were awarded the Golden Lion at the Venice Biennale 2002.

The paparazzi of architecture's new top model, like on an haute couture runway, searched for the best angle, best lighting, and best framing for a picture worthy of the narcissism of that body-object, able to catch the eye of publishers and readers alike, eager for novelty and visual excitement. The image of the immaculate work—meaning without marks of wear and time—is that which will be immortalized, as if a building could also wish for eternal youth. In that frozen image of the photographer's objective lens, the work appears to be a fetish of itself, with its clean and untouched surface, not yet eroded by the passage of time and of people. The image replaced, with certain advantages, the object itself.

In just a few days, those four photographers produced hundreds of high-quality images that began to circulate worldwide in magazines, books, and digital media. As Julius Shulman, the celebrated photographer, explained, their responsibility is rebuilding, through the medium of photography, "an image of that building in the public's mind."[2] Shulman, pioneer in introducing architectural images into the commercial media world, noted as early as the 1960s that it is the memorable picture, rather than the visit to the exact place, that becomes "the main link between the designer and his public."[3]

Kon was hired by the Brazilian magazine *Projeto* to supply the modest domestic Brazilian market, and perhaps to send images to foreign magazines, since he was once the leading international supplier of photographs of Brazilian architecture. The unexpected competition, however, made it difficult for him to expand his sales. "I could stay for two days only," he recalls, "while foreign photographers were prepared for a week of pictures, and therefore they could wait for the best light." Persistence is crucial to catching the image that will be immortalized in the public's mind.

Fastest among the four, however, was rising young Brazilian photographer Leonardo Finotti. He managed to obtain information from Siza's team on the exact date of the concrete stripping, even before the building's inauguration date.[4] With that information, he headed to Porto Alegre knowing he would get the exclusive. His pictures of the bare concrete structure, with the building still under construction, were an instant hit—Leonardo managed to place them in about forty magazines around the world, from Chile to China. With a more aggressive and globalized attitude, Leonardo won much of Kon's market, and has since traveled the world following newly inaugurated works to shoot, hired by several international magazines that already knew him.

Leonardo has said that the life of a global photographer of starchitecture is similar to that of a businessman. The travel routine is accompanied by the need to keep up with the network of architects and publishers in order to ensure firsthand access to information and advanced sales of exclusive images. "The architecture media circuit is pretty much based on marketing and personal relations," he says. On the other hand, there is the difficult task of capturing the perfect image: "I feel I am a laborer of photography," says Leonardo. "In the two or three days dedicated to a certain work of architecture, if I am not on-site, I am in the hotel analyzing and working on digital images in search of perfection; there is no time for sightseeing or rest, it is exhausting."

The challenge for professional photographers, according to Spanish critic Fernández-Galiano, is to overcome the "saturation of information that drugs our retinas," and manage to "cut the visual clutter with one single memorable image," which in itself is a "communicative feat."[5] In this flood of contemporary images, "specific architectures are praised only because they are more photogenic than others," explains Fernando Fuão.[6] The architectural qualities are now assessed according to their visual impact, which reinforces the importance of the appearance of skins and surfaces, as we shall see, in a new *photogenic superficiality.*

In their struggle for the memorable image, photographers cease being local professionals associated with local architects and become "global hunters of spectacular images," as Kon defines himself. They prospect novelties of interest for publishers, and become the main informants of what is happening in sophisticated architectural production. Leonardo Finotti, for example, suggests that he and other global photographers, because of their intense travels, know more about works of architecture than any architect or architecture critic: "Today we are the leading source for the publishing market."

With the rarefaction of critical thinking at all levels, photographers began to fill the role of architecture critics, not only because of the supremacy of image over text, but also because of their ability to indicate criteria for judgment of architecture, propose themes, and discover young talents. But, unlike critics who are supposedly independent, photographers are interested parties in the business. Not only do they market the pictures, but they also represent architects who want to see their work published and thus climb the ladder of the international pantheon. When the architect hires the photographer "he is making a media investment. Ninety-eight percent of my work is published in the media, nothing is for the archive," says Kon.

In such conditions, critical photography is not possible, as this type of architectural photography is always positive in relation to the object it portrays. Like the architect and the publisher, the photographer is interested in obtaining beautiful images with the highest level of technical perfection and visual acuity. If the picture reveals problems in

Photographs of the Iberê Camargo Foundation, designed by Leonardo Finotti, on the covers of *Blueprint* (UK, March 2006), *Summa +* (Argentina, November 2006), and *arq./a* (Portugal, July/August 2006).

the work, it appears to be a problem of the composition of the photograph, explains Nelson: "a critical picture is seen as a bad image taken by a bad photographer." Publishers want pristine images of the "pure work," without people, context, construction site, or history; they want, in a word, what they believe to be the restoration of a certain aura of architecture, as a masterpiece of art. The image must not only capture its aura, but, if possible, improve it. The photographer's job thus is to "beautify, make-up, gold-plate the building," continues Fuão.[7]

Thus, his task is nothing neutral or documentary, but rather is full of intentionality. Julius Shulman, the master of media-focused architectural photography, availed himself of all techniques and tricks of photography in order to obtain the best possible image of the building. He staged situations and positioned objects and people, like a director. He simulated foregrounds, focused light at strategic points, all to achieve the best effect. In front of a building in an arid environment, for example, Shulman did not hesitate to add flower vases, and even a cut tree branch fastened to a stand, to provide ambience in the foreground captured by his wide angle. Kon confirms that "it was very clear how committed he was to building a positive image of the architecture he recorded."[8]

Shulman was a pioneer in the technique of twilight photography, which had become the most desired type of image for publishers. He photographed shortly after sunset, when the light was evenly distributed between interior and exterior, avoiding the contrasts and sharp shadows of daylight. The interior of the building and its gardens were lit up, while the landscape and the western sky displayed the expressiveness proper to this time of day. The result is both a spectacular image, full of hues of colors and lights (kitsch, some would say), and a maximum of information (interior and exterior) in a single image.

The revolution of color in professional architecture photography is another topic that deserves mention. It is contemporaneous with the emergence of postmodern architecture during the 1970s, reinforcing the choice of colored surfaces, replacing the modern monochrome. Modern architecture was accompanied by a black-and-white photographic discourse, in which the volumetric play of light and shadow, the rigor of composition, and the material's texture (from rough concrete to smooth glass) were highlighted in works where color seldom played a major role (whites, concrete shades of gray, and iron or steel blacks prevailed).

Commercial and vernacular architecture, which would provide the basis for the emergence of a postmodern aesthetic, by contrast, is multicolored, decorated, neon-lit, etc. Therefore, there is a confluence of the shapes and colors of the new architecture with the transition of architecture magazines into color. A confluence, according to Robert Ewall, which was also favored by the convergence of architecture with the world of marketing and fashion, acknowledged "the merits of colour photography and its commercial benefits."[9] There are economic reasons for the profusion of colors in buildings and pictures, along with the pressure that comes from the publishing market itself.

In the early 2000s, changes in the techniques of architecture and photography, along with the progressive introduction of digital photography, gave birth to a new generation of young global photographers, almost all in their forties, such as Roland Halbe, Hélène Binet, Fernando Guerra, Duccio Malagamba, Cristobal Palma, Iwan Baan, Andreas Gursky, Richard Bryant, Alan Weintraub, Peter Aaaron, and Jeff Goldberg. They, like Finotti and Kon, developed Web sites and blogs carefully crafted to show their work and sell it in high resolution. It is through this digital media that photographers are now hired, and that magazines seek out the novelties of possible editorial interest. Photographers act as *cool hunters* of new trends in architecture—and, in this business, it is all about coming out ahead.

From the point of view of relations and means of production, this new generation of photographers is subordinate to the companies producing digital equipment and software. They are important consumers of digital equipment, computers, and image-editing software. In the digital era, according to Kon, despite the savings on film and photographic paper, the expenses of the photographer on fixed capital have increased fivefold.[10] The planned obsolescence of the equipment and the advances in digital image capture technology create a need to replace about thirty thousand U.S. dollars of equipment every two or three years. Before, this was not the case: a mechanical first-class film camera could last for decades. "But manufacturers did not make money, and once they realized that, digital was the great breakthrough of the industry," Kon states.[11] In addition, the digital treatment of the image and its search for perfection has also increased the photographer's and his assistants' working hours. According to Kon, he currently works two to three times more than he used to, and does not necessarily make more money. Rather, it is the equipment and software companies that make the money.

Although they occupy strategic positions in magazines and with the publishers they supply, photographers are generally in a subordinate status regarding budgets, contracts, art editorial choices, and copyrighting. Leonardo Finotti says his contracts with magazines arrive ready to be signed, and the photographer can hardly change a thing—from copyright to compensation, each magazine has its set of preestablished rules. As international freelancers, architectural photographers do not constitute a professional category that can make collective demands from publishers. Instead, competition among them is fierce, and at times even dishonest.

When the pictures are delivered to the editor, the photographer once again loses control over them. It is the editor who choses, cuts, enlarges, reduces, and digitally manipulates the images so as to highlight the desired effects. "The editor prefers the most spectacular [images]," says Kon, with a "predilection for twilights," with its effect of providing information on both the inside and the outside, and for scenic dramatization. To some extent, these editors end up guiding the dominant language that photographers are meant to follow, with small authorial variations.

Let us return to the nature of these images. In the series of abstractions and separations we have been observing in the sphere of architectural production, the finished work, captured through the lens of the photographer, adds an extra filter, which is that of an image that becomes autonomous from its object. Architecture thus returns to the two-dimensional representation of itself, but to obtain other results. Now the two-dimensional representation is not a code for its execution (such as floor plans, sections, and elevations); rather, the finished image is able to achieve the highest visual dramatization that architecture can provide. With this return to the two-dimensional plane and to the visual, the photographic filter flattens the social experience of architecture, in a transposition that is often naturalized by the observer.[12]

This reduction promoted by photography carries implications at various levels, including at the political level. The diverse dimensions of the social practice of architecture are minimized or suppressed in the photographic image, which favors *venustas,* the portrait of the beautiful and isolated building. The photogenic image does not enable one to see, or even hide, whether the building responds appropriately to its intended function and user needs, or if the chosen technical and structural solutions were the most appropriate, or how the construction work was carried out, who were the investors, with what sources of income and cost limitations, or the building's relationship with the city, and so on. Architecture no longer occurs in the *promenade,* in the lived experience, but rather in a static and optical hyperenhanced representation. Architecture is abstracted from its context, with its structure of complex relationships, to become an autonomous, plastic, and seductive form, which then circulates as a concept. Photography extracts from architecture a synthetic and breathtaking image, able to convey in itself attributes that stimulate what we call the "rent of form."

Obviously, one cannot demand that photography comply with the attributes of architecture and not its own. Their natures are different and even opposite, and yet can be complementary. Architectural photography already has several functions: documentary, interpretative, and artistic, and through its great photographers it has even taught us how to perceive modern architecture.[13] But in recent decades, we have witnessed a dominance of representation, or rather, the swelling of visuals to the point that architecture becomes part of the culture industry, as a medium. In this context, photography no longer fulfills a didactic and educational role in presenting architecture, but rather becomes part of the business of marketing, images, and career management.

As media agents, photographers are important players in *re*producing the meanings of this architecture and electing what should be displayed. They filter—from large, clumsy, concrete, and immobile architectural objects—images that can instantly move through digital hyperreality. Through them, buildings, their authors, and their patrons become known worldwide by millions of people. Version 7 of Microsoft's operating system (Windows 7), for example, carried in its standard configuration wallpaper images of metallic skins of the Music Experience, a project by Frank Gehry in Seattle. This choice was not accidental: the building was sponsored by Paul Allen, Bill Gates's business partner, built to house Allen's collection of rock-and-roll and science-fiction gadgets. Guggenheim Bilbao images served as background for advertisements of cars (Audi), fashion (Paco Rabanne), perfumes (Cerrutti), music videos (Smashing Pumpkins, Simple Minds), as well as for a James Bond movie (*Tomorrow Never Dies*).[14] Volkswagen did the same with Rem Koolhaas's library in Seattle, as did Audi with Norman Foster's Swiss RE, which was also the backdrop for a movie by Woody Allen.

This effect of the dissemination of images is essential to the propagation of the multiple symbolic and economic outcomes that each enterprise aims to achieve. "Post-modern buildings seem to have been designed to be photographed," or to be turned into an image of themselves, says Fredric Jameson.[15] In architecture magazines, both print and digital, images are consumed in such quantity that we begin to believe that they are things in and of themselves. The result is a self-referential loop of visuality and formalism. Architecture is now conceived from the beginning based on the images it could generate when complete.

Architects are inspired by these gaunt and uninhabited forms to conceive a new project. In many architectural firms, photographers and image specialists are already consulted in the design development phase concerning the photogenic form, and groups trained in visualization study the possible optical effects of the work, creating computer images for advanced publicity, customers, and the media.[16]

In such images, in addition to a realistic anticipation of the building's future finished image, there are often special, unrealistic effects that reinforce the magical aspect that the visual experience of the building will provide. Commenting on this, architect Martin Corullon, who worked at Foster + Partners, said that the rendered images seek to "build an atmosphere, ambience, climates, and virtues that even photographs of the finished work will not be able to achieve. Effects with light, fog, glare, reflecting pools, only made possible by virtual reality, are produced. On the computer, the solid can become transparent, one can obtain light from places that do not emit light, and colors and brightness that are not from real materials," all to generate powerful and enticing virtual images.[17] Such images, Corullon explains, "have a function and are 'actors' in the process. They help fund the design, or in getting the public's approval, for example. I have seen cases in which these images, these virtual ambiences, were created even before the design project. And after the work is finished, they were still there and were publicized."

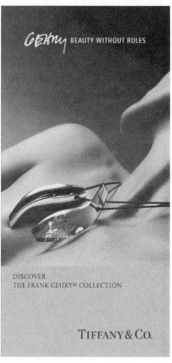

The use of "starchitecture" in advertising: Frank Gehry for Tiffany and Company, and Rem Koolhaas for Volkswagen.

The Parisian office Artefactory, for example, specializes in the creation of special effects for works by the star system. They produce fantastic images, "manipulating them in a fictional manner and introducing metaphors,"[18] such as computer graphics for an animated film. The goal is "to create an insatiable desire to see more and dive into the experience." Their presentations are decisive for the show architects create when presenting their designs to clients or judges—usually associated with raising money for design or construction. They are dramatic scenes, with effects of light and color, which alter the very status of the architectural object.

Thus, the inflation of images is at the beginning and the end of the design and construction cycle. The flattening of architecture as pure visuality is not just a feat of the photographer, but is a result of the relentless pursuit of originality, and of the gains arising from the "rent of form." Architecture becomes a monad, the complexity of which is only formal and constructive; it is the ideal object to be emptied and turned back into an image, for it was born to be a sign of itself.

Therefore, the image of architecture transformed into architecture as image contains a paradox. As Éric Alliez affirms, it is about "one image that dominates the thing being represented in such a way that virtuality dominates actuality, turning the very notion of reality around, which goes off the rails in that which Paul Virilio has named 'the bewilderment of representation.'"[19] This detachment between object and image, which corresponds to the dissociation between value and price, belongs to an advanced stage of commodity production—and finds its figurations in the architectonic output of the star system. The image that folds over on itself, which is at the beginning and end of the process, conditions the sphere of production to follow its dictates. It is no longer production that determines its own development, it is the external force of circulation that conditions the orientation of productive forces.[20] The new cycle is centered on demands of circulation, constructive juggling not intrinsic to the logic of production, but derived from the power of the image to generate additional rent.

As Guy Debord described, this advanced stage is "capital accumulated to the point that it becomes image"[21]—in other words, it becomes fictitious capital. The separation between what is experienced and what is represented is consummated in the form of autonomous images that are presented as though they are society itself. However, the society of the spectacle is not just a set of images; rather, it is "a social relationship mediated by images," which overlaps and replaces the previous reality. A new unity is established in the split between reality and image, under the command of capital in its spectacle form.

The monopoly of the appearance establishes a tautological relationship whose enormous positivity says nothing other than "what appears is good; what is good appears"—a catch-phrase known by many architects. Such tautology controls the entire circuit of architectural production: design, photography, publications, and exhibitions. The outcome is the prevalence of the image, and its exchange value is the rent of form, while the contents of architecture are emptied. This is what Debord called the "*falling rate* of use value," which corresponds to the ascent of the spectacle.[22] The hypertrophy of representation over reality produces this submission of the actual experience, as a new kind of privatization and emptying.

This ghostly proliferation of detached images, reintegrated by capital in its advanced form, promotes an "autonomous movement of the non-life."[23] This phenomenon correlates with the apparently autonomous movement of capital under the dominance of finance. In this last form, the increase in value seems to dispense with labor. The fetish of capital is money reproduced autonomously without the need of living labor. Architecture that multiplies and dissolves itself in the image-form also appears to dispense with labor. And this is how architecture reaches the hands of students, heavily flipped through in magazines in libraries and offices, on Web sites, and on social media.

THE BILBAO EFFECT

We started by analyzing the production, circulation, and consumption of *architectural images* that occur during the age of spectacle and marketing through the photographer-architecture firm system. This nonaccidental choice is derived from the tendency toward the dissolution of the architectural object into the very image that emerges from it, a phenomenon inherent in advanced capitalism and its financial and symbolic forms of reproduction, both fictional and visual. Now let us continue analyzing architecture itself, its recent metamorphoses, and its elective affinity with the world of brands.

Images obviously have not become totally autonomous from the architectural body, but rather the latter underwent dramatic mutations. Architecture in the digital-financial age has greatly expanded its repertoire of forms and techniques. The modernist cube was dismantled, and in its place, a profusion of irregular volumes and complex forms have occupied the scene. New digital technologies of design and production, new materials and design commissions, always demanding novelty from architects, allowed for the execution of works that a few decades before were unimaginable. Boosting this process is the injection of capital and public funds aiming at speculative gains of a new kind, generated from the effect of attraction that these buildings produce—or what we have been calling the rent of form.

Themes such as mass production and city planning, recurrent in the time of modern architecture, have dropped off the agenda. In the postutopian society, capital no longer finds opponents, and the ideology of planning gives way to the spectacular effects of isolated buildings that alone are supposed to activate ailing economies, attract tourists and investors, and redefine the identity of entire societies. To that end, renowned architects reject mass production and seek out uniqueness at all costs, in single works of great symbolic power in which the new power of the political economy of culture and the crisis of the welfare system are concomitantly expressed.

Even though it has been widely discussed at length, we cannot refrain from beginning with the work that, on many levels, remains the symbol of this shift: Frank Gehry's Guggenheim Museum Bilbao. This work will reappear in all of the chapters of this book because it unites innovations in form, in design technique, in production at the construction site, in the dissemination of images in media, and in the way symbolic and material gains are obtained by the various agents involved. The multiplication of the "Bilbao Effect" has taken place on a global scale.

We will analyze how architecture shifts toward the logic of branding in its production of immaterial values of economic significance. Architects of museums are also called upon to conceive designer shops, and to visually consolidate the attributes of each brand. Affinities between "starchitecture" and high fashion occur at various levels, including the progressive dissociation of authorship in favor of branding, as it

View of the Guggenheim Museum Bilbao from the Nervión River, which cuts through the city. La Salve Bridge can be seen at left. Photograph by Ardfern, Creative Commons 1.0.

Guggenheim Museum Bilbao, designed by Frank Gehry. Photograph by Zarateman, Creative Commons CC0 1.0 Universal Public Domain Dedication.

occurs in the luxury industry. Not only does architecture serve brands, but architects themselves have also become brands, lending their names to the products of large firms and, in the case we analyze, under the tutelage of an investment fund.

Function in architecture also expands until it reaches progressively less utilitarian sensory dimensions. Architecture must provide unique and memorable experiences as part of its business model. For this, a wide range of materials, building skins, chromatic effects, lighting systems, and digital ornaments are mobilized. We will see how this new architectural commodity, which differs fundamentally from the precepts of a previous modern period of production, is investigated from the point of view of fetish formation and its economic bases, which combine rent and value in a singular way.

Therefore, let us begin, without dwelling on a description of the object already thoroughly dissected by critics, by focusing on the motivations and cascading effects of the Guggenheim-Bilbao City Hall initiative. In the 1980s, the Basque Country was undergoing a major crisis, a recession that saw the closing of shipyards and an unemployment rate of 25 percent, in addition to violent separatist actions by the ETA group. The strategic planning and city marketing model of Barcelona, the neighboring capital, were then adopted by the Basque capital in its postindustrial city plan and named *Bilbao Metrópoli 30*. According to the guidebook of this kind of urban entrepreneurship, "the city commodity, the *selling of cities,* has become one of the basic functions of local governments," claims Jordi Borja, and, therefore, "the city should be promoted *abroad,* developing a strong and positive image supported by a supply of infrastructure and services, which attracts investors, visitors, and *solvent* users of the city, and which facilitates its exports (of goods and services, and professionals)."[24]

Brazilian sociologist Carlos Vainer considers this agenda to be the perfect unfolding in cities of so-called neoliberal policies of opening up and deregulating national economies. In them, urbanism is no longer thought of in political terms, but in management terms, through consensus building that is above all depoliticizing because it denies the existence of divergent and unequal interests, and their conflicts. The motto of unity among all, for operations of this kind, is precisely the "sense of acute crisis," material and symbolic, which favors the mobilization of vulnerable citizens, hostages of the crisis, around strategic consensus. This is when administrators must foster a "civic patriotism," according to Borja, in which, "trust and belief in the future of the metropolis rely on visible works and services, both those of monumental and symbolic character as well as those aimed at improving the quality of the public spaces and the well-being of the population."[25]

The success of strategic planning hinges on the implementation of large, iconic projects that have the potential for urban revitalization and the promotion of the city's image. Bilbao Ría-2000, a semipublic urban development agency, coordinated the projects, and each of them was operated by a management company along the lines of public–private partnerships.[26] Public and private investments were made in new commercial, governmental, and cultural buildings, in parks and the redesigning of riverbanks, and in new transportation infrastructures, including the expansion and renovation of the subway, the main railway station, and the airport. All are design projects signed by starchitects such as Foster, Santiago Calatrava, Cesar Pelli, Michael Wilford and James Stirling, I. M. Pei, Rafael Moneo, etc. Among these projects, the core attraction was an internationally visible new museum, a spectacular building.[27]

The Basque administration saw the offer to build a Guggenheim branch in Bilbao, knocking at its door after a series of refusals from other European cities, as an opportunity to reverse the crisis situation and change the image of the city. The goal was to present itself as an important and renewed financial center in the Iberian Peninsula and attract yuppies and tourists.[28] As Bilbao does not have beaches, mountains, or snow, writes anthropologist Joseba Zulaika, the option was to invest in the arts and culture as a way to attract visitors and finance executives (the same mix as Frankfurt, which was used as an example of a city of banks and museums). And the opportunity consisted not only of increasing the attractiveness for banking and cultural tourism investments, but also in the promotion of the real-estate industry by renovating the Nervión River waterfront, moreover promoting a moderate Basque patriotism, at once proud and cosmopolitan, opposed to radical separatism.

In the case of Bilbao, as well as other cities, negotiations for this type of museum were not conducted in the Department of Culture but directly with mayors and secretaries of finance—"I know nothing of the arts, but I approve of it," supposedly said the economist who ran Bilbao's finances, according to Zulaika.[29] The museum's curatorial aspect and cultural goals were not thoroughly discussed and evaluated, and were not even part of local cultural policies. The negotiations were conducted in secret, far from public debate. Secrecy that assures the exclusivity of the operation and its ability to generate additional monopoly rent is part of doing business. The prevailing interests, even from the point of view of public managers, are mercantile, stimulating businesses through a promotional investment and activating the local economy by attracting solvent companies and people.

The final project, estimated at one hundred million euros, had to be approved by museum director Thomas Krens and Bilbao's representatives on Wall Street—where the Guggenheim's and the art market's investors could be found. The operation of exporting the Guggenheim as a multinational company needed the market's endorsement. Would it be beneficial or not to the value of the Guggenheim brand? How would locational decisions such as this affect the art market? What dividends would it bring to Wall Street? To seek approval from Wall Street was not considered a humiliating act of subordination by the Basque managers, but rather a chance to strengthen their own local stock exchange: "Merrill Lynch now knows where Bilbao is."[30]

After its opening, the museum attracted about a million visitors a year, ten times more than the New York Guggenheim, and according to official data the investment was returned to the public coffers, in the form of increase in revenues, in four years. American critic Hal Foster goes so far as to say that after this project, architecture was no longer the same, and that each subsequent project of its kind has a "Bilbao Effect," in which each city seeks to build a spectacle of similar magnitude in order to attract new capital flows.[31] The museum is the most successful outcome of urban *co-branding* in recent decades, combining the brands of the Guggenheim, Bilbao, and Gehry in a joint media-leveraging venture. As stated by Zulaika, "the Guggenheim Museum has become more a matter of money, power, and prestige than art."[32]

Gehry's work is thus doubly successful, not only as an amazing technical/aesthetic apparatus, but also, or above all, as a highly profitable financial strategy. When disseminated via media channels as the apex of recent architectural production, it generated fabulous monopoly rents

The atrium of the Guggenheim Museum Bilbao, designed by Frank Gehry.
Photograph by Ardfern, Creative Commons-SA 3.0.

for the various actors involved. As David Harvey has already observed, urban interventions have become specialized in building exclusive places able to exert the power of attraction of capital flows.[33] In this sense, they are operations of an eminently rentier character, which mobilize the most unusual architectural forms to attract attention and wealth from all over the world. Gehry's work was instrumental in transforming the decadent and dark Basque capital, which had been suffering the effects of deindustrialization and separatist violence, into one of the world's tourist attractions. This does not mean producing better and more equitable cities, but rather building projects and places that constitute rent magnets.

The Guggenheim revives the ideology of place, but in the degraded form of "cultural entertainment." Degraded because it is devoid of the utopian component and, therefore, clearly pro-market, as explains philosopher Otília Arantes, "a euphoria that combines the relationship of finance, culture, and media with the glamorization of the market economy, after the fall of real socialism, and the progressive dismantling of the welfare state."[34] New museums and cultural centers appear as a compensatory fantasy in the face of the corrosion of social protection and labor systems. Investment in culture is thus a way to animate a weakened social body (hence the paradox, or cynicism). If social protection mechanisms are no longer renewed according to historical patterns, the state engages in a politics of heritage recycling and cultural appropriation, "centered on the autonomy of citizens (including in relation to social protection)." According to the author's formulation: "the de-aestheticization of art is followed by a moment of aestheticization of the social."[35]

From the architects' standpoint, cultural buildings, and museums in particular, became the desired work of free imagination (as opposed to neutral museums in service of artworks, as desired by the modernists). Hence, "all the architects of today want to leave their signatures on a museum," and "to create a total work of art."[36] Neither does Otília Arantes fail to acknowledge in architects a category that benefits and legitimizes the substitutional influx of the cultural over the social. The work of free imagination moves from the specific architecture of museums to any kind of building signed by a new genre of starchitect, a star system of authors and authorities that began reigning in the "architecture world after the disintegration of the modernist creed."[37]

Faced with the explosive pyrotechnic success of the Guggenheim Museum Bilbao, one can easily identify its antecedents in the "Beaubourg Effect," from twenty years earlier. The construction of the Centre Georges Pompidou was part of the process of urban revitalization of the Marais district in Paris in the early 1970s, during the ambiguous climate of the post-68 aftermath, in which a rundown neighborhood was slowly appropriated by young artists and galleries. The building, with its metal structures and tubes resembling obscenely exposed bowels, is a rectangular prism. Its filling is conventional, but presented in the form of a promotional tool. The monumentality of the Beaubourg, as well as other *Grands Projets* of the Mitterrand years, is based on pure forms (like the Louvre's pyramid or the cube of the arch of La Défense), according to a set of ideas in which "formal purity and social rationality seem to hold hands, but exclusively on the level of representation."[38]

This formalism, which still holds some promise of social intervention, even if ideological, is totally deprived of any minimally civilizing perspective in the case of the Bilbao operation, conceived under the strictest rules of management. Gehry's promotional building, with its seemingly random volumes, was strategically planned as a commercial operation, devoid of any higher aspirations. And in the absence of prismatic shapes (such as in the French case), it is filled by a formal instability that reveals the context of the dominance of speculation under which it was produced.

Cultural entertainment, in this case, is nothing more than this very ostentatious event in its direct symbolism of a city run as a business to do business. In this context, the urban planner becomes his or her opposite, that is, the real-estate developer, and acts "as a poacher"—in Peter Hall's words—hunting for opportunities and occasions to do business. Planning cities in this "end-of-the-line urbanism" means defining a spatial configuration conducive to patrimonial valorization. In this new stage of city-business, profitability and cultural architectural heritage walk hand in hand. Thus, culture is mobilized "as the new business password, a new label in the affluent society of the fashion world," a society that claims to have "dethroned the primacy of relations of production on behalf of relations of 'seduction,'" in Lipovetsky's expression.[39]

The architects and planners thus start acting as seeders of "cultural bait" for capital, by means of recovering the symbolic wealth of form—as opposed to the functional monotony of modernism, for example. In ultramodernity, the request is to build "spectral prisms in which the mythical image of the profitable is crystallized."[40] Ultimately, we witness the "glamorous convergence between high culture and big business," and once again architecture is a privileged field to analyze this fusion. Culture is not only the soul of the business, but also the role of the "last civilizing trench of capital in the face of the supposed barbarism of the losers" falls upon culture and its emancipatory claims. The allegedly autonomous realm of culture has not only become autonomous a second time (as the financial economy itself also did), it has also become generalized "to the point of ultimately enthroning the culturalist scheme for the explanation of society" and the inequalities among classes and nations.[41]

A new elite begins to define society's norms and values, no longer the bourgeoisie and the owning class—the cultural intermediaries, especially including starchitects and designers, whose power lies in the intangible assets they possess: "knowledge, creativity, the artistic sensibility and talents of cultural entrepreneurs, professional expertise, and business acumen."[42]

The architecture of museums, in its contemporary metamorphoses, is allegorical of a larger scale process. The museum, "by definition, a civilizing resource, in whatever historical form it is presented," was converted into "a media center of economic attraction and valuation," the expression of a sort of "culturalist reproduction of capital and of its *soft* domination." Culture enacts "all syndromes inherent to large speculative businesses: low quality, repetition, exorbitant prices, bluffs in regard to originality, intrusion, intellectual terrorism, standardization . . . Every product must be simple, clear, definable in a few sentences. The work is its own logo, as opaque and simplified as packaging."[43]

In short, the disorganization of the managed society of the previous historical cycle, from the ideology of planning to the welfare state, gave rise to a culture and economy running "toward each other, giving the impression that the new centrality of culture is economic, and that the old centrality of the economy became cultural, and capitalism a cultural form among rivals." Today "culture is not the other, nor even the counterpart, neutral instrument regarding marketing practices, but today it is a decisive part of the business world, and is big business."[44]

The success of the partnership between the Guggenheim and Gehry was such that in the year following the opening of Bilbao, New York intended to build itself a machine to generate money through culture. The chosen venues were piers 9, 13, and 14 located south of the Brooklyn Bridge, in Manhattan. Mayor Rudolph Giuliani had agreed to provide $68 million of public funds, and yet, the resources allocated were insufficient for the venture. The Guggenheim project in New York was much larger than that of Bilbao, with titanium flowers that reached more than a hundred meters high, at the scale of Manhattan's waterfront and skyscrapers. The museum's size was extraordinary, eight times taller than Frank Lloyd Wright's Guggenheim. Furthermore, the increase in the international price of titanium increased the cost considerably, which was estimated at $950 million, seven times the value of Bilbao.

The fact was that the Guggenheim Foundation could not rely solely on public funds for its new venture and had to raise funds from Wall Street investors. The impact of the September 11, 2001, terrorist attacks on tourism, on public opinion, and on priorities for reconstruction in Manhattan drew attention away from the project. The Guggenheim alone could not carry forward this initiative. Its SoHo branch, designed by Arata Isosaki in 1991, was barely able to pay its bills, and had to give half of its space to the Italian fashion brand Prada, in a store designed by Rem Koolhaas. The chairman of the Guggenheim, Peter Lewis, conceded defeat: "I still remain personally committed to support an extraordinary architectural and cultural project for Lower Manhattan, but I'm trying to see this new project on another scale, and also probably elsewhere, in the years to come."[45]

Gehry and Krens's attentions thus turned toward countries with money to spend, which could make even more impactful works than Bilbao feasible. The two went knocking on the doors of sheiks in Abu Dhabi, capital of the United Arab Emirates and paradigmatic enclave of the new rentier economy, as Mike Davis well described.[46] Gehry could then work without budgetary constraints, openly wanting to surpass Bilbao, at Thomas Krens's and oil magnates' request. The project, located on the Persian Gulf peninsula (which has received several other American-powered interventions), is a repetition of previous "deconstructivist" formulas, but on a much larger scale—not failing to remember the bombing of Baghdad. The project is part of the transfer of oil income (at a high at the time,[47] but extinct at some point) to new forms of rent, such as theme parks, spectacular hotels, new museums, designer shops, fantasy islands, money-laundering financial centers, etc. And the other side of works like this one is the brutal extraction of surplus value: the Emirates' construction sites are true semi-slave labor camps (and in that the new Guggenheim is no exception), populated by immigrants deprived of any rights, or labor union protection, as we shall see in the third chapter.

The Abu Dhabi project had not yet materialized and the 2008 global crisis seemed to affect its viability.[48] Gehry, impatient with the defeat in New York and the waiting in the Emirates, sought to move away from the obsession of producing a new Guggenheim. So did Krens, realizing that Gehry was repeating his successful design formulas—which for the museum was not the best way to extract monopoly gains from exclusive buildings associated with its brand. Krens then started to request designs from other architects associated with the star system, sometimes even promoting competitions among them by invitation. Within a few years, projects were popping up around the world: there were Guggenheim branches in Salzburg and Vienna (designed by Hans Hollein), in Berlin (by Richard Gluckman), in Venice (by Vittorio Gregotti), in Las Vegas (by Rem Koolhaas), in Tokyo (by Shigeru Ban, Jean Nouvel, and Zaha Hadid), in Rio de Janeiro (by Nouvel), in Taichung (by Hadid), in Guadalajara (by Nouvel, Asymptote, and Enrique Norten), in Singapore (by Hadid), and in Vilnius (by Daniel Libeskind, Hadid, and Massimiliano Fuksas). Almost none of them, however, came to fruition, and some of the buildings eventually closed their doors, either totally (Las Vegas) or partially (the SoHo branch).

Thomas Krens's international pilgrimage to sell Guggenheim branches gave rise to the nickname "McGuggenheim"[49] as an allegory of the museum franchise being sold as cultural fast food. When George Ritzer wrote about the "McDonaldization of society" in 1995 his attempt was to describe a phenomenon spreading far beyond shopping malls' food courts. Inspired by Max Weber's notion of instrumental reason, he realized that the principles of fast-food rationality were becoming dominant in various sectors of American society and around the world, affecting areas of health, education, tourism, leisure, family, and even politics.[50]

Seen in this light, the sale of Guggenheim franchises was not only a strategy to raise funds to support its loss-making headquarters in New York. It was about a broader phenomenon backed by the extreme commodification of art, and businesses centered on immaterial values. Like McDonald's, in each franchise what is being sold is the brand name, intangible corporate values, concepts, rather than products. The brand does not make any material investments in each of its franchises (as in the case of a multinational corporation when expanding its factories), but it only lends its name, attributes, and know-how. Each Guggenheim franchise costs between $20 and $50 million, and the local authorities bear the construction costs and operational deficits of the implemented museum. But unlike McDonald's, the Guggenheim cannot repeat the architecture of its buildings as a stamp. It is part of its business to favor the unique, authorial, and unexpected, as an additional form of rentier gains.

BRANDS OF ARCHITECTURE AND THE ARCHITECTURE OF BRANDS

Before analyzing the shift in the course of architecture toward the logic of brands, we must remember that since its early manifestos in the 1920s, modern architecture defined a program that elected industrial capital as its main ally and example to be followed—and further on, the state itself, and, on the periphery of industrial capitalism, the national bourgeoisie and its developmentalist governments. From engineering to industrial aesthetics, a machinist and rationalist inspiration guided both modern architecture's constructive and urban experiences. Even if experimental, their designs could nearly always be replicated at a mass scale, hence their affinity with industrial serialization, though little serialization was realized in practice. Concrete, steel, and glass were the new materials applied in prismatic forms, usually orthogonal and abstract, stripped of ornament. Research was conducted and designs developed on industrial buildings, offices, large infrastructure, workers' houses ("machines for living")—components of the fixed capital and site of workforce reproduction that form part of the production process inherent to capitalist accumulation. The city, in turn, was considered a relatively uniform urban fabric, separated only by function—a model in which the intraurban income differential could, theoretically, tend toward zero.

Industrial capital and wage labor represented the modern, and the landowner and his land rent (a legacy of the old regime and upholder of urban irrationality), the archaic. In the dispute over the allocation of surplus value, modern architecture allied itself with the productive sectors, with capital as its function more than as property. However, such symbiosis with the most advanced industrial sectors, mainly the automotive sector, which was more stylized than effective, occurred, in fact, among the large construction sector and modernizing governments, in whose construction sites the most retrograde exploitation prevailed.

In contemporary architecture, if the alliance is once again with the dominant sectors, that is, the most dynamic and hegemonic sectors of the economy, it is now occurring with rentier capital, and, more specifically, with the entertainment industry, brands, and the new digital-financial economy.

Architecture has always associated itself with the owners of power and money, mainly with those who own private property, land, and capital. Architecture has a tendency to cling to income and rent given its fixity and high costs.[51] It is almost its natural fate to reiterate property and finance, even if not voluntarily. Because of its exclusive character, architecture inevitably retains some monopoly rent. In modern architecture, there was an opposing trend that sought to minimize the power of rent and finance, associating itself with productive sectors and modernizing national governments, but in the age of financial globalization, there is no longer any force contrary to this power. The implications in terms of the constructive and social dimensions of architecture are profound: rentier architecture gives up certain capacities in favor of unproductive uses,[52] typical of the sphere of circulation and consumption (shopping malls, airports, hotels, spas, stadiums, museums, designer shops, concert halls, theme parks, etc.). There is no longer a wish for serialization and mass production, but for differentiation and exclusivity. As we shall see in the third chapter, in the sphere of production, this new architecture finds elective affinities with supposedly flexible post-Fordist accumulation.

At the turn of the twenty-first century, starchitects started to develop increasingly elaborate images to represent power and money. As Jacques

Herzog, one of the architects responsible for the Tate Modern project and Beijing's Bird's Nest, claimed: "We work with the physical materiality of architecture because only in this way we can transcend, advance, and even reach the immaterial."[53] To reach the "immaterial" by means of the most tectonic of the arts, architecture—obvious nonsense[54]—is to produce an intangible, but socially verifiable, value as a representation of corporate power (government, company, religious order, or country). The difference is that now this spectacular force of architecture not only is a prerequisite of absolutist, autocratic, or fascist regimes, but also of large business strategies, associated with tourism, cultural and sporting events, urban marketing, and the promotion of corporate identities. This is what Herzog acknowledges, without mincing words: "If now art and architecture are more than ever political instruments, it is because they are increasingly closer to the universe of brands."[55] The fact is that almost no modern architect, in the face of their (now) prosaic boxes in glass, steel, and concrete, could have anticipated the degree of technical sophistication and formal exuberance that brand architecture would reach.

Perhaps the main exception among modern architects was Oscar Niemeyer, awarded the Pritzker Prize in 1988, whose plastic, fluid, white, and curvilinear forms sought to explore the use of concrete to the limit, creating almost a brand, easily recognizable around the world, and generally praised by this new generation of starchitects for his boldness. But the context was not the same, and his works were usually conceived as icons of the power of a modernizing and developmentalist state, such as Brazil—for example, in works like the National Congress in Brasília, and palaces such as the Planalto, Alvorada, and Itamaraty. The same can be noted of Niemeyer's most famous parks, such as Pampulha, Ibirapuera, and the Latin America Memorial, or his huge residential building that marks the landscape of São Paulo, the Copan. His work has always been about giving shape to something that could express the local reality and be identified as "Brazilian architecture." Maybe, in some of his most recent works, such as the museums of Niteroi and Curitiba, he might have given in to the temptation of designing according to the standards imposed by the "new international museums," that is, the pure and simple affirmation of their visual identity—to give them their very own architectural form. However, the strength of his design, an architect whose gestures are similar to a graphic designer's in their tracing of synthetic lines with powerful visual forsight, and who, in a sense, anticipates many of the formal jugglings of recent flashy architecture, does not correspond to the same contemporary logic of brand architecture of the company-cities engaged in global competitions. Niemeyer's official and "national" architecture is directly associated with the developmentalist cycle of an underdeveloped country, imbued with the need for an accelerated process of economic and social modernization, and for its urban and architectural forms.

From capital's point of view, the contemporary rise of branding, even in companies producing tangible commodities, is mainly associated with the new financial hegemony in which image and brand overlap with the labor value of the goods produced (or outsourced) by the company, adding a new kind of value: a sort of rent of representation of their own goods. As an image separated from the object's prosaic body, these brands take on a function similar to the abstraction of money. The brand's differential of exclusivity aims at creating a form of property that cannot be generalized. The monopoly over its use is a form of rent, and for this reason it is patented and, similar to land, protected by legal (and sometimes real) fences to control access. This automation of the forms of property produces, at the same time, an automation of the form as pure property. The form becomes capital through an imagetic phenomenon in which it is remunerated as symbolic capital by the "rent of form."

Certainly, this relationship between physical object and intangible values does not occur only in the sphere of ideology. It has productive bases and is part of a process of appreciation for this new kind of capital. Currently, all major companies know how to make similar products with the same technical expertise. The difference, however, lies in the intangible values each product incorporates, through marketing, branding, and design strategies. Naomi Klein explains how large corporations have quickly realized that "everyone can make products," and also that "this ignoble task may be delegated to third parties," preferably to peripheral countries where there are low wages, deregulated labor, low environmental supervision, and high tax incentives. "Headquarters, meanwhile, is free to focus on the real business at hand—creating a corporate mythology powerful enough to infuse meaning into these raw objects just by signing its name."[56]

This search for corporate transcendence is a relatively recent phenomenon, coming about when a select group of companies realized that building and strengthening their brand image in a race for weightlessness was the correct strategy to achieve a new type of profitability.[57] "These pioneers made the bold claim that producing goods was only an incidental part of their operations," says Klein, for their "real goal [is] divestment of the world of things." Or, to try to "make believe that each product had acquired a higher status than that of *thing*," as if it had a soul, a spiritual core.[58]

The strategy was working out well, because companies that invested in their brands' names began inflating like balloons, worth several times more on the market than on paper—in an impressive fictitious capitalization. Although they continued to produce—increasingly less directly—tangible commodities, profits increased high above average because they had become true "meaning-producing agents," as if they were part of the culture industry. The world of brands thus appears as a synthesis between financial and aesthetic logics, searching for ways to obtain rent appreciation based on distinction and differentiation.

According to Isleide Fontenelle, we seem to be witnessing a displacement or change in the status of the commodity-form.[59] In addition to generating surplus value through work, this form increasingly earns rents, assuming the status of cultural commodity—by nature distinct from everyday commodities—and therefore carrying an additional rent of a monopolistic type.[60] Additionally, the fact that each company produces supposedly exclusive commodities limits the possibility for comparison between products and equivalent labor. The very measure of socially necessary labor time would cease to express value, and in turn, suffer from a kind of excess.[61]

The articulation between rent and profit within commodities introduces a new dynamic in the logic of production, a rentier feature that should not be underestimated.[62] Not coincidentally, brand management has become the field of expertise concerned exactly with defining the optimal point of combination between profit and rent.

In architecture, it is no different. The architects of the digital-financial age, unlike modern architects, do not seek the reproduction of universal solutions on a large scale—which would definitely reduce the potential for monopoly rent by commodities. The goal is to produce exclusivity, a unique work associated with the designers' brands, and the brands of their bosses. And the race for uniqueness is a contract item,[63] as clients request exclusive work throughout all details from the architect: facade solutions, surfaces, and structures must not be repeated.

The resounding success of some of the projects and their architects, however, ends up stimulating the repetition of the same design formulas, reducing their ability to generate rents from exclusivity. Brand architecture thus has a commercial limit, which requires it to adopt unusual and increasingly showy solutions. If several cities long for a work by Frank Gehry following the Bilbao model, for example, they will progressively lose the ability to capture value by means of such projects. Thomas Krens, the director of the Guggenheim franchise, identifies this risk, but his choice of hiring other starchitects may not be enough to reverse the trendline for rentier gains in the multiplying operations of the *logomuseum* around the world.

Not only museums, but also luxury brands in the fashion world and the automobile industry have hired star system architects to design iconic stores that express the transcendental meaning of their brands. As Otília Arantes states, those are "contaminations" between the worlds of art and commerce, between the spaces of museums and designer shops.[64] The same architects who design the most prestigious cultural venues are invited to enhance the aura of brands in new buildings and shops. The environment in which consumers relate to the brand must emulate what happens in museums in relation to the art. Therefore, sale and display spaces for important brands are now designed, paradoxically, to have an anticommercial appeal when it comes to consumption, promoting a disinterested purchase. What are sold are not strictly commodities, but transcendental experiences, desires, lifestyles, and immaterial values.

Examples multiply. The French brand Hermès hired Renzo Piano to design its store in Tokyo, a true feat of ornamentation in an apparently simple building, with a continuous glass-block facade that shines at night as a unique fragment, a huge gem. Also in Tokyo—the current luxury mecca—the Mikimoto brand, known for its jewelry with cultured pearls, built a plain white tower with irregular openings on its facade designed by Toyo Ito. An even bolder variant of this composition of exposed concrete was designed by Ito for the brand Tod's. The Italian Prada sought the famous Swiss firm of Herzog & de Meuron for its megastore, also in Tokyo, a building whose facade is made of a black metal frame structured in the shape of hollow trapezoids, over which flat, concave, or convex glass is applied. The different geometries create faceted reflections that cause the observer, both inside and outside, to see "constantly changing pictures and almost cinematographic perspectives of Prada products, the city and themselves."[65] In Manhattan, Christian de Portzamparc, before the disaster of the music palace in Rio de Janeiro, designed an elegant chamfered volume of green glass for the French luxury conglomerate LVMH (Moët Hennessy Louis Vuitton SE). Meanwhile, in New York, Jean Nouvel designed the Versace boutique, and Gehry did the store display design for stylist Issey Miyake, with clouds made of sheet metal. In Berlin, Nouvel designed the new Galeries Lafayette, with two immense glass cones crossing the central span and lighting the space. For Armani, Tadao Ando planned an exposed concrete store with a precise and elegant design, elevating the space to the status of a (brand's) temple, etc.

Three German automotive companies, BMW, Mercedes, and Porsche, completed buildings of spectacular architecture for their main showrooms, factories, and even museums. In 2002, BMW held a design competition for the BMW World building, in which 275 architectural firms participated. The winner was the Austrian group Coop Himmelb(l)au. The space was conceived to transmit the intangible values and prestige of the brand to the consumers. Entertainment activities, virtual reality, test-drives, and the purchasing of cars make the building a tourist destination that attracts more than half a million people a year. In order to accommodate all of this, the Austrian architects built a steel truss pavilion with complex geometry inspired by clouds and atmospheric formations, as well as a spectacular point of convergence when the covering forms a toroid and leans on the trunk of a cone. This strictly defined form can only be calculated and executed thanks to new parametric design software. The glass structure is theatrically lit in blue and lilac. BMW also hired Zaha Hadid to expand its plant in Leipzig, a huge marquee that connects three industrial buildings. It serves as the main access and circulation, home to new administrative and social areas and, above all, it produces a dynamic spectacle[66] for all employees to see, thus reinforcing the company's commitment to high design and innovation.

Maison Hermès in Tokyo, designed by Italian architecture firm Renzo Piano Building Workshop (RPBW), 1998–2001. Photograph by Wiiii, Creative Commons.

BMW Welt and Museum in Munich, designed by the Austrian firm Coop
Himmelb(l)au, 2003–7. Photograph by Diego Delso, Creative Commons by SA.

Mercedes-Benz built a museum for its brand in Stuttgart, designed
by UN Studio. The building simulates an immense aerodynamic helmet, deconstructed by folds and cuts. In its interior, a spiral of ramps is
reminiscent of Wright's Guggenheim, only here the ramps are tracks for
displaying the cars. The futuristic facade is constituted by unique pieces:
the windows are composed of 1,800 distinct triangular pieces of glass, a
feat of construction only possible with the use of flexible, robotic manufacturing, as we will see in later chapters. In 2008, it was Porsche's turn
to inaugurate its museum, another spectacular building in Stuttgart, designed by the Viennese duo Delungan and Meissl. Together with BMW
and Mercedes, these buildings, more so than museums, are temples of
fetishistic automobile celebration. The automotive community is vener-
ated there, leaving no room, evidently, for consideration of the negative
consequences—be they urban, social, environmental, or public health–
related—of multiplying individual motorized transport.

The main co-branding operation between the world of brands and
that of starchitecture seems to have been the marriage between Prada

and Rem Koolhaas. Unlike any other case, here Dutch architect Koolhaas was hired to engage deeply with the branding of Prada in order to design its new stores in New York, Los Angeles, San Francisco, and London. His approach, therefore, goes far beyond simply shaping the form of the building, and starts to resemble that of a brand manager. It is from this standpoint that he establishes new key concepts to guide the design of the stores: shopping cannot be an indistinguishable act; there should be a variety of spaces inside a shop; it should promote the feeling of exclusivity; the brand's shop should become a host for the city; the architect should know how to combine the maintenance of the brand's identity with its constant transformation in time; it shall preserve the intimacy of a small company; and, above all, it should introduce non-commercial typologies inside the store, such as cultural events and other activities not related to sales.[67] According to Koolhaas, if "Museums, libraries, airports, hospitals, and schools are becoming increasingly indistinguishable from the act of shopping" and treat people like consumers, a brand with "attitude" must propose the reverse equation, that is, to enrich the shopping experience to the point of encompassing distinct and unique activities in order to bring authenticity back into people's life.[68] In this way, elements such as bleachers, stages, debates and video projections, cafés, small bookstores, large murals, devices for digital interaction, rough and soft surfaces for tactile experiences, wall mirrors that deform and project images, etc. became part of the store's program of use.

However, Koolhaas's stores evidently do not call forth the demercantilization of life. As he intends to cover all the various social activities in a single commercial environment, under the seal of the brand, mercantilization seeks to fill every pore of existence. The act of buying is no longer a mechanical and functional experience, but begins to demand total surrender, of body and mind, from the consumer. Its counterpart is the richness of the new cultural experience of shopping, thoroughly planned by the architect, as opposed to the poverty and vulgarity of shopping malls. And, moreover, according to the architect, shops will turn out to be the last places of public life.[69] The cynical apology by Koolhaas disguised as manager actually re-creates the degraded terms of cultural entertainment, which, as we have seen, are the compensatory fantasy that the market proposes in the face of the crises of social and labor protection systems, and of public life itself.

Let us consider one last relationship between architects and brands. In starchitecture, as in high fashion, authorship is not strictly corporate (as it is with Nike shoes), but is attributed to the unique signature of an artist who had supposedly designed the products and given them authenticity. More recently, the artist's personal authorship, even in luxury boutiques, has been absorbed by the brand's industrial creation. In the beginning, all creation in the fashion world was centered on great couturiers, free and independent creators, whom Lipovetsky has called "demiurge couturiers."[70] Insofar as luxury goods have acquired their own personality and provided identity to major boutiques, the aura of the name began to detach itself from its creator and to transcend the artist himself. Thus, high fashion became an industry of creation, even though part of the production is still handmade. The old luxury boutiques became global giants, international groups traded on stock exchanges. Authorship morphed into brand management portfolios operated by marketers. The latter study how the expansion of luxury brands can be extended nearly to the loss of the brand's identity, in search of the optimum appreciation point between rentier gains through exclusivity and production profits from serialized manufacturing. As Lipovetsky points out, the old struggles for recognition and prestige are now supplanted by "mergers and acquisitions operations, concentration and restructuring movements in order to establish international industrial empires."[71] At the same time, while the creation of new products and brand management are increasingly concentrated at the top, the material production of goods is largely being transferred to peripheral countries at the base, where poor conditions of work and remuneration are readily found.[72] This same phenomenon can be found at the construction sites of works of "starchitecture," as we shall see in the third chapter.

The main example of an architect who became a brand name and who mobilized a production machine for design projects dissociated from his material authorship is the British architect Norman Foster. At one point his office employed 1,300 professionals and developed about two hundred projects per year. The company is divided internally into six major design teams, with a lead designer in each of them.[73] In addition to these vertical groups, there are crosscutting teams, which include the three-dimensional modeling and rendering team that produces spectacular images, and the traditional departments, such as management and finance, human resources, and public relations. Foster's participation in these two hundred annual design projects is obviously restricted, and his degree of involvement varies according to the client's importance and proximity. Whenever possible, however, Foster is the showman responsible for the presentation of the designs to clients, judges, and the general public, as if he were indeed the projects' author. Behind the scenes are interdisciplinary teams, from experienced professionals to young trainees, as well as numerous consultants, all involved in the production, who, nonetheless, are barely visible and rarely mentioned. The authorship remains publicly attributed to the unique creative genius, Sir Norman Foster, who individually receives the awards for the office's work.

Foster knew how to use steel technology in order to produce strong and emblematic images with his buildings—which were not always justifiable by technical requirements, but rather were required by overlapping forms that commanded the resulting high-tech solutions. His office produced brand logo towers, such as HSBC in Hong Kong, and, more recently, the insurance agency Swiss RE's building, known as the London "Gherkin"; iconic airports, such as the "dragon" in Beijing; and also branding for governments, such as the Reichstag dome in Berlin and the Greater London Authority headquarters, in the shape of a teardrop, located on the edge of the Thames River. His forms, which maintain an industrial appearance, at times hide a highly customized and handcrafted assembly system. Paul Goldberger, for example, notes that the structural jugglings of the HSBC building are a "highly exaggerated, almost baroque expression."[74] In these cases, Foster's architecture is more about a high-tech visual expression than its actual effectiveness. Unified by the need for a production and appreciation of eye-catching brands, the often-vaunted distinction between high-tech architects and luxury set designers may be less than meets the eye.[75]

But let's go back to the problem of Foster's megafirm producing projects that continue to be attributed to a single architect. Certain qualities can be associated with Foster's brand, which are handled without the necessary direct intervention of the architect: an ostentatious use of technology, growing environmental concerns, formal exploration with toroids and curved shapes (increasingly distinct from orthogonal boxes), a capacity to build strong images for corporate or governmental

At right, the Swiss RE Building, designed by Foster + Partners for the insurance company's headquarters in London, 1997–2004. Public domain photograph by Arpingstone.

identities, etc. Each client seeks architecture firms with specific attributes in mind, more than others. In this way, the six major teams in Foster's firm have different specializations (more environmentally, technically, or commercially oriented) in order to cover the various personalities of the brand. Within each group, there are specializations in the tasks developed as well as the encouragement of different approaches, especially among the younger members. The company's partners and most experienced architects are still those who make key design decisions and judge the various options presented by the team, but they generally don't put their hands on the work. Those who design are a team of young architects coming from all over the world; many of them were trained at prestigious and cosmopolitan universities and are in tune with new developments in the field. Not only that, they seek out references in other cultural, geographical, and technological fields, looking for elements that can bring unprecedented and surprising qualities to the designs. Glass tubes from the chemical industry, for example, were being tested to provide special lighting effects on a facade.[76] Young architects acting as "coolhunters" seek to transform Foster's brand into something fashionable. These professionals, like the photographers we analyzed, seek to "arrive at the trends of the source, find out where they come from. By knowing this, it is possible to dinstinguish oneself—and that means a lot in the business world."[77] The circle closes when "cool" people (a group known as "alpha consumers" by marketers) start to recognize the brand as equally cool and want to relate themselves with it, as in the emblematic case of the megabrand Apple.[78]

The Foster brand has begun to attract the interest of hedge funds and private equities. Investing in large design companies seems to be a profitable niche. In a study conducted by the Department of Economics at the University of Chicago, Professor Kevin Murphy assesses that not only does investing in a good design greatly increase the profitability of a business, but also that the firms and design consultants themselves should be seen as interesting targets for financial investments.[79] His example, not by chance, is Foster + Partners—among the architects who have won the Pritzker Prize, Foster's firm is the largest in size, turnover, and profit. In 2007, 85 percent of Foster's participation, the equivalent of 40 percent of the company's shares, was sold to the 3i investment fund for the amount of 350 million pounds. 3i has a varied portfolio, which in England alone ranges from construction companies to ones managing ocular surgery, from software to plastic injection factories. In the same year, 3i led the implementation of a plan for the reorganization of the administrative structure and the expansion of the firm, increasing from nine hundred to 1,300 employees of fifty different nationalities. In 2008, Foster + Partners operated in twenty countries with the goal of acquiring commissions in emerging markets and with high liquidity. In the second year of 3i's presence, the firm earned 191 million pounds, with a profit of forty-nine million pounds, of which more than 80 percent came from abroad.[80] The boom was remarkable and perhaps unsustainable. In 2008, Foster + Partners led the ranking of the one hundred most profitable British companies owned by investment funds, with an annual growth of 147 percent.[81] But in 2009, it was strongly affected by the economic crisis, along with a financial scandal, which we will address in the conclusion.

FLUID SURFACES AND TATTOOED SKINS

The dominant tendency in architecture's star system is undoubtedly one of lightness, transparency, or translucency, toward the limits of matter's disappearance. Let us recapitulate the declaration-manifesto by Jacques Herzog: "to work on the materiality of architecture in order to transcend it, to go beyond, and even reach the immaterial."[82]

The modern revolution of steel and glass was the first step in the pursuit of lightness and transparency, as it allowed for the separation of the facade's surface from its structural function, disconnecting, in this way as independent elements, the structural skeleton from the glass curtain. However, Fordist serialization and standardization, partially assimilated into modern architecture, ultimately resulted in conventional solutions of smooth glass towers and boxes, which nevertheless retained undeniable physical presence. One cannot say that a work such as the Seagram Building by Mies van der Rohe has reached what contemporary architects call immaterial materiality.

Transparent glass is a paradoxical element: it is invisible by nature and, therefore, while offering no obstacles to vision, highlights elements that confirm the materiality of architecture: floor slabs, columns, furniture, curtains, people etc. The new immateriality will be conquered by materials whose effects differ from those of glass in modern architecture: reflections and translucency instead of transparency, or organic and even elastic forms rather than flat and inelastic ones. It is in this respect—with the prevalence of the exterior over the interior—that building skins can be conceived, superimposed on structural skeletons nontransparently and, in this way, promote a relative autonomization of the surface.

Thus, surfaces may become fluid and tend to the immaterial, even if they house relatively conventional and heavy structures underneath. They can acquire these characteristics thanks to new design possibilities and the digital fabrication of complex forms, as we will see in later chapters. This is also thanks to the materials that are now available or used in innovative ways in the construction industry: polymers, polycarbonates, glass, ceramics, metal, and other hybrids, which can be molded industrially into desired forms, textures, and opacities, in addition to the new paints, films, and printing methods applied to them.[83]

In order to enhance the effects of the new skins, specialist-designed lighting has been incorporated. Unlike the glass building, whose facade was lit up when the interior spaces were being used, or when its lights were kept on, the new lighting concept is independent from the dynamics of building use, thus creating its own rhetorical effect. The lighting is designed to emphasize the elastic depth and the relative autonomy of the skin from the rest of the building. The most emblematic cases, as we will see, are the lighting effects internal to the skin, that is, lighting systems, some multicolored, inserted into the very surface or immediately behind it. Its activity and variable chromatic effects are programmed and controlled by computers.

This growing visual prevalence of surfaces in relation to structures is what allows for current architectural dematerialization's magic and for its transformation into a media image. It enables the "breaking of mass, density, and the apparent weight of gigantic buildings," according to Charles Jencks.[84] The new architecture wishes to reduce mass and weight while emphasizing volume and contour—"the difference between the brick and the balloon," in the words of Fredric Jameson—or the difference between heavy modernity and light or liquid modernity, in Zygmunt Bauman's terms. These principles are already partially present in modern architecture, but they are now designed in an entirely disparate spatial world, no longer operating in accordance with modern binary oppositions, explains Jameson.

Wolfgang Fritz Haug, in analyzing abstraction in commodity aesthetics, precisely points out the surface element as the fundamental component in fetish formation. According to him, there is a structural differentiation that allows the surface to be released from any functionality in order to adhere to the commodity as a skin, beautifully prepared, operating not only as protective envelope, but also as the "real countenance shown first instead of the body of the commodity."[85] The surface will be converted into a new commodity, explains Haug, "incomparably more perfect than the first," and will disconnect from it, disembodying itself and traveling the world as "a multicolored spirit of the commodity" circulating with no strings attached.[86] No longer will anyone be safe from its enticing looks, because this abstracted (or staged) appearance is always technically perfect. Smooth, untouched, and immaterially oriented, it attracts to the same degree that it erases the traces of the work that gave rise to it in the first place.

The duo Herzog & de Meuron is probably the firm that has undertaken the most daring experiments with the architectural epidermis, conceiving of it in increasingly unusual and immaterial ways. They went from a more monolithic architectural experience, with stone, copper, and rusted plate textures to ever lighter and high-tech envelopes, made with colorful polymer plates, silk-screen glass, and inflatable membranes, such as the Allianz Arena in Munich, which hosted the opening of the 2006 World Cup. The latter is one of the most spectacular and polished examples designed by the Swiss architects. Jacques Herzog says that the stadium became a model of "Logo-Design for a country or a club, a tool to enter a market."[87] The stadium was the most media-laden sports building ever built for a major event (surpassed only by the duo themselves in Beijing), with its surprising image that resembles a giant illuminated tire (blue, red, or white), incessantly spinning outward to the four corners of the globe.

The images of the arena under construction reveal the technique of abstraction used in the design.[88] After all, how can we turn a very heavy stadium into something as light as a balloon? The internal structure is relatively conventional: reinforced concrete stands covered by a metal structure. Nothing very different from the generation of stadiums built across Europe in recent decades. The surprise comes thanks to the moment in which the inflatable and illuminated surface starts to be applied onto the body of the building, producing a magical aura. When the covering membrane, made of a plastic similar to Teflon, starts enveloping the whole concrete structure, the effect is complete. Lighting that in the other stadiums focuses on the interior, here is also directed to the outside—inside, the sports spectacle, outside, the architectural spectacle—capitalizing on the city of Munich, on German high technology, and on the architects themselves.

A similar effect was adopted at the Beijing National Aquatics Center, known as the Water Cube, for the Beijing Olympics, designed by the Australian firm PTW. The cube structure that houses the Olympic pools is inspired by soap bubbles aggregated into a lather. The geometry of the metal structure is a simulated computer reproduction of this physical form, with twenty-two thousand beams that make up the sparkling walls and roof, in a single system. The gaps between the beams are closed by the same type of double membrane as at the Allianz Arena,

Allianz Arena, a soccer stadium in Munich designed by Herzog & de Meuron, inaugurated at the 2006 World Cup. Photograph by Diego Delso, delso.photo. License CC-BY-SA.

Allianz Arena, designed by Herzog & de Meuron. Photograph by Christian Horvat, Creative Commons by SA 3.0.

giving the building its characteristic image. The membranes are inflated like air mattresses and receive tens of thousands of multicolored LED lamps that can be activated in different digitally controlled chromatic combinations. The dramatic effect of the membrane in this project, as in the Munich stadium, is not limited to spectacle alone. It also responds to functional, structural, and energy demands. The system of metal trusses used to span the large distance of the pools and bleachers is a smart, lightweight solution. The double membrane coverage favors thermal and acoustic insulation and diffused natural lighting, complementing the artificial system. The hot air trapped inside the inflated membrane is used to heat the water for the swimming pool. Intelligent systems of eco-efficient surfaces have been increasingly studied and implemented in other projects, to demonstrate that their benefits are not only related to mass media. In any case, today "environmental friendliness" is already part of any successful building's architectural program.

The balloon effect, of course, can also be produced without the use of inflatable elements. Several designs inspired by organic and biomorphic forms, always with the support of new software, have produced surfaces with similar effects. The Selfridges shopping center in Birmingham, designed by Future Systems Group, achieves organic and inflated forms with hard surfaces. The volume is curved in all directions, and its roof and side enclosures form a single continuous surface. Its skin consists of fifteen thousand identical disks of polished, anodized aluminum fixed onto curved concrete walls, which are coated with insulating material. The building, in complete contrast with its context, has become the new icon of the city, acting as a catalyst for the urban renewal of Birmingham's Digbeth district.

This undeniable obsession with innovative skins in contemporary architecture has ended up bringing back the taste for ornament (now called "digital ornament")[89] that had been rejected as taboo by modern architects since the famous 1908 manifesto by Adolf Loos, "Ornament and Crime." According to the Austrian architect, the decorative epidemic was a regression for modern man. In the disenchanted world of new rationality, ornament—in its degraded state at the time—integrated into mass production, should be understood as a disease of degenerate aristocrats, in this case, or criminals with tattooed skin. Loos saw ornament as both moral and economic delinquency. His rejection of ornament stretched to erotic symbolism and the principle of deified pleasure with the same vehemence, as impulses opposed to rationalist objectivity. Pleasure, according to the prevailing work ethic, was a waste of energy, as was the case with ornament in construction. Thus, ornate furniture, clothing, and buildings were a crime against the economy, and an immoral reverie that destroyed human labor, money, and materials.[90] The text by Loos and the formulations that followed defined modern architecture within the realm of severe, clean, and durable forms, contrary to fads and conspicuous consumption, from the lacey design, to the carved woods and tattooed walls. Loos described the new man as the personification of the spirit of simplicity, work, and savings—basic elements of a Puritan ethic—whose affinity with the relentless spirit of capitalist accumulation was concurrently pointed out by Max Weber.[91]

Postmodernism brought ornament back once again, but as a quotation, often ironically, in contexts that were blatantly contrary to modern asceticism. Not coincidentally, the most representative architects of this tendency, pejoratively nicknamed craftsmen of facades, made their joint public presentation in the *Strada Novissima,* an artificial street designed by Paolo Portoghesi for the Venice Biennale in 1980 in which the whole street was made of simulated facades, the compositions of which generally did not distinguish between constructive or ornamental elements. Except for a few architects of the postmodern group (Léon Krier, for example, an uncompromising advocate of neoclassicism), the revival maintained something both provocative and playful, a big joke with the architecture of the past. Or perhaps it was an attitude inspired by the Pop movement that valued the vulgarity of conventional or commercial architecture—for this very reason, *Learning from Las Vegas* was considered the first major postmodern manifesto, with its defense of the commercial strip.[92]

But the rehabilitation of ornament that we are witnessing has nothing to do with buildings' intentionally fake facades (such as the precast palaces of Bofill, among others) or postmodern quotations. Now it is about a different bond, fully assertive and positive, with the new spirit of capitalism, which, owing to the *cash nexus,* is expressed naturally and with structural coherence in technologies that enable the ornament's digital design and production, dissociating it from its basic foundation: craftsmanship.

While Loos focused his criticism on ornament as a degraded, parasitic product attaching itself to the cycle of economic growth, a few decades earlier the notion of ornament—for William Morris, for example—was confused with real freedom from manual labor. Its essence, explains Sérgio Ferro, is the "laboring hand that allows its technical gesture to derive pleasure from itself." Therefore, "it always is, if authentic, the broadening, the 'didactization,' the explicitness, the review of this gesture, the expression of joy at work, as Morris used to say."[93] Hence Sérgio Ferro's explanation for the disappearance of ornament in modern architecture is not only of a programmatic order, but derives from class struggle at the construction site. "The working hand becomes dangerous when, through its song in the ornament, it supports the worker's demand for self-determination, the demand of the moment. It is necessary that the working hand fades . . ."[94]

The uncovering of this symbolic violence that turns out to be to ornamentation needs to be explained by the same objective conditions that have since defined the defeat of the workers at the construction site. These are the circumstances that allow "the return to overt forms of ornament, up to postmodern kitsch, following the slope of annihilation of the workers' struggle." But for new ornament, "the working hand now is only the architect's," as Ferro recognizes, and "it becomes euphoric in the face of its plots, alignments, modules, its language games, the elegance or brutality of its lines: its 'ego' explodes like fireworks."[95]

In the digital age, ornament is produced entirely inside architectural offices with the aid of computer programs. The information is then transmitted to the industrial manufacturer, sometimes with the aid of ornamentalist robots. In this regard, the pedagogical experiences of the Department of Architecture at the Zurich Institute of Technology (ETH Zurich) are exemplary. The most elaborate computer-aided ornamental designs are executed using different materials made by a robot, with a precision not reproducible by human labor. Executed millimeter by millmeter on the machine are extremely difficult brick apparatuses, complex fittings of wood pieces, carvings in various materials, or special cuts in polystyrene molds for concrete ornamental panels. Regarding these experiences and what it means to suppress the worker who executes the job, we will deal more closely when R-O-B enters the scene, in the third chapter.

But ornament was rehabilitated only owing to the new objective conditions of technology use, corresponding to that new subjectivity that is mobilized and fomented by capital reproduction in its current phase. The catalog of a widely attended exhibition held in Basel in 2008, "Re-Sampling Ornament" (so, just before the outbreak of the global crisis), states that "in our era of conspicuous consumption, brand culture has become a welcome resource for the architecture of ornament in all its opulence," and goes on to introduce design projects of decorative finishes and luxury brand environments.[96] Oliver Domeisen and Francesca Ferguson, curators of the exhibition, recognize in ornament those same aspects rejected by Loos—eroticism and waste—that became trendy once again in a society that nourishes narcissism and accelerated consumerism. Its game of beauty and sensuality and its tactile appeal are requirements for an architecture that hypertrophies the sensory stimulation response. The new ornament is not based on work; it is a lie by definition, a transgressive act, a visual narrative (or a fable) produced by the architect as a "method of subsuming anything to the architectural language: human bodies, plants, microscopic standards, fantastic beasts."[97]

The digital rehabilitation of ornament promotes a simultaneous enlargement and emptying of the universe of forms available to architects. These forms are available to create increasingly seductive buildings in superficial terms, according to a postutopian world. As Koolhaas

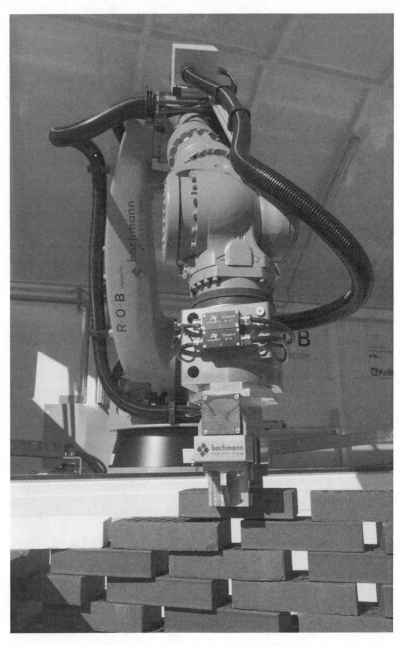

R-O-B, an industrial robotic arm in a container. Copyright Gramazio Kohler
Research, ETH Zurich.

Wall created by R-O-B for the Eleventh Venice Architectural Biennale. Copyright Gramazio Kohler Research, ETH Zurich.

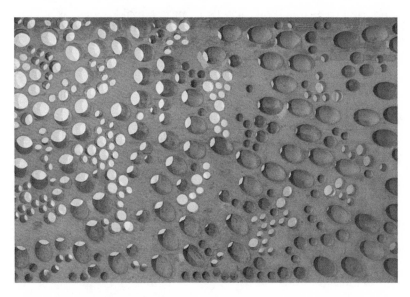

Close-up of a concrete wall fabricated by a digitally controlled robot. Students: Chris Keller, Lorenz Weingart. Copyright Gramazio Kohler Research, ETH Zurich.

states: "I do not see any utopian model still functioning in which the architect could orient himself. So what is left to the architect but to design beautiful ornaments? Period."[98]

The application of films or industrial silk screening on glass or plastic is one of the most recurrent surfaces. Colored films producing ornamental effects were used by Koolhaas at the McCormick Campus Center in Chicago and at the Dutch embassy in Berlin, both designed in 2003. The (also Dutch) architects Neutelings and Riedijk created a multichromatic facade at the Institute of Sound and Vision, in Hilversum. The glass that makes up the facade created by Jaap Drupsteen was industrially melted by Saint-Gobain and is composed of colored patches simulating blurred TV pixels. UN Studio created designs with silk-screened musical motifs for the Graz Music Theater. The theater's red tint is almost imperceptible in daylight, but dazzles at night thanks to artificial lighting. Herzog & de Meuron used serigraphs in the library of organic forms located at Brandenburg University, as well as at the Ricola box factory, in Mulhouse. In a hospital in Basel, the Swiss duo overlaid the facade with glass imprints of green balls, producing a holographic effect, changing the visual perception of the orthogonal building's rigid form required by the hospital program. The Eberswalde Library is another decorated box, with photographs printed directly onto concrete slabs, or applied onto glass panels, taking up the entire facade with a strictly decorative effect. At dusk, the imprints on concrete disappear and the images on glass become visible like illuminated frames from a movie.

Metal skins are experimental features for architects like Frank Gehry, who explores new types of folds, scales, textures, and colors in each work. The ornamental use of metal as a fabric composed of warps, wefts, and irregular reflections was explored by Dominik Dreiner in a suite of offices built in Heilbronn, Germany. Herzog & de Meuron also designed pixel-derived ornaments, such as the decomposed image of the Tenerife ocean, executed at the Espacio de las Artes in Santa Cruz. The museum's concrete facade is perforated according to a pixel diagram obtained through successive reductions in the resolution and an increase in the contrast of the images. There could not be anything more pointedly gratuitous.

Ornaments are not effects on the outer surface only. In the Casa da Música designed by Koolhaas in Porto, Portugal, all the internal voids and spaces for use are decorated, with the exception of circulation areas. There are rooms with velvet walls, ornamental glasses, tiles with abstract and concrete designs, or figurative ones with references to the Pombaline style. The climax is the gold-plated wooden surfaces of the main concert hall. Its designs were derived from pixels of amplified gold grains, granting a new effect to the material only achievable with the use of digital instruments. The ripples of pixels on the wooden surfaces also simulate the approximate pattern of sound waves.

Muslim motifs and graphics open another field of exploration for digital ornament. Arabesques have been adopted by Jean Nouvel in three design projects in the Middle East, though without the technical functionality of the diaphragms regulating the passing of light at the Arab World Institute in Paris. In Doha, Qatar, he reproduces the Agbar tower of Barcelona, but with a surface composed of octagons and squares providing a monochratic and lacy appearance. The immense flattened dome that covers the Louvre Abu Dhabi Museum is also formed by the overlapping of geometric patterns, in a complex web of Arab inspiration. The culmination of such effects is reached in the Dubai Opera, the tectonic character of which is overshadowed by the truly lacy cloud covering the building (of conventional structure, by the way). This decorative smoke emerges atmospherically, providing the building with a sense of movement and instability, a sort of antifixity index. The effect is obtained by two three-dimensional lateral blades along with layers of irregular surfaces articulated with the solid central tower, forming veils of ornamental arabesques. Filters of opacity and transparency are created by the multiformed-lacy pattern of these textures, here applied not as a contextual element, but rather, as a performative one. During the day, light penetrates from the outside, and at night, the opposite occurs, providing a visual show of lights.

Arabesques are also adopted by Herzog & de Meuron in their design for the city of flamenco, in Jerez de La Frontera. The building's boundary walls and its central tower combine Islamic-inspired designs (the basis of flamenco), with modern graphic symbolism, inspired by rock, punk, and graffiti artists' signatures. The result is an entanglement of linear and hollow elements, designed using a computer and composed of concrete structural and decorative elements. This experiment is at the origin of the large-scale solution the duo later adopted at the

Beijing National Stadium. There, structure, skin, and ornament merge into a single system. A succession of tangled and stiff wires forms a texture similar to a bird's nest or a straw basket. The building is hollow, though its interior is not visible from the outside, with only the roof wrapped by a membrane whose sole function is to protect the stands from the weather. In the "Nest," what counts is the structure itself made into a great ornament. In addition, it allows for the radiation of yellow and red lights onto the outside like a big explosion of fireworks, as in the opening of the 2008 Olympic Games.

In contrast to ornate skin stiffened in the form of a structure, architect Mark Goulthorpe executes a moving surface controlled by computers. His Aegis Hyposurface experimental project is a multifaceted deformable surface, similar to a rubber membrane, composed of articulated metal triangles that move by means of thousands of micropistons. The command is not provided directly by the machines; the surface receives stimuli captured by optical and electrical motion detectors from the movement of people, or from the levels of sound and light, interacting with them in real time. According Goulthorpe, the project "marks the transition from autoplastic space (determinate) to alloplastic (interactive, indeterminate) space."[99] The dynamic and sensorial form, adaptable to environmental stimuli, indicates one of the limits that decorative exploration of fluid surfaces and tattooed skin has reached so far.

Once again, scenographic experiences reach the limits of disappearance of the architectural artifact, as in the Blur Building by Diller & Scofidio, though these are no longer about blurring of experience, but about illusionism. Architect Toyo Ito produced a building resembling architecture of light in Yokohama, the Tower of Winds. It was built around an abandoned chimney, to which computer-controlled neon rings were fastened together with a sequence of light cannons positioned on the ground. A screen veils the metal cylinder and the neon from top to bottom. It reflects the light projected from the ground at night, simulating the existence of a real building, otherwise disappearing when internal neon lights are triggered. Similar to the mobile surface by Goulthorpe, the system reacts when externally stimulated by sound, wind, and the movement of city traffic. Lighting can remain static or pulsating, according to such interference, appearing as a sort of visual music

The Aegis Hyposurface, a digitally manipulated wall. Experimental design by Mark Goulthorpe for the Birmingham Hippodrome, England, 1999. Photograph courtesy of Mark Goulthorpe.

of the environment.[100] With the commands turned off, the building disappears abruptly. Architecture is only a skin of light, but it can be misleading. Euphoric proliferation in the use of media surfaces and digital ornaments to turn architecture into an increasingly immaterial experience can lead it to the zero degree of existence, as pure form.

THE TOURISM OF THE AURA

After observing the dematerialization of architecture and the various features it uses to multiply its symbolic reverberations within its own field, let us go back to the issue of the political economy pervading this entire process: the effective generation of rent through form and the redistribution of its extraordinary gains to a chain of agents who surf this wave of speculation—architects, construction companies, governments, entrepreneurs, property owners, computer companies, publishers, universities, hotels, travel agencies, airlines, etc. A complex system we have named "rent distribution," promoted by starchitecture and inseparable from

Tower of Winds, an illuminated, cylindrical structure mounted on an old concrete building in Yokohama, Japan, designed by Toyo Ito and Associates, 1986. Photograph by Forgemind ArchiMedia, Creative Commons CC BY 2.0.

the democratization of rent, is a mechanism of concentration, in certain agents and spaces, of socially produced surplus value.

Thus, the cycle of the architecture-image is only completed in its return to concrete materiality, when the immaterial reproducibility of brand architecture returns to its physical condition as the built object, with pilgrimages to the original work. The "rent of form" benefits from a symbiotic relationship between the copy and the original, between the image that circulates and the building as such, which attracts wealth produced socially in other territories in such a way that one stimulates the rentier's gain of the other, and vice versa.

If, as we have seen, the circulation of images maximizes the rent of the form and remunerates several intermediate agents (from publishers and photographers to all those who benefit from the consumption of the image itself), its economic achievement for entrepreneurs and the local economy becomes effective only when it attracts companies and diluting agents that are able to invest or spend funds locally. Though not entirely, a significant portion of those gains stems from tourism. As we shall see, the bonds between the seduction of the spectacular image and the buying and selling of unique experiences within tourism are closely associated.

The increase in the virtual circulation of images and information through new digital and communication technologies, contrary to what might be inferred, did not correspond to a withdrawal from the physical circulation of goods and people. According to Pierre Lévy, "the acceleration of communications is contemporaneous with an enormous growth in physical mobility. Both are part of the *same* wave of virtualization. Tourism is currently the number one global industry in terms of annual turnover."[101] In the case of tourism, people pay for the real experiences that the virtual world is not (yet) able to provide with the same level of satisfaction. In *The Age of Access,* Jeremy Rifkin states that tourism is "increasingly transforming cultural resources into paid-for personal experiences and entertainments."[102] Similar to the entertainment industry, it is an experience industry, but whose specificity is the sale of authentic and memorable experiences—which are, however, increasingly artificially produced.

The idea of authenticity is in direct relationship with the unique qualities of a place, its personality—sources, precisely, of the exploitation of its monopoly rent. In this case, the landscape, or the architecture, is what provides the actual physical basis for the sale of an "authentic experience" and its monopoly rent. And yet, one cannot say that the destiny of architecture is very different from that which other arts have to face from the moment they start being technically reproduced. That is, the producer–receiver relationship, mediated by technical objects of an increasingly massified consumption, removes its privilege of auratic distance and eliminates the reserve and reverence that cult value imposes upon those who contemplate it in its unique apparition. Dissolution of aura can only be reversed, so to speak, artificially, as Walter Benjamin explained in reference to the bastard aura of film actors—precisely the sector par excellence of the then-incipient cultural industry, in which this phenomenon of transformation of aesthetic reception took place—a radical shift increasingly observed in all realms of art, and which, in fact, is the complete expression of a historic mutation in the very perceptive structures of an entire era. Now, in the case of cinema, itself an art that was already technically produced (that is, produced to be reproduced), the issue of originality and cult relationship is not relevant. But paradoxically, it is precisely architecture, the oldest of the arts, that gives Benjamin the matrix for this relationship that was so minimally aesthetic, in the traditional sense. It was the first art of the masses, of a mass distracted by routine use. Thus, its reception, according to Benjamin, occurs more on a tactile level, on the level of habit, than on the level of concentrated and reverential attention—contemplative or optical—inherent in the experience of auratic art, such as when we look at a painting in an exhibition. If this interpretation is suitable for everyday "experience," it may not be for another type of eminently optical architectural reception, according to the seclusion model, which is that of the dumbfounded traveler in front of a renowned building—in Benjamin's characterization.[103]

In this sense, is it possible to speak about the existence of an aura inherent to monumental buildings? Is that what is perceived when observing works such as Brunelleschi's or Michelangelo's in Florence at close quarters? In this way, one could assume that the existence of the original work of architecture, and of its presence, prevents the complete dissolution of the aura of architecture after all. But, currently, the encounter with these originals hardly occurs without all the mediations to which we have referred that are part of an increasingly sophisticated and comprehensive cultural industry.

At the same time, if rent maximization occurs with the acceleration of image circulation, architecture is never purely reproducible. The original can be visited, enjoyed in its concreteness, in its place of origin—which could allow the return of repressed quality, in short, of something that at least resembles the attributes of a unique work of art. After all, one of the unavoidable specifics of architecture is its inseparability from place. On the other hand, we can wonder about the authenticity of that aura, increasingly manufactured to obtain the desired effects—among which the economic is not the least—produced through aggressive city marketing and the promotion of corporate brands. It is therefore an aura born already tainted by mercantile calculations, which, accordingly, cannot be mixed with the aura of the ancient work of art that kept a distance and a difference from the material world—a certain autonomy, even if only partial. But if the aura of media architecture is commercially produced, it is only convincing in that it mimics something endemic to artistic creation: authorial freedom, which confers upon it the necessary prestige in the market of cultural experiences, even though its protagonists are conditioned to be as creative as a marketer hunting for an idea, or a fashion designer searching for a concept, etc. It is, therefore, an empty freedom, a freedom lacking the critical and liberating potential of the great work of art. In short, it is architecture circumscribed by economic calculations, which is, in turn, the only thing able to give it social meaning.

Fabrication of the aura is not only an external act of capital with regard to architectural creation. Since the very first moments of a project, as we have seen, architecture firms are studying the visual effect of the work and its ability to attract. The paparazzi take their first pictures as soon as the building starts to emerge on-site. The spiral of images rises to a crescendo, moving from specialized magazines to the general media, including ads that adopt the buildings as backdrops for their products. Potential travelers are bombarded by photogenic images trying to attract them, acting as bait in search of money. Images of tourist destinations, as well as narratives of the experiences they offer, are crucial in the decision-making process of the contemporary tourist. According to Jan

Specht, "for an industry that sells products that can only be consumed in their own place, and that cannot be touched or tested before being bought, a reliable image at hand becomes a crucial advantage in global competition."[104] Tourists pay to see from up close, increasing the fascination caused by certain images, in order to mobilize all of their senses. As Rifkin warns, in the case of artworks and monumental buildings, they pay to have access to a trace of the aura that the unique object can convey, though they already arrive so conditioned by marketing that the experience they think they are having is also completely predetermined.

The construction of a tourist destination's brand (brand destination) is associated with repetitive symbols, collectively memorized, which become representative of each place and culture: in London, it is Big Ben or the red buses; in Paris, the Eiffel Tower; in Sydney, the Opera House; in New York, the Manhattan skyline; in Rio de Janeiro, the Sugar Loaf, and so on. Destinations "without a perceptible face, without a clear image," explains Jan Specht, "do indeed have a difficult position in global competition."[105] Hence faceless cities have the desire to build postcard places that can be recognizable worldwide. For a more sophisticated consumer, the cultural tourist, these central cities are perceived through a more complex system of images, places, and experiences, beyond their most obvious icons.

Images should present positive values that act as forces of attraction to travelers, stronger than the repulsive forces that the destination might eventually evoke (such as slums and urban violence). In this way, the images are partial and display only what arouses pleasure. They are narratives of a pacified, positive world, without conflicts—as an advertising fable, interpreted by Jean Baudrillard.[106] The photogenic imperative is thus a way to reconstruct the history of places from the perspective of the winners and their business world. The result is that the product becomes artificial and demands that certain parts of the country and the culture be turned into restricted areas, as Rifkin states, "reserved for those who can afford to pay for the privilege of experiencing someone else's culture."[107]

The defeat that the tourist industry imposes on the losers takes place on various levels, from the subordination of places, cultures, and workers, at the service of monetary subjects with (a lot of) money, to the emergence of a new leisure culture and its correspondent class (the new leisure class)—for whom work is something worthless. Tourism is a social and economic experience that has impressive affinities with rentierism and not with production. Businesses and local economies compete for tourists as a way to attract the wealth produced elsewhere in the world, proving that rent appropriation is dominant in the tourist industry. Its qualities "differ from the world of work both spatially and conceptually," explains Kevin Meethan.[108] Furthermore, Jeremy Rifkin warns, "although tourism brings money and jobs to communities and countries around the world, studies show that little of the money filters down to the mass of people living there. Most of the hotels, airlines, vacation clubs, tour companies, and chain restaurants are parts of international companies, many of whom are headquartered in a handful of world-class cities in the G-7 nations . . . Leakage for most Third World countries is generally around 55 percent, according to Lindberg."[109]

Cultural tourism of museums, concerts, and great works of architecture, in turn, is an asset of central countries through which to direct flows of rent to themselves. The "Beaubourg Effect," which preceded the "Bilbao Effect," was a pioneering initiative that favored the policy of great museums of the Mitterrand era, when culture began to be managed as if it were "the oil of France."[110] Unlike exotic tourism (of strange cultures and landscapes) that usually focuses on third-world countries, here central countries also vie for tourists to reassert their dominance in cultural production. Only cities with cultural facilities and more sophisticated programming can attract tourists who want to expand their cultural capital, including the elites of emerging peripheries.

The creative class, or class of symbolic analysts, whose importance increases in the knowledge economy,[111] has become a disputed group among cultural tourist destinations. Their investment in travel is differentiated because "the distinction between recreation and work has become blurred . . . using travel as a means of improving his or her intellectual competencies."[112] Tourists of the creative economy or, more broadly, cultural tourists are especially desired by tourist destinations because "they are motivated by the cultural benefits of the trip," "they are more educated," "spend more money," and choose their targets in search of "excellence" and not bargains.[113] Thus such tourists favor the building of brands and attributes of destinations that are able to snatch up larger shares of socially produced wealth.

It is in this context that countries, cities, and institutions vie against one another in the global tourism market, "such as in the global investment market," says Kevin Meethan. In this competition, "a dominant role is played by architecture, from historical monuments to contemporary structures," explains Jan Specht.[114] Tourism stimulated by emblematic buildings is not a recent phenomenon. What is new is its massification and management in order to obtain short-term financial and symbolic returns—today works are built with the goal of attracting tourists. Great historical monuments were not built for this purpose; rather, each, in its own way, dissolved into a long-term social and cultural experience. Current iconic works have to forge identities at high speed; their relations with the local context are fragile and artificial, constructed through marketing scams. Their magnetic effects of attraction depend on their unique and distinctive character, in a global and instantaneous dimension. Hence originality and formal complexity do not arise only from new technical and creative possibilities, but are the very deep economic base of this type of operation.

Terminals of arrival at the destination of choice are also always undergoing changes. If, in the 1980s, Marc Augé pointed out airports as examples of "nonplaces"—homogeneous spaces of global capitalism similar to shopping malls, devoid of those meanings that give sense to the experience of the place in each context[115]—today they too, like train or subway stations, are being signed by renowned architects and thereby are acquiring identities of their own, and obeying the demands of the spectacle. These are structural challenges, allegorical forms, the unusual use of colors and light, a festival of technology and formal exuberance. Look at the airports designed by Foster (Hong Kong, Beijing, and Amman), Santiago Calatrava (Bilbao and Lyon), Renzo Piano (Osaka), Richard Rogers (Madrid and Marseille), Helmut Jahn (Bangkok), Massimiliano Fuksas (Shenzen), Rafael Viñoly (Montevideo), etc.—almost all the so-called high-tech architects, unlike the luxury artisans such as Gehry, Nouvel, Christian de Portzamparc, Zaha Hadid, and Koolhaas.

Arrival terminals, with their sophisticated designs and increasingly light and bold roofs, rather than mere generic hubs that mimic malls, have become the first statement of a city's symbolic and magnetic power for those arriving there. Rogers contends, for example, that the brief of the commission for the expansion of the Shanghai Airport explicitly requested "an iconic design that reflects the importance of Shanghai in the global scene as one of the major commercial cities in the world, and the economic center currently undergoing the most rapid development."[116] Circulation infrastructure, mainly associated with the flow of tourists, has been designed with requirements for originality and formal exuberance, similar to cultural and sports buildings that attract visitors.

Whether in the brand-new terminal with its high architecture, or when arriving in front of the coveted buildings featured in photographs, visitors are inevitably in shock when in touch with the real object. But what is most curious is that the "wow factor" is programmed in such an excessive way that it may end up producing the opposite result: frustration. With such exquisite and even enhanced photographic images, as we have seen, the original sometimes suffers from inferiority in relation to the copy. As Fernando Fuão recalls, "we often see in pictures buildings that look fantastic, when in reality they are quite different and unattractive. Many are the reports of travelers who were disappointed when faced with buildings previously published in the magazines."[117] Deception is only counterbalanced because, for better or worse, one stands before the actual building, which can be traveled through, experienced, touched, and ultimately tested by the reality principle.

The Guggenheim Bilbao was able to attract a flow of about one million visitors a year, ten times more than the visits to the Guggenheim New York at the end of the 1990s. According to official data, in its first year of operation, this accounted for an increase of approximately 25 percent in the flow of tourists to the city.[118] However, evaluations of the museum's economic impact are controversial. One cannot accurately measure its participation in the increase in tourism and in consumption at hotels and restaurants, and consequently, its contribution to the increase in tax collection. Factors such as the ETA cease-fire were not evaluated, or, for example, the consequences of September 11 for global tourism as a whole. The difficulty of measuring the impact the museum generated did not prevent advertising it to the world as a success, however. Gehry, for example, calls his Guggenheim a "money machine."[119]

It was precisely its supposed success and the success of other secondary experiences that triggered the global race for iconic buildings, magnetized by money. Kurt Forster, architecture critic and juror of the megaproject for the Galicia City of Culture, said that he was convinced by Eisenman's statement: "I am imagining 'bus lines' spitting out tourists to visit the mountains . . . crowds will travel to the City of Culture, and will leave with the memory of having visited Rome or Athens—a true magnet to attract investments."[120]

But the flood of new buildings that followed, thanks to the abundance of fictitious capital circulating in the pre-2008 crisis years, caused everyone's rent to begin to fall. Hence, the fear of the copy or of the multiplication effect is induced by the very success of the experience. The snake seems to eat its own tail: the more one repeats successful practices, the lower their effects of profitability. Replicability compromises its own profitability. Reproduction of spectacular buildings and museums in dozens of cities, however different they may be, tends to destroy the qualities of scarcity required of these works in order to attract tourists. It is the same limit verified in the massification of luxury brands, because the higher their capacity to be duplicated, or even pirated, the lower their ability to generate monopoly rent.[121] Competition among cities will take place within increasingly narrower margins of return on investment in megaprojects, and many are already collecting losses.

The risk of reduction in monopoly gains resulting from the very success of the Bilbao model is noted by its supporters, such as Beatriz Plaza, who believes it is quite possible that "Bilbao loses its current advantage."[122] Researcher María Gómez shows that in 1999, the Basque government predicted a decrease of 32 percent in the value added by the museum for subsequent years.[123] The cancellation and delay in the construction of the Guggenheims in Manhattan and in Abu Dhabi, similar projects by Gehry that were even more daring than Bilbao, however, prolonged Bilbao's monopoly gains.

Peter Hall, the well-known English city planner, evaluates how the frantic race for iconic buildings led to a zero-sum game.[124] In fact, the rent in tourism generated from circulation does not produce additional value, unless secondarily, in the construction of the building itself or in the improvement of tourism infrastructure. The goal is to achieve the biggest gain with the lowest investment (which is not small at all),[125] in the race to suck the value produced elsewhere through the architectural straws of rent suction.

The saturation of gaudy works may find its market expression in minimalist magnetic projects, such as the Therme Vals by Peter Zumthor.

His Pritzker Prize coincided with the 2008–9 crisis and the supposed "end of the waste age," as Gehry himself predicted.[126] According to Jan Specht, "spectacular does not necessarily mean 'loud,' but can just as well impress in silent reticence."[127] Tourism specialized for students, architects, and architecture lovers has already been reflecting this race for the discreet, according to companies Architecttours and Pro-Viaggi Architettura.

Despite the fact that tourism of the new architectural wonders seeks monopoly gains, its dividends are distributed among various agents. If, on the one hand, it attracts and appropriates a mass of social surplus value produced in other sectors and regions, on the other, it distributes a wave of rent among a large chain of intermediaries. Accordingly, it monopolizes wealth and distributes it at the same time. Projects such as those we are analyzing produce a propagation of rent captured by agents prepared to reap the benefits of the cash flow it provides.

In this distribution, many benefit individually: the industry of tourism, transportation, property owners, local and international businesses, the media, the publishing market, universities, architecture and engineering firms, information technology, advertising companies, etc. New jobs are created, new infrastructure is built, and the symbolic capital of cities and entire regions is increased thanks to its new marks of distinction. This is what is called the synergistic effect of the signature architecture, a real window of opportunity in which everyone wins and no one apparently loses.

Governments assume the role of investors in projects such as these in order to trigger the financial boost that will benefit a portion of the local economy. The state is the decisive agent, for it bears the risks and costs of the operation, which private entrepreneurs would not take under the same conditions. This means that it is the state that pours in large amounts of resources, often canceling other less media-oriented and more socially important investments in order to assume an active role in the rentier hunt for circulating wealth. If the operation results in a loss, most of the time, the public funds bear this alone—as has been the case in several cities, even before the 2008 crisis.

As we have said, studies on the economic impact of projects planned to attract money are controversial and have come under question. The information presented by the Basque government on the impact of the

Guggenheim is favorable, of course; after all, it is the principal case of worldwide success. Accordingly, the investment costs of the museum have returned to the public coffers in four years' time through taxes, and generated in the same period (1997–2000), 485 million euros to the local GDP: a return rate of more than 20 percent, taking into account only the costs of construction. Although I am not an economist, I can verify that, in the available studies, the calculations and results are presented in a simplified manner, making it difficult to consider them correct. The investment amount is often added to the cost of the construction work only, 97 million euros, and does not compute the price of the land, the royalties paid to the Guggenheim, the mobilization of public technicians, the interest on fixed capital, the required expansion of infrastructure, etc. Construction costs aside, in the same four years, for example, the direct costs of the museum's maintenance, according to studies commissioned by the government, were 28 percent higher than the local generated GDP,[128] which means the museum provides less wealth locally than it exports (because it pays royalties and hires foreign companies for exhibitions, insurance, specialized teams, transportation, etc). This data proves the interpretation of Joseba Zulaika, who says that the museum franchise exists to generate rent, first and foremost—a deal that the president of the Basque Country made a point of announcing on Wall Street.[129] Fears of this type of investment caused other worldwide branches of the Guggenheim to be canceled.

To confirm the hypothesis that the economic impact of such works—supposedly their biggest asset—is controversial and might be negative, I analyzed another study devoted to the impact of the new Central Library in Seattle, designed by Rem Koolhaas's team and inaugurated in 2004.[130] The information obtained is also inaccurate, and at times, laughable. The dissemination of the positive economic effects to other agents is described by responses from local restaurants and hotel managers. The estimates range from an increase in sales of 40 percent to others who have seen no changes at all. The study itself acknowledges that the three years of disorder caused by the construction and the temporary displacement of the library collection affected the results of the research. However, the conclusion could not be more different: "There is a consensus that the new Central Library is an economic benefit to Downtown businesses."[131]

If the tangible effects on the economy are difficult to measure and the available data is not fully reliable, the dividends provided by the new cultural assets in terms of intangible capital, also not measurable, are taken for granted. In the case of the library, it is stated that profits from its image began "with no marketing effort." Media coverage was "extraordinarily high," not because it was one more library, but because "the physical design of the building was of primary importance." The result, according to Kate Joncas, the Downtown Seattle Association's director, is that "the greatest economic development impact of the new Central Library is the coolness factor. It makes us cool on an international stage."[132] This is an attribute that contributes to attracting not only tourists, but also the "creative class," to live and work in Seattle, favoring its reputation as a "place of thinking, learning, creativity, and innovation."[133]

If public resources are consumed with more, less, or even with no financial return, this does not prevent the Keynesian-type of multiplying effect from occurring in the activation of the economy, once many agents are remunerated with public investment. Tourists attracted by the seductive image of the new buildings will come, to a greater or lesser extent, and will benefit the economic activities of so many other agents. Even if the building brings harm to the public coffers (after all, cultural buildings should not be built to profit governments), it favors dozens of well-positioned intermediaries to capture additional gains—starting with the architects.

After all, how much does it cost to produce a *cool* attribute for a city or the new architectural brand for modern China? The price is not calculated according to the hours worked by design teams, of course. Not coincidentally, the architects are the first to be remunerated with the increase of their clients' symbolic capital, and the rent it promises to boost. Their contracts, on the order of tens of millions of dollars, are not remunerations for the value of their labor, but part of the distribution of future gains. Not by chance, many of them, especially the most professional ones, have become highly profitable companies and have been acquired by international investment funds, as we saw in Foster's case. With an eye on this type of price formation disassociated from value, the other agents involved in construction, whenever possible, want to seize a share of the future rent—taking advantage of the disproportion of these millimetrically designed works, always prone to financial imbalances borne by public funds, as we have already discussed.

By the time construction is complete and the law of labor value exits the scene, a circuit of low-flying promotional agents circulates around the building: media, photographers, publishers, exhibitions, tourist agencies, institutional public relations, etc. What is being prepared is the global launch of a magnetic image to attract wealth from all over the world and remunerate all of its intermediaries in the process. Finally, when the flow of investment and tourists begins to arrive, hotel chains, restaurants, aviation companies, real-estate investors, in addition to cultural companies that run the show, begin to reap their rewards.

This often speaks to imponderable results, without exact calculation, of controversial measurement, depending on both local and international injunctions. The novelty effect may dry up or lose exclusivity; disaffected local groups or separatist-terrorist attacks (from ETA, for example) may even affect investments. On the other hand, international flows of capital and tourists might suddenly change according to economic cycles and the herd movements of investors. Instability and unpredictability become the rule. The architecture of rent is thus a risky operation given its speculative character.

In times of economic growth, there is a swelling of rent, natural to the domain of forms of fictitious capital, whose territorial materiality is expressed in the architecture of the spectacle. During times of crisis, the speculative rent balloon may deflate, as has happened in Dubai. In one year, the price of the city's real-estate properties fell 50 percent. In November 2009, Dubai World, a real-estate and infrastructure investment conglomerate and the country's wealthiest company, declared a debt moratorium on its $60 billion in liabilities.[134] With empty hotels and airports, investors accumulating losses, workers dismissed and repatriated, the crisis in Dubai produced a process of boomerang reversal of rentier gains.

Finally, the rent distribution we speak of here seems to be the opposite of the social policies of income distribution. In our case, it is concentrating, electing agents to benefit and others to lose. Before grabbing the rent, works of architecture that are sponsored by the government grab public funds, and prioritize some investments to the detriment of others. Not coincidentally, the shift toward policies of city spectacular-ization through iconic speculative works occurred simultaneously with the reduction of social policies and the reversal of rent distribution in favor of workers.

Otília Arantes, referring to the Great Projects of the Mitterrand era, associated architecture's "will to monumentalize" with the crisis of the welfare state and the increase in social disparities resulting from the financialization of the economy. According to the hypothesis of the author, "the greater the gap between the political reform program and its effective implementation, the greater the space for rhetorical-monumental entertainment."[135] Thus the formalism of this simulated architecture would not be a transient aberration, but rather the develop-ment of a process of form and image autonomization in relation to the effective contents (the social reforms), which are then concealed. In the conservative offensive, for example, no more social housing is built as part of the public welfare program—a program that is invisible to the current dominant architecture field.

In this reverse income distribution, what is seen is the capture of social surplus in favor of certain well-positioned agents. They are specific hotel groups,[136] airlines and tourism companies, builders, real-estate entrepreneurs, speculative investors, almost all of them of international-ized capital. On the other hand, portions of the population that depend on different public policies other than pyrotechnical investments may find themselves in a fragile situation with fewer resources allocated to them. If they are residents in the vicinity of the construction, they can still be targets for eviction and removal, either by the police or by the market, in the latter case owing to the rising prices of land and rent.

The increase in the value of property surrounding these projects is one of the most expected consequences, even if not fully measurable and predictable (once again)—because the investments are concentrated in one place rather than scattered throughout the city. Large cultural buildings have served as anchors for processes of urban renewal and the replacement of populations in degraded neighborhoods, at least since the early 1980s.[137] They are bait to attract higher-income groups and investors who are interested in the surrounding area. In any given city, these grand projects are often concentrated in the same region to favor the visualization of the urban transformation (in terms of real estate and iconicity). It is about the strategy of building new centralities or clusters of attractions close to each other. In Bilbao, the old industrial district of Abondaibarra, on the banks of the Nervion River, has become its new center, connecting cultural buildings (the Guggenheim, the Museum of Fine Arts, the Opera House, and the University of Deusto), government buildings (the Palace of the Congress), and new business and trade centers.

In São Paulo, in 2008, for example, Herzog & de Meuron were hired to design a cultural building that gathers dance rooms, an opera, and ballet and music schools to add to the city's cultural cluster in the Luz region (already including the Sala São Paulo concert hall, the Pinacoteca do Estado museum, the Memorial da Resistência cultural center housed in the former Department of Political and Social Order (DOPS), and the Museum of the Portuguese Language), and to where the headquarters of the São Paulo state government and some of its secretariats would move. The development is close to so-called Crackland (Cracolândia), a region that was being renovated under the marketing name of "Nova Luz" (New Light), with the goal of attracting information technology companies and universities through fiscal incentives.[138] Although the Herzog & de Meuron building is conceived as a plaza on various levels in which the cultural equipment is arranged, the ground floor is controlled by turnstiles, and the main access to concert spaces is accessible through an intimidating monumental ramp, or through paid parking lots, for those arriving by car. The result, despite the most generous aims of the architects, is an architecture that segregates and chooses its audience of interest. As stated by the then secretary of culture, João Sayad, "we are afraid of making a building open to the city, like in the European style, afraid that drug addicts in the area will take up the spaces; maybe we should build a castle."[139] The project was suspended judicially, the architects were required to return the more than $10 million they had received, and the secretary of culture was convicted for irregular hiring, without public tender or bid.

In the project of the City of Music in Rio de Janeiro, by French architect Christian de Portzamparc, winner of the 1994 Pritzker Prize, the mega-investment was not associated with a renovation of central areas, but with adding value to the most dynamic area of the real-estate market of the city: the neighborhood of Barra da Tijuca. There, one mostly finds gated communities, shopping malls, and apartment build-ings with balconies, in the best Miami style. Barra is a neighborhood devoid of urban landmarks, monuments, and historic buildings when compared to the rest of the city. It was with the intention of marking it as a distinctive architectural icon of international prestige that the mayor and the architect justified their choice of place. Ana Paula Pontes, archi-tect with the Portzamparc team, comments that to legitimize the invest-ment they asserted that "important cities such as Rio must always show signs of vitality, and projects such as this reaffirm, worldwide, that Rio is alive and cosmopolitan."[140] In his press release on the project, Port-zamparc strives for grandiloquent rhetoric: "The City of Music must have strong personality and great visibility; it must be magnetic, attrac-tive. It must be conceived as an urban symbol. An equivalent of the Arc de Triomphe and the Eiffel Tower in Paris or the Brandenburg Gate in Berlin."[141] The truth is that the work is a huge operation of rent con-centration in an already upscale neighborhood, where new real-estate developments abound. The work began in 2003 but was completed four years behind schedule, costing approximately $250 million.[142]

Once again, the same sequence of agents is remunerated, almost all of them considered creative—those who capture the distributed rent—while the population as a whole continues to be penalized by the weak-ening of policies for social protection, health, and education. After all, they are not part of the spectacle, and rentier gains arising from cultural tourism dispense with these subjects, except in the subaltern condition of the service industry (receptionists, waiters, housekeepers, security guards, drivers, janitors, etc.) or still in the miserable work of building these monumental works.

Not only them, but also entire cities and regions are completely excluded from this type of business, although they sometimes contrib-ute with migrant construction workers. These are third-world cities, without protected access areas for the cultural experiences available to tourism, cities that are more characterized as a planet of favelas, without the resources to sweeten a magical world at the tourists' disposal. Viewed on a global scale, this distribution-concentration of rent is even more perverse. Only a few cities compete with each other, while others sink in an ocean of hardship, in which basic issues of sanitation and housing are far from being resolved.

RENT, INTEREST, AND FETISH

In characterizing the society of the spectacle as the advanced stage of capitalism in which all things had turned into representation, Guy Debord was pointing precisely to the autonomization of images in relation to social praxis. At the same time, "lived reality suffers the material assaults of the spectacle's mechanisms of contemplation, incorporating the spectacular order and lending that order positive support."[143] Images dissociate themselves from life and return to it as if they were the real world. It is about a tautological movement in which the means get mixed up with the ends, an operation of the maximum breadth of the conditions of existence by a second, immaterial, separated, but integrated reality. The term "spectacle" had already been adopted by Benjamin to define the aestheticization of politics as the central practice of fascism. Debord, however, completes the argument by defining spectacle not only as the manifestation of totalitarian regimes, but of capital itself. In its most well-known definition: "Spectacle is capital accumulated to the point that it becomes images."[144]

The description that came to be generalized since the 1970s is that we would go through a transition from modernity to so-called postmodernity—and a corresponding transition from the centrality of an economic logic of production to one of circulation and consumption. The ability to accurately control form and image is therefore a decisive element. Thus, we are witnessing the dizzying inflation of design. This is "the practical extension of the system of exchange value to the whole domain of signs, forms, and objects . . . in the name of design," says Baudrillard. Image and product can circulate as one single thing: product-image as a sign of exchange value.[145] According to Hal Foster, in these conditions the product is no longer an object, but a piece of data to be manipulated.[146]

This transformation is contemporaneous with the expansion of financialization as a global hegemonic phenomenon. This is when the logic of fictitious capital takes over the command of real productive forces. Time and forms of interest-bearing capital are imposed upon others and serve as the new measure. On the one hand, time is projected forward, with interests dictatorially commanding the expectation of future profits and decisions of the present. On the other hand, the money-form is no longer articulated with its content, disengaging itself from its foundation. Capital wants to disengage from labor and institute total domination with no subjects.

Regarding commodity production, as this is still what we are discussing, the expansion of the logic of interest-bearing capital over all other spheres of economy and culture is expressed through an autonomization of meaning in relation to the hard materiality of commodities. In the production of commodities, the rationality of fictitious capital is expressed by the exchange of an imaginary product (like "brand name" or "experience") for money—that is, the transformation into capital of what originally was not. In its financial form, this is the possibility that capital finds to increase its value, disengaging from the hard materiality of products.

What we are witnessing is an advanced manifestation of commodity fetishism, for it is not only the separation between product and producer, but also between the real product and its image as an imaginary product—which begins to circulate and to be valued with autonomy. Fetish in its first manifestation, commodity fetishism, is the separation between the act of producing and the product, the autonomization of the product in relation to the producer. The enchantment of the commodity, which seems to have been born of its own initiative, denying its origin, is a first abstraction. The fetish of the first degree is associated with the formation of value in the production of commodities, tangible goods that crystallize the energy of physical labor.

Now fetishism in the society of the spectacle goes beyond this initial alienation, it is a form of autonomization of property and its representation. This abstraction is no longer internal to the commodity, as in the first case, but appears as an external force. In the fetishism of financial capital, money seems to generate more money, despite production and labor, as if value were born of circulation itself. This abstraction begins to overdetermine its productive forms, as a more finished form of exploitation. At that moment the fetish finds its "pure form" and "carries no scar, no mark of its birth."[147]

It can be said that an automation of the image occurs in a similar manner in relation to the object. Image also becomes a financial asset, like rent that acquires a figuration. As Debord says, "The spectacle is another facet of money, which is the abstract general equivalent of all commodities ... The spectacle is money for contemplation only, for here the totality of use has already been bartered for the totality of abstract representation."[148]

If the first fetish was still bound to the production of value and to the world of Prometheus—that is, the release of productive forces, the "fire of labour," which licks inanimate matters awakening them[149]—for the fetish in its most advanced form, the kingdom of Midas (or Gehry's kingdom) prevails: everything that money touches shines as its image and at the same time dehumanizes itself, because the process of accumulation means detaching from its foundations.

In the production of culture, and in the case of architecture, the passage from one type of fetishism to another has important consequences. Fredric Jameson points to a "radical difference between that structural role of abstraction in postmodernism and the kinds of abstractions at work in what we now call modernism, or, if you prefer, the various modernisms."[150] Postmodern abstraction is associated with a financialization that finds real-estate speculation and its rents, in the sphere of the production of the space, as the closely linked equivalent of interest-bearing capital. The problem posed by Jameson is to define the new mediations between the financial/rentier economy and cultural inflation, taking into account the specifics of architecture.

Commodity fetishism, in architecture criticism, is truly taboo and taken on by few. I believe we owe to Brazilian architect Sérgio Ferro the most forceful interpretation of this real interdiction in his essay "O canteiro e o desenho" (Design and Construction Site, in a free literal translation).[151] The difficulty is in defining architecture as a fusion between art and commodity, as a protagonist in the production of value. The critique of the commodity fetish in the production of architecture has allowed us to glimpse a hitherto hidden space: the construction site. The design-construction site contradiction, which is at the basis of the separation between producers and their product, is the motto of Sérgio Ferro's criticism, which we will discuss in chapters 2 and 3.

Ferro also notes that the change in the nature of the fetish finds the criticism of the producer's alienation insufficient to explain contemporary production. Modern utopias, according to him, adeptly or poorly, have always been constructive and in line with the advancement of the industry and engineering. Architectural designs of today, however, scoff at conventional constructive precepts with their aberrations: jumbled wefts, non-Euclidean geometries, sloping pillars, oblique curves, irregular volumes, and cascades of random shapes. A bottomless pit of formal autonomy that finds, in the new technological tools of design, the possibility of transferring the artistic gesture into a viable productive process on the construction site. Designing on the computer increases its potency and enables figures previously unfeasible with a ruler and compass. Architecture tends toward the sculptural, and the image of the finished work becomes a media event.

In this context, there is an exacerbation of formalism, a rehabilitation of the frivolous, a predominance of the signifier over the signified, and finally, we are faced with an architecture in which the futile assumes metaphysical proportions.[152] Formal jugglings converted into an advertising apotheosis give rise to a tectonic no longer related to the human scale and the static equilibrium of the objects. According to Peter Fuller, it is about a "constant stream of advertising images which, as Sontag has suggested, appear almost more real than reality itself," giving "the impression of a physical world in which things have been dematerialized or reduced to surfaces."[153] The design of commodities, from the simplest objects to the most complex buildings, goes through an expansion of the aesthetics of appearance, of ever more sophisticated and flashy packagings and skins, as an "*obscene* flat kingdom of surfaces," in Otília Arantes's expression, in which a mere provocation of the image melts away any constructive purpose.

The economic foundation for these metamorphoses in the field of iconic architecture is, above all, the search for what we are naming the "rent of form." That is, the use of architecture to obtain monopolistic gains, derived from the attraction provided by its unique and impressing forms. In these works, the visual effect, noisy in a Gehry or quieter in a Zumthor, heavy in a Siza or light in a Herzog & de Meuron, cool in a Koolhaas or high-tech in a Foster, must be able to generate the "wow factor," that is, the ability to impress, attract the observer, and make him or her retain that unique architectural object in his or her memory. The identification of the work with certain intangible attributes guarantees the alchemical capacity to convey, through large inert objects permanently attached to the ground, immaterial values to cities, governments, and corporations. This is how iconic architecture collaborates to increase symbolic and economic capital for its entrepreneurs and beneficiaries, along with increasing their competitive advantages.

It is a mode of monopoly rent similar to that of the art market, of tourism, and of the valuation of brands, as we have seen.[154] What is being sold is not the product, but the concept and experience it provides. It can be paid for directly (by visitors purchasing the entrance ticket or by public and private funds paying for the promise of future income arising from the project), or indirectly, to the extent that the forms circulate and attract businesses related to the icons they represent. They impact the publishing market and the tourism industry, attract investors, increase the value of land and tax collection, collaborate to forge identities and even to expand the ability to generate fictitious capital for companies, cities, and countries in the sales of their stocks and bonds.

For the operation to be successful, in the case of public works (but not exclusively), the building should not only be designed according to the requirements for a good form of rent, but must also correspond to a strategy that articulates local and international interests. In this way, iconic works are often part of strategic urban planning, which defines public policies according to the criteria of business governance. Governments start to bet on works and investments that have rates of return at least equivalent to the cost of the interest-bearing capital, in a conception of public action that is increasingly financialized.[155]

The rent of form, in this context, appears as yet another automation of property and its representation. As in capital fetishism, its image seems to generate more money, regardless of production and of labor, as if value were born of the circulation itself. The buildings seem to disconnect from the ground and from the work that gave rise to them, like balloons—hence the constant disposition of the most rewarded architects to bring architecture to a zero degree of existence, to pure form. However, such total dematerialization is not possible as it is in other branches of the culture industry and knowledge economy. Therefore, an interpretation of the political economy of architecture restores its material foundations and shows that the production of this rent is still based, directly or indirectly, on the production of space by labor.

In the next two chapters, we will investigate the productive forces behind this immaterial architecture in an attempt to explain how it is produced. However, we must acknowledge that the main gains, which drive the entrepreneurs of the works we are analyzing, come from rent—as appropriation of the surplus value produced in other sectors. Its buildings function as magnets that attract wealth generated elsewhere, which is appropriated as remuneration for its unique properties. Hence, the production of value starts to be conditioned by this external logic.

The agents who dominate and control the process of execution of these works are not construction companies or real-estate developers strictly speaking. Those who commission architectural works for the star system—almost always the same governments, cultural institutions, and private corporations—are in search of the valuation of their brands. That is, they do not seek to obtain dividends directly from the immediate process of production (though they still depend on it, even to account for the immense amount of work deposited in their treasuries, as we shall see). Their interest is directed at the gains derived from the very exhibition of the architectural form, as a corporeal manifestation capable of expressing intangible values, concepts, identities, and attributes to which they want to be linked—and, at the same time, to attract tourists and investors.

In the cases we are analyzing—unlike in the production directed at the conventional housing market—land rent, or location rent, is not the main renumeration, although the mechanism of private leeching of social wealth might be similar. The works analyzed (museums, spas, hotels, designer stores, corporate headquarters, stadiums, concert halls, etc.) favor the rents that are not immediately derived from the increase in the price of land, as is the case of traditional real-estate development. They are almost always indifferent to the land laws of each city, even in the case of private works, because they are approved as exceptions, according to the competitions that gave rise to them, owing to the lobbies in favor of the development, or for being part of strategic plans fostering these exceptional projects. Their gains, therefore, are not constrained or limited by the land-use regulation of each city. These works seem to hover over these factors of production, like speculative investments passing through several stock exchanges without any concern for the frameworks conditioning the productive system of each country.

They obtain their monopoly gains in a differentiated segment of the real-estate market, and their processes of appreciation are equally different. Iconic architecture is required when the desire is to produce baits to attract foreign currency and intangible gains for brands and cities, for that is the only way to generate this sort of special urban phenomenon. These are buildings with monopolistic qualities intrinsic to the form, not dependent on the place they are located, like an artwork, but without properly being one (though aspiring to it). This is a type of rent generation derived from the imagistic power of the built form, unreachable (or even undesirable) by ordinary mercantile real-estate products still attached to the land—though increasingly financialized by mortgages and investment funds.

Even if works by Gehry, Herzog, Koolhaas, or Foster can land in any city that pays for them, these works do not literally hover in the air but are, in fact, inserted into specific urban contexts, many of them awaiting the side effects of real-estate renovation in degraded or impoverished areas. The great majority of these works are already commissioned with the goal of generating a wave of land appreciation (or of reverse rent distribution, as we have described) of major consequence for the structure of the area and for real-estate gains in its immediate and extended surroundings. In this sense, if, at its limit, the rent of form can dispense with place, it cannot escape from it, inasmuch as it becomes effective only as a built work. This is the only way it distributes its dividends to certain agents well placed to capture those gains where spectacular architecture lands.

Similarly, these works are not literally immaterial images, as their physical dissolution into increasingly ethereal surfaces might imply. Cyberspace still has no substitute for the concreteness of the built work, and this concreteness remains as residue and truth of a valuation that wants to dissociate from work and social praxis. As we shall see in the next chapters, it is from the intersecting cracks in the contradiction between material production and immaterial valuation that one can perceive the meaning of the social production of space by starchitecture in the digital-financial age.

2

PROGRAMMED DESIGN

WHAT ARE THE TECHNICAL AND MATERIAL BASES that permit the design and execution of branded architecture's irregular volumes and formless surfaces? What new instruments are harnessed to deal with the complex geometries that boost rent? Which abstractions will the act of design suffer under the cybernetic turn? What are architects morphing into, and what are the limits of their creations? Finally, what are the main transformations seen in productive forces and relations of production in the starchitecture of the digital age?

In this chapter and the next, we will enter into the sphere of production—first, as we investigate what has changed in design and its techniques so we can then analyze how design takes physical shape at the construction site. We will see how architects, draftsmen, and construction workers acquire new (or old) responsibilities, which obliges each of them, in their own particular way, to partially redefine relationships, hierarchies, and skills.

The transformations we will now discuss cannot be attributed to one single factor, such as the digitization of design, but stem rather from a set of more or less simultaneous events: the rise of the system of accumulation dominated by finance and rent; the networking and flexible accumulation of post-Fordist production with changes in the working world; the collapse of the socialist bloc; the welfare crisis and increase in social inequalities; new forms of U.S. hegemony; the spread of new digital and information technologies; the consolidation of an epistemological shift in science, linguistics, and philosophy, and so on. Thus, even though our focus is initially on the digitization of design, it will be contextualized, whenever possible, through the relationships it establishes with other factors.

AN UNFEASIBLE WORK OF ARCHITECTURE AT THE HEART OF ADVANCED CAPITALISM?

The Berlin Wall fell in 1989. Since then, Western architecture has sought to construct new icons of global capitalism (now unopposed). That very same year, the Walt Disney Corporation, not coincidentally one of the most powerful machines for producing visual and discursive pro-systemic meanings, hired Frank Gehry to design a building that was supposed to be the most innovative in American architecture, located in Los Angeles: the Walt Disney Concert Hall. This was also a building that could finally provide a "civic identity"[1] for the capital of the entertainment industry, the fastest growing metropolis in the advanced industrial world.

This proved to be a civic identity whose democratic principle lasted for just a short time. Urban uprisings, already frequent in the polarized and racially charged city of Los Angeles, broke out again in 1992 and led Gehry to alter the design. It would no longer have a covered courtyard accessible to the public, which the architect called "the city's living room," but would be enclosed like a fortress. The result is a building whose defensive character leads one to interpret its steel armor as an urban shield. According to Diane Ghirardo, the Disney Concert Hall became a design entrenched against possible urban revolt, in deference to middle-class paranoia.[2]

This paranoia was built into the city itself by real-estate developers, as Mike Davis has explained: "the *eutopic* (literally no-place) logic of their subdivisions, in sterilized sites stripped bare of nature and history . . . repackaging myth (the good life in the suburbs) . . . [and] also pandering to a new, burgeoning fear of the city."[3] The "fortress effect" of the Disney Concert Hall is therefore in line with the history of that damaged metropolis, contrary to the architect's recurring claims that he designs for democracy and liberal American values.[4] The works of Gehry in Los Angeles, says Mike Davis, are "powerful metaphors for the retreat from the street and the introversion of space that characterized the design backlash against the urban insurrections."[5]

However, my point here is not to judge the close relationships between the new monuments of starchitecture and their brokerage by the ruling classes in order to trigger, by means of large works, processes of urban renewal and the expansion of social control. The focus, rather, is on how Frank Gehry's design for the Walt Disney Concert Hall poses a new problem for the architecture and construction industries in the United States: the iconic building initially proved to be unbuildable. What's more, at that point in the development of productive forces in the construction industry, the building of a new urban identity was unrepresentable in a drawing, and was impossible to properly calculate and budget for. It was rejected by firms and construction companies as unfeasible.

The urban landscape's "Disneyfication," as Sharon Zukin calls it—a form of a "symbolic economy based on media, real estate, and artistic display"[6]—here reached its limit from the point of view of its material base: the challenge seemed greater than the objective conditions of architectural production. It was part of Disney's business to create fanciful shapes, but when they emerged from movie screens and into concrete reality, the animation effects must pass the test of constructability. Gehry said that he received inspiration for his composition from the dancing forms of Disney cartoons, but in architecture, images require tectonics.

In 1989, Gehry's office had only two computers, one for word processing and another for accounting.[7] The drawings were still all done by hand (as described in the next section). It was a complex project and the architects and engineers contracted for the construction drawings ended up refusing to finish the project, thus avoiding technical and professional liability. The questions they all posed were "How do we build this, from what materials and systems?"[8] When the drawings were 85 percent finished, the team realized that they could not be successfully completed with traditional methods.[9] The estimators had difficulties predicting costs and ended up overestimating them.

Gehry's spectacular architecture, whose surprising forms could express the new age of the American and world economy, had met its material limitations. Victory in the competition proved that the project was accepted on subjective conditions, but the objective conditions for the building's construction were still not at the center of advanced capitalism in the mid-1990s.

Gehry's team itself went out in search of solutions, as we shall see, until the project was able to be represented, calculated, budgeted, built, and finally inaugurated in 2003. The impasse described here caused a somersault of starchitecture in the digital world. This was a world in which Gehry Partners was one of the major "agents of innovation,"[10] associated with large software, hardware, civil and military construction companies, and financed by public and private funds.

The apologetic narrative describes Gehry's rise as a major case of technological success in architecture. It is about the transformation of an architect-craftsman with links to the California counterculture and Pop Art artists and sculptors into today's top *digital master builder*,[11] with a first-class portfolio of clients in government, art institutions, the entertainment industry, hotels, and universities. Our purpose is to find, behind this fireworks display, a story whose unbiased meaning shows

Sketch by Frank Gehry of the Walt Disney Concert Hall, May 1991. Courtesy of Gehry Partners, LLP.

evidence of the real changes taking place. As we shall see, not only did Gehry's office expand tenfold in order to spread its fluid, unstable, and metallic forms across the world, but he also expanded his business to become a software developer with the creation of Gehry Technologies.[12]

Our route in this chapter is to follow the thread of the Gehry Partners office, which will eventually lead us to Peter Eisenman, who seems to have gone furthest in automating the creation process, using the computer as a decisive agent in defining design features, almost entirely diluting authorship, and in the end proposing an automation of morphogenesis.

THE DRAWING SITE

Sérgio Ferro has thoroughly examined the notion of the "separate design" as a system of information and transmission of external orders imposed on workers at the construction site.[13] A decisive historical transition took place in modernity when the unity between the drawing and the construction site was broken, in the transition from the simple cooperation of craft guilds to manufacturing governed by a heteronomous force. It is at this point that the architect was emancipated from the construction site, following the trend of division between intellectual and manual labor, and became increasingly closer to those with power and money. From then on, workers underwent a progressive loss of knowledge and influence over the means and ends of production. This decisive fracture was inaugurated during the Renaissance when the scientific system of coding and representing architecture was created—inaugurated by Filippo Brunelleschi and largely preserved over the following centuries, having received improvements through subsequent treatises, the most famous of which being Gaspard Monge's descriptive geometry in the nineteenth century.[14]

The externalization of knowledge by agents specifically assigned to concentrate it was, at the same time, a sign of "progress—no one can doubt it," as Sérgio Ferro recognizes.[15] On one side, as drawing entered into the relations of production, abstracting (separating, distancing) the worker from his knowledge and relative self-determination—the work itself became abstract. Commanded by a heteronomous design-destiny, this disqualification of individual knowledge occurred in association with artistic and technical progress in architecture, and not with its regression. As Giulio Carlo Argan explains, the dome of Santa Maria del Fiore was a "clamorous technical-formal novelty," a project that inaugurated modern spatiality.[16] Or, in Manfredo Tafuri's interpretation, Brunelleschi produced "an autonomous and absolute architectural object, destined to intervene in the city's structures and change its meanings. A symbolic and constructive self-sufficiency of the new spatiality, giving it a value of rational order."[17]

Thanks to the abstraction that gave rise to it, the dome itself had become a "giant perspective machine" capable of representing spatiality in its totality. Abstraction thus produced a double movement: alienation from work and the development of productive, technical, and artistic forces. From the standpoint of capital accumulation, the abstraction of the drawing in relation to the construction site is the path required for the extraction of surplus value, in a manner similar to any other drawing for the production of goods. It is up to the separate design to provide ligature, to serve as the mold and measure for the heteronomous work to be coagulated into an object, thus becoming more of a mold than a form. The drawing, as an instrument for the command of capital, reunites, in a forced whole, the parceled workers into the "collective labor" that, when set in motion, adds value to capital.

The combination of techniques of production and of domination, singular to capitalism, is more openly perceived at building construction sites than in heavy industry, maintains Ferro, because the absence of mechanical mediation allows one to see clearly the arbitrary command of exploitation. The specificity of the division of labor in construction entails, therefore, unrelenting violence and instability in a sector that should theoretically seek stability and the accumulation of experience and knowledge. In turn, in the absence of distances imposed by the mechanization of industry, other distances are established, again through drawing: "architectural mediation" (formalism, play of volumes, textures) and the erasure of the marks of the production process, especially through the camouflage of coverings and claddings ("whose secret is to make the concrete work abstract").[18]

It is in the design/construction site contradiction that the "separate design," even at the center of the intellectual work, reveals its handicraft: the manual production of the drawing with the aid of various instruments. Similar to workers at the construction site, architects, engineers, and draftsmen are subdivided into specialties and layers of professionalization, which together create a typical collective laborer in manufacturing.[19] The artisan's skill is fractured and inserted into the division of labor that separates the professional from a portion of their knowledge. Without taking part in the decisions made a priori that shape the project, most professionals design fragments of the product. These are drawings of electrical and hydraulic installations, structures and foundations, landscapes, retaining walls, details of all kinds, or even the standardization of lettering and stamps. Only the chief architect and his immediate associates, who control and coordinate the partial work of conception and representation, have a complete idea of what is being executed—they are the definers, together with their clients, of the architectural "parti."

Before moving forward toward the world of the digital drawing, let us examine how design presentation boards were previously hand-made—an experience of practical knowledge that is no longer part of the architect's university training, nor the imaginary of the computer-assisted design (CAD) generation—despite the fact that the entire operative language of conventional design software is still based on the practice of the drawing board.

If the starting point of the design, as Ferro states, was once the "artist's loose hand movements," the "tortured line in a drawing competition," it was then followed by technical and methodical graphic representation: "the line without deviation, accurate angles, the sharp meter, black on white."[20] The artisanal craft of board preparation was a miniature construction site, a physical experience with materials, of rigorous control of body movements and drawing instruments. All architects had to go through this experience, to varying degrees and depths, occupying different positions within the process. This "choreography" of rhythms and gestures that was the manufacturing of architectural drawings has been almost entirely replaced by drawing on the computer, which has established a new relationship with the body of the draftsman, less elaborate and convoluted, and more repetitive: myriad mouse clicks and keyboard commands on CAD.

The perfection and cleanliness of this work became another sort of violence internal to norms of representation, which was often aimed at the apprentice or draftsman—the linemen of design. Similar to the claddings' artisan, described by Ferro, who with "his trained hand, light with the load of so much wisdom, caresses, until polished, the surface on which he disappears,"[21] the draftsman could also not leave any vestige of his presence. The draftman's is the amputated hand, skilled nonetheless, of the world of drawing. Any trace, although contained and precise, still retained the mark of manual skill, in the framing of the drawing, in the options of the "flavors" and graphics of the boards, in the care of the trace, in the colorful shades in which drawing artisans recognized their own styles, even if muted. The skilled draftsman transformed mere instruction boards into detailed graphic objects, whose artisinal quality expressed the constructive geometry of the very architecture represented by them.

On the drawing board, the architect-draftsman worked with tools, chemicals, and papers.[22] The rule of measurement and trace was given by rulers, set squares, compasses, and the architect's scale. The drawing pens, cleaned after the last drawing, had their mechanisms checked and their ink refilled. Before starting the drawing on the tracing paper—the basis for future blueprints—the board was verified for stability, cleanliness, that the cables of the parallel ruler were stretched for alignment, and that the connections of the old drafting machine were adjusted. Tracing paper, thanks to its transparency, was superimposed onto another drawing, which was then redrawn. The practice of redrawing was carried out successively: in the early stages with pencil on a more simple and rough parchment paper, and then on the tracing paper, until the final presentation could be made on a sheet of greater weight and resistance (such as a Schoeller, for example).

Positioned on a white table, the tracing paper was then cleaned with a cotton swab soaked in benzene so that the oiliness of the hand did not produce areas impermeable to the Naquin ink. Benzene was often retraced onto rulers, and even onto the paper itself, when the hand inadvertently touched beyond the passage of the squares and the ruler. The light hand should not touch the paper, and it should always be impeccably clean. Pens with specific widths were used for each different line thickness and then replaced with care. The stroke should be uniform, always with the pen strictly perpendicular and with the same pressure throughout the process to avoid irregularities and the formation of ink bubbles. Tiny Nankin ink bubbles would generally arise at line intersections or careless stopping points of the pen after slipping; they had to be avoided and wiped, as they are slow to dry and could potentially blur the drawing. The most careful draftsmen used to draw the corners beforehand using a finer pen in order to surround the area in which the ink from the thicker pen would be contained, without overflowing.

After each stroke, one needed to wait long enough for it to dry so that the parallel rule and square could slide over without producing ink traces. The drawing was planned in such way that the rule would always slide in the same direction, while lines continued to dry. Nonstandard angles required the use of mobile squares regulated by a protractor with a threaded portion, nicknamed the "alligator." Before the invention of this instrument and even after, the most orthodox designers used loose squares, larger or smaller, in order to construct each angle manually, with the aid of the protractor. Circles and their sections were traced using compasses with pens fixed to an end, and the dry point positioned with care not to pierce the sheet or slide. Templates were used for drawing circles with small and standardized radii. Curves composed of segments of circles and more complex organic forms were designed with a different template called the French curve. Lines without geometric ruling, such as contour lines, required the firm hand of the draftsman, or the use of flexible rulers guiding the trace of the drawing pen.

Hatches could be made one by one by slightly displacing the squares, or else using expensive Letraset decals, a translucent sheet containing hatches, designs, symbols, and printed letters to be applied graphically. Irregular shapes such as trees, human-scale figures, and cars were stamped onto the drawing using wood blocks dampened in ink pads. Lettering and annotation were made using a stencil, the "spiders," or templates for each drawing scale—another delicate craft to avoid smudges. The old "spiders" slid one of their dry-tipped pens onto the low relief of carved letters of any of the several possible rulers chosen according to the desired font and size, while the other leg carried the technical drawing pen that executed the line, also in the chosen width, compatible with the font size of the letter to be drawn.

Colored areas were used to highlight portions of the drawing, made by masking sections with adhesive tape and then dispersing a substance, either shoe polish applied with cotton or oil pastel evenly spread on the back of tracing paper using cotton soaked in solvent. These areas were made with special color pens; nonetheless, their execution was likewise meticulous in order to hide the overlapping of paint layers or the paint direction. Also, both board margins and stamps were objects of the draftsman's design. In the case of stamps, their layout, readability, and graphic quality were highly valued. Offices with their own logo had it drawn or stamped on all of their boards.

The care given to this whole process was also a consequence of the tiring work of correcting a simple mistake. In black ink, a mistake could not be easily erased with an eraser. The line or smudge would be removed by gently scraping the paper with a razor blade in different directions. The paper damaged by the blade had to then be smoothed out with the use of special erasers. Depending on the weight of the paper, the scratch of the blade was often visible on the tracing paper, but disappeared in the copy.

At the end of this whole choreography, there was the original, which received a final cleansing with benzene and was then archived. From it, blueprints were made, which were produced on paper sensitive to certain light spectra, and developed in an ammonia-based solution. The result was a blueish, reddish, or black reproduction, sometimes with little contrast in the case of older machines, which gave off a terrible odor. All workers executing such reproductions, usually in basement workshops with little ventilation, were exposed to ammonia toxicity.

When copies were returned for revision, the original was again attacked by the razor blade, sometimes to the point of tearing it. Hence, various offices would prefer to use graphite, even for the final drawings. Pencil drawing with mechanical pencils of different gauges also required special techniques. Despite the ease of correcting mistakes with an eraser, and not having to wait for ink to dry, the necessary care to avoid grime and the way of sliding the rulers and keeping them clean were similar. There was added difficulty owing to the fact that graphite, when making a stroke on tracing paper, drops a powder that adheres to the back of the hand and rulers, which needed to be constantly cleaned to avoid smudging the paper. Moreover, graphite was irregularly polished at its tip during drawing, which needed to be carefully observed so that the lines did not become unbalanced. The mechanical pencil also had to be wielded in an upright position, so the width of the whole line corresponded to the chosen gauge.

Scale change in manual drawings also demanded new exercises. In the case of regular, orthogonal drawings, each measure was transposed onto the new drawing by means of the architect's scale. But when the base was irregular, such as in the contour lines of a piece of land or even in an irregular perimeter, the entire drawing had to be graded using a square grid and each line segment transposed onto the grid of the new scale. This was possible to do with the help of another device, the pantograph scale.

Three-dimensional drawings were almost exclusively axonometric projections, which were simpler than perspectives with one or more vanishing points, whose depth distortion is complex to realize to scale and unnecessary in technical drawing representations for service orders. · In an axonometric projection, the floor plan is projected obliquely by means of parallel lines, drawn point by point through sliding the set squares. Another challenge here was handling instruments so that the ink didn't smudge. The projection of shading in an axonometric elevation was also complex, the filling of which was done by the color masks technique.

Perspectives with vanishing points could be ruled geometrically or freely and artistically. In the first case, all techniques for transferring measurements, by means of compasses, with the use of set squares, required a complex exercise of descriptive precision. In free perspectives, both for study and for presentation, architects and draftsmen could emphasize certain aspects of the design, with small optical distortions, or through the use of elements and focuses of attention in the drawing. Colors were also used freely, usually with watercolor. Freehand drawing could also show the uses intended by the designer, according to the way groups of people and their activities, shaded areas, trees, landscapes, and horizons were drawn. Perspectives, because they were more laborious, were limited in number and sought specific points of view to be pictured. The construction of the environment through perspective drawing was handicraft work by architects and draftsmen as well.

Wooden models were also part of the design craft. They provided the architect physical contact with his or her design, as a built artifact. In its execution, some geometric principles of composition and even structural performance could be verified. In the case of models, and even for office archiving for later display, sobriety and neutrality were a must—with the exception of those made for client presentation, which were often more realistic and colorful. The chosen woods were usually thin sheets of plywood or balsa wood, as they are light and easy to cut. Massive blocks, however, could also be cut by mechanized saws, such as a jigsaw. Hacksaws, files, and craft knifes were used for cutting wooden plates and sheets after all of the parts were gridded. Cut pieces were checked and sanded, sometimes using different sandpaper thicknesses, until the wood was even and smooth to the touch. Pieces were then carefully assembled with adhesives or with fittings. In the case of wood glues, which have a strong toxic odor, they would be precisely spread so that they didn't seep out of the contact points. The finished models were kept in raw wood or protected with a coat of sealant or matte varnish, or even painted white, with all the care that this required. The main offices had teams of model makers, and rooms with workbenches and machines to execute them. Similar to what used to happen with drawings, however, all architects, at some point in their training, to varying degrees and depths, had to learn the craft of making models. As we will see, models, like drawings, are now "automated" through laser cutting or even through complete digital execution using 3-D printers.

In this way, the drawing encompasses the construction site, in that there is intellectual and manual labor, either unified in the figure of the architect-craftsman or in the manufactured form of production of design projects as in the case of larger architecture offices in which a more advanced division of labor takes place. The product obtained, however, is not an end in itself, as is the case with the work of an artist. It is a means, an instruction for the execution of the final object: the constructed building. The set of blueprints, models, and perspectives, however, does not fail to be a commodity—even before architecture becomes the building. The use value of this commodity-drawing is the instruction and command of the separate work of transforming matter into built artifact.

Because this type of work does not entail design instructions for mass production, as in the case of heavy industry, requirements for accuracy and automation are lower. Architectural design analyzes each unique case so as to boost the developers' gains—extracted from the surplus value of the work and through the appropriation of rent—be they related to land, real-estate development, or the form of rent we are investigating in this book, the "rent of form." Therefore, the archaic drawing site for the development of architectural drawings is not some kind of irrationality within the circuit of capital accumulation in the production of cities. The artisanal execution of drawing is suited to the demand of maximum appreciation of each new design project, which requires that research be conducted on the most appropriate building type for extracting from each parcel of land the maximum wealth, whether in the form of rent, profit, or interest. This does not, however, prevent the drawing from entering the digital age in search of additional gains.

THE DIGITAL DRAWING BOARD AND THE CLICK OF THE MOUSE

Recent metamorphoses in drawing have enabled changes in the mode of representation to stimulate transformations in the mode of design and in the results obtained by the new buildings of starchitects. If the so-to-speak artisanal nature of design remained almost the same for five hundred years since the emergence of the "separate design" in the Renaissance period, it has been changing in increasingly greater breadth and depth over the last two decades. Its geometric, instrumental, and technical representational limitations were, at the same time, limitations of the possibilities of design conception. As we shall see, changes in architectural drawings' mode of production in the digital age, associated with broader changes in the capitalist regime of accumulation, in technology, and in materials, will allow for changes in the productive forces in the field of architecture, aiming at boosting rentiers' gains. There is a rupture in the "consulate of representation" in the moment it is incorporated in the cybernetic turn, that is, in the passage from form to information, in its purely operational nature.[23]

The introduction of computers into the drawing of architecture as of the 1980s produced changes in two ways, initially in the practice of representation and then in buildings' possibilities of design, calculation, and construction. Although both modifications are interrelated, for analytic purposes we will discuss the changes produced in representation techniques, in which the Euclidean paradigm in geometry and the Mongean paradigm in the decoupage of the architectural object (floor plan, section, and elevation) were kept. In what follows, we will examine how the computer has changed morphogenesis itself, allowing, through vectors and algorithms, the creation of complex architectural forms hitherto unimaginable, ideologically supported by the epistemological shift represented by complexity theory and by modifications in the dominant forms of capital reproduction.

Programming technology for interactive graphical computer interfaces dates back to the 1960s, when the first principles of computer-assisted design, or CAD, were created.[24] This technology was originally adopted by major industries (such as the aerospace and automotive industries), which benefited from the accuracy of information in order to integrate design and execution through automated machines, while software development was being conducted in partnership with research centers at American universities, before becoming commercially viable. The first CAD software for personal computers adopted by design offices—and not just in industrial environments—began to be sold in 1982. There was not a specific software for architecture and construction, which, lagging behind in technological innovation, adopted programs from other sectors of industrial production in simplified and two-dimensional versions. Thus, CAD programs used for architectural design functioned as nonspecific digital drawing boards qualified to execute general technical drawings.

Since then, the continuous, dull murmur of the mouse and keyboard clicks quickly spread within architectural firms: low-cost peripherals were generalized as main input devices, in place of expensive digitizing pads. The old atelier increasingly resembled a data-processing company, or even the desktops of financial market operators. Offices underwent a kind of sterilization, with boards almost always clean and desks populated with computers. In the click of a mouse, as a repetitive motion, there is an atrophy of the architect-draftsman's gesture, even causing new work-related diseases. The drawing position is static and the eye is constantly required to find lines and points not always clearly distinguishable on the screen.

Conventional architectural CAD is the digital version of what used to be done by hand, so it does not deeply change the previous design rationale, but rather the means of obtaining graphic representations by partially automating them. That is, it brings cybernetic advantages without qualitatively changing the existing relations of production. Its goal is to "free the designer from the repetitive, tedious, and time-consuming tasks . . . of manual drawing."[25] Conventional CAD, here designated as a digital drawing board in order to highlight its simultaneous change and continuity, remains the software used (legally or illegally) in almost all architecture firms and schools. Chief among these products has been AutoCAD from Autodesk Company, with a share (in 2003) of about 70 percent of the architecture software market.[26] Its number of licenses grew exponentially in less than a decade, going from fifty thousand units in 1986 to 1.3 million in 1995, reflecting the rapid spread of digital drawing technology, accompanied by a fall in computer prices.[27]

Let us look at some of the computer-assisted architectural drawing's advances.[28] The drawing of lines is clearly dissociated from the movement of the pen and ink accompanied by rulers and compasses. The geometry of the drawing, even if still Euclidean, is built through commands, keyboard shortcuts, or mouse clicks. It creates a vocabulary specific to digital drawing, in English, which becomes the only CAD user language. There are commands to execute parallel, perpendicular, and oblique lines, angles and sizes are typed, and any point is coordinated by the same relationship of angle and distance of translation, rotation, and reflection operations, thus eliminating the architect's scales and protractors that once accompanied the draftsman at every stroke. Aspects of the drawing that entail repetition or symmetry can be composed through multiplying or mirroring the original element.

Drawings are made one by one, as on the conventional drawing board. Graphic patterns are conventional, but are now inserted digitally and with high precision. The tools are the same, but all of them are virtual: pens of all widths, color pencils, hatches, solids, transparencies, gradations, pantones, blocks. They can be used with relative ease, allowing the person to try options such as cut-and-paste, stretch, reverse, overlay, copy, paint, erase, undo, multiply, print, redesign over, incorporate external images, insert text, quantify and size (linear, area, and volumetric), set parameters, calculate, etc.

Cleaning the drawing is no longer an obsession as it was for the draftsman. Deleting lines or even undoing or redoing the last drawing operations are actions performed through one or two commands. Entering texts with the desired size and font also eliminates the suffering of the stencil. Hatches and colored masks are made by outlining the polygon to be highlighted. Types of strokes (dashed, dashed dot, dotted), which were part of the skill and practice of the draftsman, are standardized line type patterns in CAD, as are thicknesses. Stamps are applied to a model board, after which you only need to change the number and title for each drawing. Human figures, trees, and furniture are all inserted through drawing blocks taken from a virtual library, which can also be created by the CAD operator. Change in scale is performed by a simple on-screen zoom, or through an indication on the print command. No more scaling and redoing the drawing manually in order to study it at different scales.

The main change introduced by CAD is the layers of drawing. Either by overlapping or separating groups of elements, the layers allow the draftsperson to filter, isolate, and regroup them according to what he or she wishes to highlight in each drawing (structure, masonry, roofing, facilities, etc.). The drawing accumulates layers upon layers, as if these were sheets of tracing paper, but which can be linked together or separated in order to alter any of them, which is a procedure that makes verification and coordination among various designers and their designs easier. Their communications now spare the exchange of paper, because drawing files are sent and received through the Internet. The drawing that returns is then added as one or more layers to the base file for verification, and then displayed on the specific construction boards.

The "originals," drawings in the form of bytes, are stored digitally and can be deployed when any correction, revision, or reproduction is needed. Printing is done at a print shop, sometimes the same one that used to do the old blueprints and which now has large plotters. Final copies are no longer bluish and smelly, but clean and high contrast. Their appearance, however, as a prescribed code of service at the construction site, is very similar to the handmade artisanal board.

Perspectives have also undergone partial automation. Axonometric elevations can be drawn with the same CAD program. Yet, particularly since the second half of the 1990s, perspectives with vanishing points and other graphic elements, such as colors, textures, and lighting, have been created in commercial three-dimensional modeling programs. After the basic modeling of volumes, made with meshed structures, the rendering is made—including the application of the desired qualities on each surface, such as textures, colors, opacities, and transparencies. Ambience is also added with three-dimensional blocks of furniture, focused spotlights, shading, and brightness. Unlike the manual approach, in which an a priori choice of focus defined the entire image construction, view angles can be chosen by changing the viewpoint. Now, with the computer, one can analyze the design from various angles, including in motion, simulating a trajectory. When the perspective is produced for clients or for dissemination, it usually acquires an increasingly greater mediatic and spectacular effect.

Physical models have also undergone changes in their manufacturing process. Not only do most offices increasingly outsource them, but they also, since the 1990s, have relied on laser-cutting machines to cut their parts. The information is directly transmitted from digital drawing files to the cutting machine, in a process similar to the production of numerical control machines, which we will cover in the next chapter. The model maker has to glue the parts based on the assembly map, and complete the finishing. More recently, and with larger investments, it is

The London studio of Foster + Partners. Photograph courtesy of and copyright Nigel Young/Foster + Partners.

Studio of Gehry Partners, LLP in Los Angeles. Courtesy of Gehry Partners, LLP.

also possible to execute the entire model on computers, using special stereolithography machines. These are 3-D printers based on the use of liquid polymers that solidify when exposed to laser beams.[29] These machines, which have been used for more than twenty years to execute industrial mockups, are increasingly common in large architecture offices and schools, thus releasing architects and students from hands-on work in order to have a physical model of their digital designs.[30] Hardened polymer provides artificial tectonics, which is no longer experimentally tested by the architect during the production of the model. Here there is an evident loss of tactile and relational knowledge regarding design and constructive choices. The model automatically generated by the machine with its thousands of laser pulses no longer provides any parallel with the work experience needed to generate that form, even as a reduced model transcribed to other materials.

The design knowledge that used to pass through the hands of architects is becoming increasingly automated, and will advance to the point of questioning the strictly human dimension of the act of design, as we shall see in the coming sections. The unity between the head and the hand in the creation of the architect has changed with the introduction of machines and is limited to more restricted time periods than before, when architects used to execute, as craftsmen, their design-commodity.

Richard Sennett wonders whether these "fractured skills" historically associated with the architect's practice won't bring unstructured consequences to the discipline. According to him, one must "addresses what gets lost mentally when screen work replaces physical drawing."[31] As he states, "drawing in bricks by hand, tedious though the process is, prompts the designer to think about their materiality, to engage with their solidity as against the blank, unmarked space on paper of a window."[32] In technical drawings, perspectives, and models, all increasingly automated, there is a practice that decouples from materiality, in a "disconnection between simulation and reality," notes Sennett, as much as from the experience of the craftsman's skill, which once brought the architect closer to the working world, and in some way to the very experience of work at the jobsite, to which he once organically belonged.[33]

Often operated by newly graduated architects and draftsman with no construction experience, CAD drawing broadens the separation between the logic of jobsite production and that of digital representation. The way to inform the design is different, mainly through zooming in and out, overlapping scales, and information commands. The dive of the zoom into the empty space of the screen, the observation of the design through fragments (such as under a microscope) sometimes disorients and hinders apprehension of the whole. On a drawing sheet fastened to a drawing board, representation is produced and understood as a small, complete narrative, even when partial (a section, an elevation). The drawing emerges from the paper in its constructive logic, delimitation of axes, structural bearing points, main alignments, etc. In CAD, the same drawing contains several layers and several scales, which usually results in some excessively informed areas and others with gaps (often owing to acceleration and reduction of design time). The drawing process happens nonlinearly, through fragments, comings and goings, like pieces of a puzzle—exhibiting a similarity to the postmodern fragmentation of language itself.

At the same time, this software cannot be fetishized. It was programmed by professionals and companies, which define certain parameters that guide the design practice. They are the ones who decide what the possible operations are, or are not, that architects and CAD operators will have at their disposal. In this sense, the software overlays a heteronomous layer on the architect's design deliberations. Or, if not heteronomous, its autonomy is restricted to solutions that have already been foreseen. MIT professor and CAD expert William Mitchell makes the point of stating that the "software is in fact a deeply conservative force. One tends to think of it as a liberating tool, but mostly it is anything but."[34] This is because one cannot ignore the commercial logic that drives the development of the software: "you privilege those practices and you marginalize other practices simply by making the ones that you support with software much more efficient, much faster, much easier; so, you introduce this kind of distinction between the practices . . . reinforced by another kind of dynamic commercial software."[35]

Some architecture offices have begun to produce their own programs[36] and have even set up software companies, such as Gehry's. At Carnegie Mellon University, Ulrich Fleming adopts the pedagogy of opening design software together with his architecture students to show that "the program is a crafted artifact like many other crafted artifacts that can be crafted well (or less well). Given that, I would suggest that the only software worth using is one that you can program, that you can customize."[37] Would that be a regressive way of understanding the software industry or the path toward what Sennett has defined as a challenge to modern society: "how to think like craftsmen in making good use of technology?"[38]

The fact is that we are facing a new moment in the abstraction of architectural design and construction work. Again, it is a contradictory abstraction, with simultaneous progression and regression. Digital design, by increasingly distancing itself from the artisanal vestige of material making, approaches the notion of design as "ideation," as *cosa mentale,* without physical restraints. The act of design thus reduces its drawing gestures in order to focus on "programming" sequences of instructions—first to the machine and then to builders. In this way, design detaches itself from its material analog to advance what is inherently most essential to it: prescription. In this sense, the computer, as the architect's instrument, increases the power of command, allowing drawings to become more precise, rigorous, and ultimately, more fully determined as work orders, without breaches.

We must also assess the capital gains arising from the introduction of CAD. In offices, computer-assisted design promotes time saving and increased productivity. The introduction of machines and software, as in other sectors, represents a change in the composition of organic capital and in the very process of production. Offices invest more in tools available to designers: instead of rulers and pens, now computers, printers, and programs. The increase in fixed capital (machines and software) corresponds to a decrease in variable capital. From capital's point of view, saving time means reducing the number of employees while changes occur in their specific skills. This is the effect of automation, which affects various sectors, particularly banking.[39]

The architect's class situation, whether self-employed, employer, or employee, is not directly modified with the introduction of the computer, but can change with the overall reorganization of the sector. The growth of studio-businesses, increasingly computerized and productive, might imply a reduction in the feasibility of small studios of self-employed architects, and hence an increase in wage relations. At the same time, the possibility of outsourcing CAD drawings over the Internet has allowed for the hiring of virtual draftspersons in various parts of the globe. This is an increasingly widespread form of precarious labor relations, as the overseas/offshore hiring of third-world CAD promotes a general lowering of remuneration for these professionals.[40] Associated with low union membership and the loss of craft skills, there is a symbolic break in the profession's aura, at least for those who have become the "info-proletariat."[41] In the United States, young architects who sell their labor power in this way call themselves, in a self-deprecating manner, "CAD monkeys."[42] Psychic and motor consequences are studied. As neurologist Frank R. Wilson stated when visiting a workplace, "They were young, talented, educated, motivated, healthy and physically active, vigilant and self-critical, etc. What was wrong? My answer: eaten up by the machine; complete loss of autonomy. They weren't artists and designers anymore; as far as the company was concerned, they were computer operators."[43]

With automation, the software industry has become an increasingly important element in the economics of architectural design. According to French architect Bernard Cache, "building software is also part of the business in this field."[44] Its license (in the range of thousands of dollars)—which has to be paid per machine for the use of each program, many of which must be renewed annually and with periodic updated versions—is a form of rentier gain. The license controls access to patented software and acts as a fence to protect the knowledge stored within. In this way, "knowledge rent" maintains some similarities with land ownership rent: it is a form of monopoly rent.[45]

In 2007, revenue from the commercialization of CAD software was $5.23 billion, with a growth of 15 to 20 percent in previous years. There were 5.3 million users worldwide, 63 percent using two-dimensional programs and 37 percent three-dimensional ones.[46] Nevertheless, sales of three-dimensional programs were significantly higher (53 percent of the total), which demonstrates a lucrative and growing market.

Piracy affects this sector on a large scale. A report by the company SolidWorks highlights differentiated regional dynamics: while piracy in the United States is between 10 and 15 percent, in India it can reach 70 percent, and in China and Russia, 90 percent.[47] According to Autodesk information, about 50 percent of machines use pirated programs.[48] However, Autodesk itself has partly benefited from this piracy because the widespread use of its file formats (dwg, dxf, rvt), even if illegal, at offices of all sizes, construction companies, output shops, and by both students and professionals has garnered it the largest share of the market, because it is network-dependent on the same software to transmit open data.

There does not seem to be any free CAD software with programming open for users.[49] The dozens of "free" versions, leased for a limited period of time, or as bait for people to purchase the paid and enhanced versions, are obviously not free software. There is no version of AutoCAD for Linux by Autodesk, for instance, in a deliberate policy to boycott the free operating system and Windows competitor.

STEEL FLOWERS ARE BORN

Let us now return to our main character, Frank Gehry, and his journey to construct the spectacular forms of the Walt Disney Concert Hall. The official version tells us that, dissatisfied with the collapse of the Los Angeles project, Gehry and his team started researching, together with software companies, for ways to execute his sculptures—and certainly not with conventional CAD programs. The first failed attempt was conducted with the Massachusetts Institute of Technology. The resulting three-dimensional modeling program used triangles to build surfaces, which displeased Gehry, who wanted smooth and continuous surfaces.[50]

Looking for alternatives in industry at large, the team came across software called CATIA (Computer Aided Three-Dimensional Interactive Application), made by the French company Dessault Systèmes, which in the late 1980s was already a leader in the automotive and aircraft industry market.[51] CATIA was developed by Dessault in the late 1970s for the production of military jets and became one of the most successful softwares for three-dimensional industrial projects. The 1988 commercial version three of CATIA allowed for parametric drawing of irregular forms using smooth continuous membranes, as Gehry wanted, built from Bezier curves and algorithmic surfaces. CATIA adopted the IBM UNIX platform and, given its success in several leading industries, it entered a joint venture with IBM in 1992.

Just in case, Gehry's team first tested the program on a huge metallic sculpture rather than on a building. The sculpture in question was the "Fish," located at the entrance of Barcelona's Olympic Village, completed in 1991.[52] Their choice was not accidental: what the office wanted to test was the computer's performance in assisting with the description and calculation of complex geometries, nothing more.[53] The sculpture was the best test because it allowed for an evaluation of the constructability of an irregular surface and its support structures without concerns regarding its use, facilities, environmental comfort, and so on. This experience was emblematic of the architecture to come.

The "Fish" project was fully executed in a 3-D model using CATIA, and all the coordinates for cutting the parts were transmitted paperlessly, through computer numerical control machines (CNCs) to an Italian workshop. Jim Glymph, the head of execution and Gehry's associate, stayed in the factory at Permasteelisa until his computer, which ran the CATIA platform, had transferred its database to machines executing the laser parts. Taken to Barcelona, they were assembled in a few weeks, while the rest of the Olympic village's conventional steel construction suffered from delays and the reworking of metallic elements.[54]

Glymph characterizes this successful experience as a "paradigm shift" in several senses: the design was able accommodate geometric complexity; it was completed within the planned budget and time frame; it initiated a new process of design documentation; the direct collaboration with the Italian workshop avoided the common dissociation between architect and manufacturer.[55] Its application to other buildings was immediate, first, at the Nationale Nederlanden in Prague, and soon after, at the Guggenheim Museum Bilbao, which confirmed the success of the venture.[56] After the inauguration of Bilbao in 1997, and with the embarrassment of American construction companies for having been

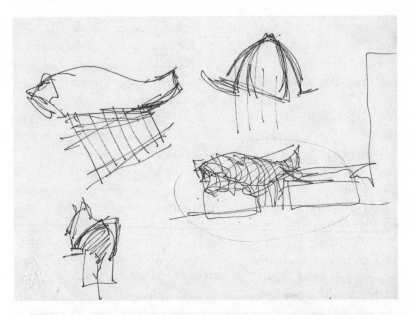

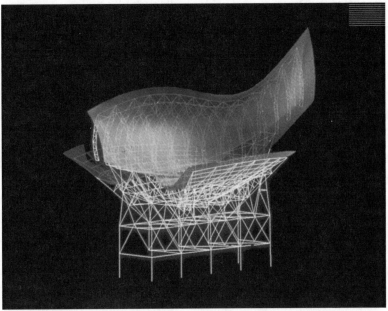

Sketches by Frank Gehry for sculpture at Vila Olímpica in Barcelona and digital model of sculpture at Vila Olímpica made with CATIA software, 1991. Courtesy of Gehry Partners, LLP.

left behind by Basque and French companies, the construction of the Walt Disney Concert Hall could finally begin (and was completed in 2003).

Let us look at the stages of the design project in order for the steel flowers to finally come into existence.[57] Because at that time Gehry's works still arose from handmade physical models using cardboard, aluminum sheets, acetate, modeling clay, and rubber rims, they needed to be transferred to the computers. To do so, there are two procedures. In less complex forms, the model is gridded, and a lazer-digitizing arm reads its intersection points. In more complex ones, the model needs to be scanned by a device similar to a medical CT scanner.

Since the 1980s, the introduction of organic, complex non-Euclidean forms into the virtual environment, modeled after existing physical objects, was one of the challenges of the film and gaming industries. It was no accident that architecture magazines began to interview animation developers in order to know what techniques and software they were using to build their virtual realities. In a 1993 issue of *Architectural Design*, Mark Dippe, the special-effects assistant director for *Terminator 2*, directed by James Cameron (the director of *Avatar*), explains the virtual morphogenesis of the silver android. According to Dippe, "it is no longer about anachronistic 'special-effects,' but 'real' images . . . of a hyperreality."[58] The procedure of scanning the actor's body by means of a reticle and the production of the android's smooth continuous surfaces in three-dimensional software is very similar to the one carried out by Gehry's office. The android, when defeated, is liquefied, and its metal, when melting, generates amorphous forms, similar to those produced by the architect in his buildings. Around this time, the software made for the film and gaming industries started to be adopted by some architectural firms that wanted to develop increasingly bold and spectacular volumetric forms.

However, structural and logistical concerns, not at all an issue in the virtual reality of film and games, required consideration. That is why cutting-edge architects had to do research on digital design environments of heavy industry, looking for programs that included calculation, parametric description, and building information of complex parts—so-called CAD/CAM programs—which are able to transpose design into computer-assisted manufacturing. A similarity regarding the design matrix was found with the aeronautical and naval industries, which produce objects with smooth and complex surfaces stiffened by ribbed structures that can be mimicked in architecture.[59] These industries produce complex, large, and expensive artifacts on a nonmassive industrial scale (unlike the automotive industry), which allows points of contact with architectural production, not only regarding 3-D modeling software, but also, as we shall see in the next chapter, with shipbuilding laborers starting to work at construction sites.

Once Gehry's physical models are scanned, surfaces begin to be parametrically ruled by CATIA. With the help of a programmer, the computer defines NURBS (Non-Uniform Rational Basis Splines) surfaces, which are continuous, soft, and deformable meshes, like a virtual rubber plate.[60] All intersections of this grid are geometrically coordinated, allowing their description to be stored in a parametric database. Three-dimensional shapes are then unfolded into two dimensions to be examined in terms of assembly, and then returned to the physical model format, now made with laser-cut pieces. This simulated transformation of the amorphous shell into two-dimensional polygons is a test to verify how these complex curvatures unfold using the CNC machines in final building construction. Ultimately, it is similar to designing patterns for cutting clothes.

The next step is deepening the three-dimensional virtual model, associated with a relational database. The design is completely developed in this model, which is not only a three-dimensional representation, but a simulation through which one can access the building output, including the temporal dimension of the life cycle: architectural design, engineering, construction stages and processes, even the building operation and its systems after the project is complete. All the elements inserted therein are parametric so as to guide quantification, budgeting, cutting, and assembling parts.

In Gehry's projects, the initial and decisive step is the detailing of irregular covering surfaces and their support structures.[61] The "skin," with all its folds, is studied by means of Gaussian analysis, which dyes the NURBS surface using different colors according to the intensity of curvature and the critical deformations it undergoes at each point. This allows for segmentation into polygons, each one having minor deformations to avoid the complexity of a double curvature in a single piece.

Under the "skin," the subsequent layers are studied—their rigidity and support, tightness and insulation—by means of a hidden metallic structure, which may be more conventional, with elements composed of straight sections, such as in Bilbao or the Disney Concert Hall, or less so, through curved ribs, like the hull of a ship or a plane, as in the Seattle project. Studies of loads and structural behavior are then conducted, including simulations of wind and snow, as well as cost analysis and the feasibility of fabrication, which may, at times, demand simplification of the more exuberant forms, until the shell's model is consolidated. As the interior of the building starts to be developed, 1:1 mock-ups are made in order to test materials, impact resistance, and exposure to weather and fire.

Subsequent definitions of the design are largely conditioned by the architect's intended surface effect. Alterations made to the covering as a result of the building program or of the installations are possible, but are avoided so as to ensure the integrity of the structural envelope. Besides the calculation and design of the structure and its three-dimensional representation, studies of the architecture and installation are conducted simultaneously, supplying the very same model online, which is then manipulated digitally by designers. Coordination of the project also occurs within three-dimensional virtual reality, so much so that problems of interference and incompatibilities between complementary designs can be more easily detected than in a two-dimensional drawings conference, or even between layers of conventional CAD. The three-dimensional model itself already shows areas of conflict, in which there is geometrical interference with the system and its envelopes in relation to others.

Because external designers and construction companies are not typically using the same three-dimensional environment as innovation agents, there is a reciprocal tension between conservative dispositions and change. On the one hand, they are pressured to acquire the most modern programs, thus promoting a software replacement ripple effect. Architectural firms, in turn, begin to internalize most of their projects—including the integration of structual and mechanical systems—and to increase in size in order to boost their digital platform, as happened in Gehry's office and the offices of other starchitects. On the other hand, conventional agents press for three-dimensional information to be unfolded in traditional two-dimensional CAD representation, which ends up happening fairly frequently, as Dennis Shelden recognizes.[62]

Another innovation stimulated and appropriated by Gehry's team, based on the software developed by Disney Imagineering with the Center for Integrated Facility Engineering at Stanford University, was visualization over time of three-dimensional models, the so-called fourth dimension.[63] Thus it became possible to simulate and analyze the sequence of construction phases on-site, their progression, and possible conflicts over time. The information obtained from this analysis began to inform the construction schedule, the coordination of the construction crews, and the right moment to order parts and materials so they arrive at the site "just-in-time."

The virtual model, now multidimensional, allows for building performance analysis, which Chris Luebkeman, CEO of the engineering company Arup Associates, has called the "fifth dimension."[64] This means going from the stage of mere representation to the stage of simulation. In performance studies, a broad range of simulations can test various aspects of the system: cost variations, energy efficiency, solar radiation and gains, wind flow and internal ventilation, optimization of mechanical systems (air conditioning, elevators, etc.), acoustic analysis, and fire management (behavior of materials, columns of smoke, and even simulation of flight reaction in the event of panic). Arup, which performs structural calculations and performance analysis for many starchitects' design projects, and which is always up-to-date on software, adopts an expanded model that includes environmental elements (air quality, sanitation, use of soil, transportation, cultural heritage, legal regulations), societal elements (public facilities, access, inclusion, comfort, safety), economic elements (viability, productivity of the occupied building, social costs and benefits, jobs, competitive effects), as well as natural resources (materials, water, energy, waste).[65]

Gehry's office has been acknowledged as pioneering the use of the multidimensional model for information management in architecture.[66] This complex model should not be mistaken for a mere three-dimensional rendering. Developed in the last decade by the commercial software industry under the name of Building Information Modeling (BIM), it was aimed at the construction industry. With BIM, project documents can be fed all types of useful information, including in non-graphic formats such as databases.[67] Working with this model means a qualitative change in design practice, which is no longer focused on drafting drawings (whether manually or digitally) to achieve a new treatment of information. All project elements are now coordinated and associated with small data packets based on their attributes. In this way, design becomes a large multidimensional and relational database, concomitantly graphic, mathematical, and textual. It can be accessed and manipulated cumulatively by the various agents engaged in the network of design and construction processes. The development of an information system is also a way to reduce the risks involved in the construction industry, an area whose difficulties in planning, coordination, and predictability are notorious.

While Gehry's team experimentally traced the course of multi-dimensional modeling to respond to challenges in the 1990s, the software industry, from then on, began to commercially develop the BIM system in order to sell a predetermined package of operations to other architects. If one cannot confirm that Gehry paved the way for the new business, which made his spectacular works possible with similar digital tools, he certainly became one of its main promoters. Gains from the new frontier of knowledge that opened up to civil engineering were immediately exploited by almost all software companies in the field (Autodesk, Revit, Graphisoft, ArchiCAD, VectorWorks, and Bentley), which started to develop BIM programs with the goal of achieving extraordinary gains.[68] As Jon Pittman, Autodesk's vice president, recognizes, "as designers through building information modeling provide more extensive, complete, and actionable data to the building enterprise, they should get paid for it."[69]

Like any other wave of innovation, BIM technology starts at the top, first being used in major capitals, until it is fully disseminated. In 2006, only 16 percent of design offices in the United States affiliated with the AIA (American Institute of Architects) used BIM technology, but 50 percent of the offices with revenues over five million a year adopted the system.[70] In 2006, the National Institute of Building Sciences in the United States initiated the process of developing national standardization parameters, the National Building Information Modeling Standard,[71] an international reference that can equally serve as the basis of assessment for environmental and performance certification.[72]

The growing digitization of architecture firms means that a substantial part of their turnover is invested in machines and programs. Since megafirms started to invest a huge amount in constant capital, it has become increasingly difficult to compete with them. Technological innovation is accompanied by a trend of monopolistic concentration in signature architecture firms or corporate-real-estate architecture.

Staying ahead in the use of new softwares also requires that programmers are able to use them to their full potential—and these people are more expensive than the abundant CAD operators. Pressure is put on universities to update their curricula and train qualified young designers, and, on the other hand, BIM operators are being sought in the Global South.[73] Another limitation for the expansion of new technology lies in the fact that until the entire chain of projects and works is integrated with the new information management model—and for that it needs to increase the profits of all agents—the lowest common denominator prevails, that is, conventional CAD programs.

The moment the articulation of all of a project's agents and information in a hyperreality is possible, the architect completes his or her transformation from archaic draftsman to programmer—intellectual work in a pure state, without any trace of motor memory, because the computer, as has been said, is "inherently a tool for the *mind*—not the hands."[74] The architect will manipulate data and no longer pens, real or virtual, circulating like a flow of information between designers and builders, between design and execution machines. Here is another step toward the abstraction of the act of design, in which ideation increasingly becomes technological programming, and, so to speak, antihistorical, as Giulio Carlo Argan predicted.[75] From the architect-programmer, one expects a "new objectivity," scientific and technological, separating him or her from roles, now retrograde, hitherto attributed to the intellectual, in which one used to recognize the very personification of a critical elaboration of reality. Thus, it is up to this new configuration of intellectual work, at the limit, as Manfredo Tafuri has already said, to "plan its own demise."[76]

At the same time, the architect is a special kind of programmer; he or she is not a technologist *stricto sensu*. The knowledge he or she

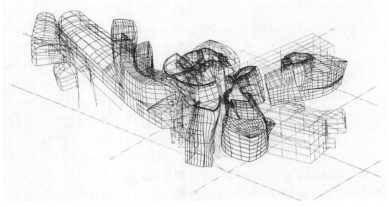

Sketches by Frank Gehry and digital model of the Guggenheim Museum Bilbao, 1993–97. Courtesy of Gehry Partners, LLP.

mobilizes and the information produced differs from computer science. As a "meaning broker"[77] or "symbolic analyst,"[78] the architect's programming involves creating cultural values with economic importance. This activity is similar to that of other producers of material and entertainment culture, such as designers, stylists, animation directors, advertisers, and so on. In this sense, the architect takes part in the creation of new lucrative forms from a priveleged position.

The possibility of concentrating information and creativity into a unique design-based/virtual model that gathers all stakeholders puts the chief programmer in a position of control over other programmers. In the face of the fragmentation of specialists' partial knowledge, one assumes that only the architect could take on the role of unification, thanks to his or her generalist and multidisciplinary training. The architect thus regains the status of master builder in the digital age,[79] regaining power over the act of building, as Brunelleschi did in his time. In this case, the most successful architect-programmers would be raised to the level of construction CEOs, while others would inhabit the underworld of data typists, the CAD- or BIM-"monkeys."

New software allows for the centralization of information and for the fragmentation and dispersion of workers, in a manner more powerful than before—including geographically, as we have seen. Its net effect is hierarchical as there is a chain of command in programming. Initial decisions made by a few will determine how all parceled agents will relate in the virtual environment of design modeling. The instantaneous power of the model allows the central head to always keep informed and updated in order to make decisions.

If there is progress in new technology, it is necessary to see its meaning and direction. Innovations, as usually occur in capitalism, are concentrated in the most profitable sectors—in the case of the construction industry, these lie in the construction of corporate and iconic buildings in competitions between cities. These are projects that promise extraordinary gains, not only in their construction, but in the form of additional rents—and that is why they attract such innovation. And even though the software is used by companies that produce mass housing, its format aims at increasing the profitability of the process more than the architectural qualities or benefits to urban conditions.

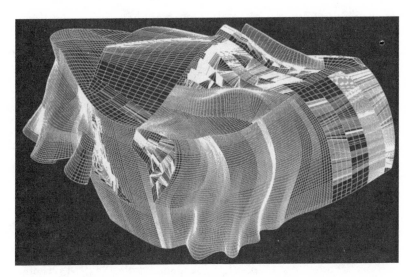

Digital model of the Experience Music Project in Seattle, designed by Frank Gehry, 1995–2000. Courtesy of Gehry Partners, LLP.

It would be interesting, in turn, to verify what possible uses—and transformations—new modeling technologies would have in works that are not entirely commercial, designed in the public sector by cooperatives or self-organized groups. In this case, the gains in design capacity could be directed toward the expansion of use value rather than capital gain. On the other hand, because virtual modeling allows for the simultaneous and networked operation of designers, rather than reinforcing the project manager's control and the designers' precarity as info-proletarians, it could promote, in a different context, horizontal and freely associated work, perhaps of craftsmen of the new economy, to use Sennett's expression.

The field of design's intense development in productive forces did not happen in the direction of the opening and democratization of these forces—which could have occurred—but rather it concentrated them according to business management models and strengthened their control on the construction site. Not only was there a gap between the pace of innovation in the field of design and in that of construction, owing to the manual laborer's continued working at low wages to curb investment in fixed capital, there was also a steep increase in the heterogeneity of the worker executing the task. The contradictions between design and production in architecture were not suppressed, as the ideologues of digital production wished, but have reached new heights. The design/ construction site *(dessin/chantier)* scheme of Sérgio Ferro and his research lab at the Grenoble School of Architecture must be revisited, an enterprise to which we aim to contribute here.[80]

Although Gehry has been our main character thus far, it is clear that this entire technological apparatus was not set in motion as a result of the self-imposed challenges of this eccentric architect. Nonetheless, he and his team were not only active and relevant agents in this whole process, they also knew how to capture and uniquely demonstrate that process as a manifestation of the spirit of the time. Not surprisingly, Frank Gehry became the first renowned architect to also explore the sale of design software. His work has served as publicity for the possibilities of software developed in his office, the Digital Project (a BIM version of CATIA adapted for the construction industry), in partnership with Dessault and IBM. Gehry Technologies promises users the chance to create with the same freedom that made Gehry a myth, something that the software of competitors cannot. But if this is not the case, the tool promises efficiency by improving productivity in conventional projects as well. By 2008, Gehry had already equipped three thousand professionals from SOM (Skidmore, Owings & Merrill), one of the world's largest architectural offices, also selling software packages in China.[81]

Despite leading the innovation, Gehry did not significantly alter his design method.[82] His exploration of form in 1989, which found objective limitations to representation and production in the Disney Concert Hall, was eventually able to move forward without further restrictions. That which was previously unrepresentable, uncalculable, unbudgetable, and unbuildable could be executed with reasonable reliability. Nonetheless, the architect did not change the focus of his formal investigation with the emergence of virtual reality. If Gehry still felt he was free to create, he did so as the craftsman of physical models handled by the architect-sculptor's hand, from the loose trace of the drawing—so that everything that followed was subsequently transformed (or promoted) by cutting-edge technology. Peter Eisenman, our next character, promised to go beyond, as he intended to set digital geometries in motion, thus eliminating much of the author's power, adding information to the

computer from the earliest stages of conception, during the generation
of forms.

THE AUTOMATION OF FORM

Digital design and its hyperreal effect do not only promote gains in
productivity and savings in time, or an infinitely superior capacity to
store and mobilize information. In information space, what occurs is
the "production and circulation of signs qualitatively different than the
previous ones."[83] According to Pierre Lévy, "virtualization" (of bodies,
technique, economy, and language) alters the perception of space-time,
of the subject–object relationship, and poses new cognitive problems.[84]
Thus, the problem of creation in art and in architecture cannot remain
unaltered.

Like other architects, Eisenman has also perceived that the digital
age has transformed the representational mode of Renaissance drawing,
which lasted for five hundred years, but this point lies in equally overcoming the monocular and anthropocentric perspectival vision.[85] The
breakdown of this perspective happens concomitantly with the loss
of centrality for the so-called Cartesian subject, which has implications
for the method and meaning of the act of drawing. According to him,
the designer must divest himself or herself from any prior positioning,
whether subjective or objective, to build signs whose physiognomy can
be grasped only a posteriori. New technologies would thus allow for the
extension of the creative act beyond the human, toward a universe of
forms unimaginable by previous rationale.

Provocatively, Peter Eisenman states, "Bilbao deals only with the
illusion of a change, instead of with real change." According to him, "one
can ask what the time-space differential might be between Bilbao and
Borromini,"[86] or between forms of starchitecture and those of baroque
architecture. Gehry's much-vaunted formalism would be inadvertently
outdated in relation to current problems, regardless of how advanced
his digital design systems are or how profitable his buildings might be.
He would be restricted to the activity of making his sculptures feasible
as architecture, which means he might have not advanced toward a new
formal creation experience that assimilates the cognitive transformations
provided by the new cybernetic paradigm.

In the 1980s, Eisenman and Gehry were part of a group of architects known as "deconstructionists."[87] At that time, they were already researching means of architectural expression consistent with contemporary indeterminacy and new spatiotemporal relations. In his sequence of experimental houses, among other design exercises throughout the 1970s and 1980s, Eisenman sought to explore the idea of a series of drawings that did not form a continuum ordered in time and space and were able to unfold to infinity. As Otília Arantes explains, "the end result is not the synthesis of a process, the result of an accumulation, but an arbitrary pause in a series that could indefinitely continue through successive displacements . . . The path is therefore more important than the objects that result from it, which makes his houses just moments along the path."[88]

At the same time, everything takes place as if the author was no more than a passive observer of the self-reflexive movement of form in search of itself. This antihumanism, which references French poststructuralist philosophy, mainly Jacques Derrida, was already investing in a sort of atrophy of the historical subject and in an unprecedented automatism of form.

His computer explorations, which date back to that period, gradually became a method and system with the emergence of new three-dimensional technologies and algorithmic drawings, introduced to him by his young disciples, including Greg Lynn.[89] Eisenman has said that with the use of "algorithms, imported from the aerospace industry, automobile production, and special effects in film may actually lead to the modification, transformation and transgression of architecture's nature."[90] An algorithm would enable him to perform, through logical expressions and mathematical operations understandable by the computer, the displacements and combinatorial games with which he was already experimenting in previous years. Thus, by "turning electronic culture into a method" of design, the algorithm creates a "new world,"[91] or at least, as he was already accustomed to saying at the time of his experimentations with serial houses, it provokes minor individual changes in perception in order to generate a different awareness of the world.[92]

For Kostas Terzidis, algorithmic language allows for "a mediator between the human mind and the computer's processing power."[93] This is where his and Eisenman's interests lie: in the border language (or common language) between human and nonhuman, which makes him advocate for the concept of otherness inherent in the man–machine relation, as distinct forms of intelligence in manipulating information and probabilities. Computer programming by the architect would not only occur unidirectionally, but would add to a cumulative but bidirectional database. This introduces a new problem regarding the notion of authorship, at least in the romantic sense of the inspired artist, now put into perspective by the random nature that was introduced by the machine and its artificial intelligence. "An algorithm is a procedure, the result of which is not necessarily credited to its creator . . . instead to an anonymous, mechanistic, and automated procedure."[94] It is as if creation slipped out of the hands of the subject through an endless series of mutations of the initial information. Algorithms allow forms to move on the computer screen until the moment they are frozen—admittedly at this time usually as a result of a decisive act (of a not entirely absent subject).

Despite the rationality of the algorithmic language, its result is unexpected, formless, complex, unstable, and everything else that follows in terms of transgressions of inherited patterns. The starting point of algorithmic programming is any post-Euclidean geometric problem: biomorphism or mimesis of any complex form that can be changed by unfathomable computations. The results are unable to be appropriated by materialistic rationality, and paradoxically imply a mystical reason, such as cosmic morphogenesis, in Pierre Lévy's definition. According to Lévy, for an artist today "it is less a question of the artist interpreting the world than of allowing existing or hypothetical biological processes, mathematical structures, social or collective dynamics, to speak directly." He calls the artist "a sculptor of the virtual" who "provide[s] a voice for cosmic creativity."[95]

Architecture would no longer be "designed," but "ejected by reality," in the words of Edmond Couchot. However, the intensity of this ejection produces its release from reality toward a "synthesized, artificial reality, with no material substrate beyond the electronic cloud of billions of micro impulses that run through the computer's electronic circuits, a reality whose sole reality is virtual."[96] In this sense, says Couchot, one can say that "the digital image-matrix does not present any adherence to the real: it frees itself from it."[97] It is therefore a confluence of technological and mystical reason.

Interestingly—since we are running counter to classical rationalism—André Gorz recalls that the Leibnizian project of *Mathesis Universalis,* in which the laws of the universe and logical processes of thought converge in a Single Calculus, is reborn in the mid-nineteenth century in the Boolean ideal of a universal language based on the binary matrix (0, 1) of a sui generis algebra in which the truth, or falsehood, of propositions could be computed as a mathematical sequence. What is surprising, however, is that when so algebraized, the operations of the spirit could finally embrace layers of reality hitherto inaccessible to concrete, nonformal thinking. It seems that the above-mentioned singular marriage of mysticism and logic was under way. In this way, continues Gorz, mathematical thinking has crossed an unexpected frontier: "to invent and carry out nonexperiential realities—which today we call 'virtual realities,' and which can be established in the world through computer science mediation."[98]

Manipulation of form by a subject that rejects its condition would happen, so the narrative continues, through the very movement (folding) of nature over itself. Eisenman passes from the Derridean "deconstructivism" of his previous phase, and from the bottomless pit of unfoldings of a continuous process of "dedifferentiation," to Deleuze's interpretations of Leibniz (and Baroque art), or René Thom, to present a non-Cartesian conception of space. According to Deleuze, space is a continuous matter that is alive, like an organism, composed of endless folds and textures. Informal art, which is not subjected to Renaissance perspectivism and planimetrics, is also made through folded forms and textures, like origami, in which morphogenesis is always a matter of folding. The notion of linear time is inflected by that of a "happening" or an "event," whose fulminant moment projects itself out into a sort of dead time, in which nothing happens, like a fold in the temporal flow. The subject under such conditions of time and space is confused with the attributes of its own folds and happenings; therefore, its perception needs to be completely rearranged.[99]

Eisenman adopts these philosophical interpretations on notions of space, time, and subject in their literal (and imagistic) sense in his formal architectural research. Each of his projects from this period starts with a conventional geometric reading of the territory and program of needs, and then with the execution of small volumetric models (digital and cardboard-made), which are progressively folded, unfolded, and refolded until the end result is reached. The folds are not completely random because they start from graphical diagrams chosen by Eisenman and his team. Such diagrams, without any concern for scale, are graphic elements superimposed as transparencies, articulated with each other by means of mathematical equations. They cannot be drawings made by architects because they must hold no authorship or historical memory. They are generally obtained from visuals of other disciplines such as mathematics, biology,[100] and physics, and bear some similarity to the design theme, as if the diagram registered a seismography of its own in each design situation. They are like physical layers of the real, electromagnetic fields that can only be conceived mathematically (or biologically), because they lack the thought ruled by optical parameters. In this way, the computer is fed with information gleaned from a non-anthropocentric universe, which will serve as instructions for the automation of morphogenesis.

Under these conditions the architect would be a mere conductor for a sort of self-consciousness of matter that folds and unfolds itself in an infinite continuum of the Leibnizian space. Authorship would be diluted in this genesis, guided, in large part, by the computer, as a post-human instrument capable of simulating or even embodying the continuous folding of matter. Its programming would already be found in itself; hence the architect must be able to make it emerge from itself.

With the discovery of the mapping of molecules and the genome as a system of codes that programs humans and nonhumans, which is at the basis of the invention of computer science, the boundaries between man and nature dissolve. The cell was cybernated as a small information unit. Reproduction could then be conceived as a copy of a message. From such analogies between biology and communication emerges the notion of the modeling and composition of organisms.[101] Because the programmer is also a program, the metabolic transfusions between subject and object (which "intermingle and hybridize"[102]) become part of the new reproduction of forms, managed by means of this new biology and cybernetics.

The successive abstractions in the act of design, which we have followed in this chapter, here reach their extreme limit. The idea of a subject who is the programmer of objects is questioned. The architect-programmer is himself a program of cells, like any other existing matter.

He is simultaneously the program, programmer, and programmed, and dissolves himself into the unique and continuous nature of the universe. Thus, the act of designing finds its ultimate abstract condition in the indetermination between subject and object, between man and nature. In the condition of programmer and programmed, in which the subject is obliterated by the autonomy of matter's self-organization, the architect is merely the sensitive element that inseminates or disrupts the genesis of form, as in an assisted reproduction. Creation escapes his hands—there is something magical, as Eisenman says, in the computer's manipulation of the schemes: "I only choose forms that it generates," I look for the "accident."[103]

In Eisenman's works, the trigger of each design theme must be that seismographic diagram. In this manner, for the Biological Research Center in Frankfurt, Eisenman chose the pattern of the protein production DNA nucleotide sequence as diagram; for the Church of the Year 2000 in Rome, he chose the formation of liquid crystals, with the understanding that its suspension between the physical states of matter symbolizes the relationship between man, God, and nature; for the design of a library in Geneva, he adopted memory frequency diagrams of brain synapses; for a software company in India, he chose the mandala shape; for the City of Culture in Santiago de Compostela, he transferred the irregular geometry of the five sacred paths of the pilgrims, and the geological layers of the terrain; and so on.[104]

Such diagrams overlap uniform reticules or terrain and are manipulated by the computer and progressively folded and unfolded until the initial Euclidean volumes are unrecognizable (and within them the program of uses initially conventionally developed). This procedure implements a movement, a diverse space-time relationship in the programming of the form. Until it is interrupted by the architects by freezing the image, even then, it continues to produce incessant micro-movements. This interruption, says Eisenman, occurs when "the picture looks less understandable to us," when the project development begins.[105]

The execution of such digital operations, and the way it is presented by the architect and his disciples in texts and lectures, confers a signature to Eisenman's design. Authorship, partially refused in morphogenesis, is replaced by the market and the economy. In the case of starchitects, Eisenman's difference lay in his somewhat automated design method, carried out with such consistency by his office. In design competitions Eisenman took advantage of this paradox: his signature was at the same time an absence of authorship in the conventional sense. He says: "upon receiving the request directly from a municipality or government, they mean: 'We want an Eisenman. Let's build one.' What makes it interesting to me in a competition is that the end result is a design hard to define as a Peter Eisenman."[106] That is, the author-creator gives way to the brand, as we saw in the first chapter.

Ultimately, we are dealing with a superficial and fetishized use of technology—pursuing the *cybernetic appearance* above all—because Eisenman is not in search of the real possibilities of the cybernetic turn for the production of architecture, a subject that Buckminster Fuller, for example, had advanced decades earlier.[107] In the end, he does not propose a new operative mode for architecture, but the use of new digital tools only as means of accelerating the already hypertrophied and exasperated manipulation of form. The system, eager for spectacular and profitable images, rewards these "genius" manipulators of forms, be they the architect-craftsman of the trained hand or one who mobilizes computational refraction.

THE IDEOLOGY AND ECONOMICS OF COMPLEX FORMS

As we have seen, new technologies lead to double-sided consequences in the production of complex forms in architecture: on the one hand, they allow volumes and surfaces hitherto unrepresentable and uncalculable to be interpreted, regulated, and made feasible; on the other hand, digital design makes possible the genesis of forms hitherto unimaginable and ungraspable by so-called Cartesian rationality. In this sense, there is an expansion of the formal and symbolic universe available to architectural creation.

From an ideological point of view, architects will seek justifications external to their discipline to arbitrate formal choices. They do research in mathematics, physics, chemistry, and biology, to find theories and images that can be incorporated into the programming of the architectural morphogenesis. At the same time, they ask philosophy for the protection of authority for their visual explorations. The incorporation of theoretical formulations and discoveries from these other fields of knowledge is almost always epidermal, as is indeed the nature of complex surfaces mimicked by the architects. But they are the ballast, the justification, and the discourse for their arbitrariness. In short, it is about the mere stylized emblem of visuals and languages that reflect new discoveries in science, using the processing power of increasingly powerful machines.

Theories of systems, games, and chaos have been freely manipulated in a single pro-complexity discourse, as follows: Modern architecture was simplistic and authoritarian, while current architecture is open to the complexity, in natural or abstract forms, of a new mathematics. From this derives a grammar of instability and amorphousness, and the vocabulary of the new tectonics, as we saw in the first chapter. But unlike scientists and philosophers, architects superficially manipulate that knowledge to satisfy a limited demand, which is usually the construction of a building.

When architects come into play, handling their models and computer programs in search of intricate shapes, a paradox and an inversion between complexity and simplification occurs. Formal research is self-referential, it folds into itself in a tautological mode, complicating geometry and simplifying the social and urban relations of the environment, annulling historical time, erasing contradictions and conflicts. Such architecture is presented as an isolated monad—a "pure sign, deprived of references other than those referring to the object itself."[108] However, as Tafuri affirms, architecture occupies a specific field of "complex structures," though this complexity is not derived from entangled form-related confrontations, but stems rather from the way various structures converging through it interrelate with one another: social life, history, city, political, symbolic, and technical systems, etc.[109]

The architecture of complex forms, derived from thoughts seemingly induced by singularly formal analogies, masks a simplified insertion of the object in its context, usually through refraction. From this comes its behavior as self-referential monad, enclave, and fortress. But then, on what is the choice of complex forms hovering in the air based? In more or less random decisions, which do not emanate from the complex logic of the object, but from the "images detached from every aspect of life."[110] When the logic is that of the object, there is an intrinsic value, an internal consistency, a contextualized experience. But in the architecture we are examining, the choice of form motivated by extrinsic values is recurrent, in turn, a mere emblem of theories whose attraction increases according to its seemingly transgressive glamour. Hence the sense of arbitrariness that is evident in these works. Why these forms and not others? The form responds solely to its codes, to its genesis as metabolic programming. It is intended to be ahistorical and asocial, accountable only to the equation that gave rise to it, to the mathematizations of its DNA, aligned by the computer.

In search of explanations for the current flourishing of such formalism in contemporary capitalism (moreover, a congenital and recurring tendency in a system governed by abstraction, and consequent indifference to any and all content), one may encounter the same phenomenon in the most diverse areas of knowledge: in all of them reigns a sort of mystical fervor for computerized modeling. The analogy then seems to impose itself naturally: the new "machine of cybernetic symbols" comes to be the capitalist system itself, states Gorz.[111] A system whose trajectory can also be understood as a succession of "victories of the symbolic and the formal over non-computable dimensions of the social world of life, such as our life experiences."[112]

Therefore, there is an automation of form that finds matches in the automation of the economy and in the fetishism of finance capital, as we discussed in the first chapter. Social reality is dominated by abstraction at all levels. The abstraction of money contaminates several others, including the practice of design, as we have seen. According to Gorz, "the abstract has broken the boundaries of the concrete and covered the world of life with a fabric of algebraic equations that, thanks to its structural efficiency, appears more real than the living fabric of social relations."[113]

The forms that become automated rarely express the "ultimate goal" or what would be the "true meaning" of this abstraction: economic growth and capital accumulation. But, if there is a rationale in the complex form, it lies in its ability to generate benefits to all capital involved. It is precisely its insertion as monad, usually in decaying areas and adverse contexts, that allows it to propel a wave of gains distributed by various agents, from entrepreneurs and builders to the publishing and tourism sectors.

The economic reasons for the complex form are thus of the order of capital appreciation. Be they Gehry's sculptures, or Eisenman's self-generating forms, or any other from a starchitect that promotes strange and seductive forms, the more different, rare, and surprising they are, the greater their potential for further gains in the form of profit and rent. Form's "exclusivity effect" functions as technological innovation and allows for additional gains arising from its rarity and monopoly rent. As we have seen, enhancing rent is an effect of symbolic capital that increases the title deed, which in turn, allows for the capture of a larger share of social surplus value. The difficult form is equally advantageous in the generation of value at the construction site, as we shall see in the next chapter, because it produces additional gains in execution: the more difficult the work, the better for capital, as the luxury economy demonstrates.[114]

In the misshapen forms of the architects of the "digital vanguard," arbitrary, random, accidental, and partially unconscious manipulations promote complexities with clear economic meaning. Ultimately, these forms could be any, provided they are always unique, new, attractive, serving as bait for capital appreciation, and ready for any—or no—use.[115]

In turn, the ideology of complexity, or fetishized complexity, is not neutral and carries political pitfalls. Freedom of form in the limits of the random gesture, while promoting a kind of intentional "semiotic instability"—ungraspable compositions that escape visually assuring matrices—converges toward bases of the new economy and the destabilization of the working world itself. The fluidization of forms here reveals a real class dimension, if one can say what is really at stake: the frequent avant-garde allegation that such dismantling represents the end of stable and stifling references does not fail to include, as a mere detail, the dismantling of the very institutions of the working world.

The sellers of complexity present it as socially indeterminate, as derived from paradigms of science or nature, when in fact it hides a form of class domination. It is not mere abstraction, as it embraces a tangible sociohistorical specificity. According to István Mészáros, the ideology of complexity in capitalism masks the confiscation of real political power from society: its capacity for self-government. The discourse of complexity is thus a form of social control. Growing complexity is presented as "the impossibility of the autonomous productive life-activity associated producers," that is, "the real issue is *control* and not socially undetermined complexity."[116]

Therefore, Mészáros proposes that the argument of complexity is used conversely to what is ideologically presented. That is because "the increasing complexity generated by a system which cannot productively control its escalating complications is a serious liability, not an asset," while "the combined resources of the associated producers are, in principle, much more adequate for mastering the complexity proper to the genuine productive requirements of the social reproduction process."[117] Instead of the complexity of control, Mészáros proposes the "control of complexity," which means "regaining control over the labour process as a whole."[118]

The emergence of fetishized complexity as an impediment to workers' control is thus not merely an ideological phenomenon, but also a phenomenon of class struggle. It corresponds to a restructuring of production and value distribution mechanisms, as was the case with post-Fordist corporate networks. Complex architectural forms are a product of and have parallels with the emergence of new structures of accumulation, which could also be qualified as complex, simultaneously centralized and dispersed, but which actually meant a new defeat for the working class, as we will discuss in the next chapter.

A short explanatory aside: all major technical changes in productive forces, as Marx explained, respond to working-class pressure that preceded it.[119] During the thirty "glorious" years (1945–75), the years of welfare, workers had obtained a number of advantages, and capital gains were limited to the increase in relative surplus value. This was the result of several factors, and among them there is one that interests us the most: the structure of production in terms of major industries, and its correlative, collective labor. The latter leaves its abstraction as capital creation to assume a concrete body in working-class consciousness. Its largest demonstrations were the workers' strikes of 1968 in France, the largest ever in Europe, when workers demanded other relations of production and self-management.

In 1973, for example, one of the main French watch and clock companies, the LIP factory, based in Besançon, was taken over by workers and subjected to a libertarian self-management system.[120] These workers had participated in the 1968 movement, and in 1973, when layoffs and the possible closure of the factory were announced, they kidnapped some of the directors to request clarification regarding the restructuring already under way. Knowing that the factory would be liquidated, they took control of its inventories, strengthened the factory committees, organized action committees, general meetings, a newspaper (the *UnitéLip*), opened the gates of the factory to visitation and the cafeteria to the public, accepted volunteer work from supporters, and conducted a campaign for watch sales, because the stores had refused to sell them. When the police took back the factory, the workers, with nowhere to go to, extended the self-management model to the entire city—"we will occupy Besançon"—creating activities in squares, theaters, cinemas, schools, and bringing production inside the homes— "the factory is the collective of workers and not its walls." It was an act that culminated in a march of one hundred thousand people. In 1975, however, with the election of the conservative Valéry Giscard d'Estaing, the "LIP example" was economically defeated, with the elimination of contracted credit lines and the purchase of precision watches by state-owned companies, such as Renault.

Capital reacted against the wave of strikes and self-management practices that emerged in Europe (such as the 1974 Portuguese revolution) and elsewhere in the world in those years in two important ways. First, with the undermining of the workers' achievements and social protection, through dismantling the social-welfare policies and with the emergence of neoliberalism—which is, at its core, less of a coherent economic doctrine than a technology of power aimed at dismantling the class cohesion unwittingly strengthened during the Fordist period. And second, by attacking collective labor through wage individualization practices, job rotation, etc. This meant replacing large companies with networked production, facilitated by computers and by concentrated low-wage pockets on the periphery of capitalism, which had yet to be explored. The sequence of information and time scale that converged in centralized heavy industry was now dispersed in networked production units.

This also took place in architectural production, such as in Norman Foster's HSBC building in Hong Kong, which resorted to a worldwide network of suppliers, with parts arriving in ships, or in the case of Guggenheim Bilbao and its titanium plates, whose ore was mined in

Australia, and which were laminated in Pittsburgh, treated in France, cut in Italy, and then taken to Bilbao, Spain. Or even in the purchasing of services from digital designers at low cost in the third world, or in the migrant workers circulating through construction sites via chains of subcontractors.

The prescriptive hypercentralization we analyzed in this chapter reaches the limits of the manufacturing form, with the spreading of end suppliers and even of assemblers. Workers can no longer understand the complexity into which they are inserted. The very possibility of collective labor—the great working-class weapon of welfare—is thus annulled. Complexity at all levels is therefore a weapon of capital. This change did not occur by chance, but as a response to the threat posed by the unprecedented role of collective labor self-managed by the working class itself.

3

ONE TO ONE
FULL-SCALE
CONSTRUCTION SITE

TRANSFORMATIONS IN PRODUCTIVE FORCES and in the social relations of production, which have taken place as the architecture of starchitects has evolved, find their moment of truth in the stage of concrete production, that is, in factories and on construction sites. There are conflicts and imbalances, as we will see. The promise of flexible automation in construction, which began to obey information design models, meets resistance in its execution while being partially put into practice.

The starting point of this chapter is an evaluation of the extent to which the construction site is a productive form that anticipates aspects of so-called flexible accumulation, in part because of its versatility and capacity to produce distinct architectural works. More than was the case during the Fordist paradigm, the construction site now finds affinities with the new regime of accumulation, allowing for a convergence, for better and for worse, with the general movement of capital from a technological and organizational point of view.

Our path will now be parallel, but opposite, to the previous chapter. We will analyze the maximum point of automation with the suppression of the worker by a robot-mason: a similar and mirrored frontier with regard to the automation of forms tested by Peter Eisenman. Next, we will visit Frank Gehry's construction sites in their ideal form, examining how his team seeks to harmonize digital design with nonstandardized prefabrication and on-site assembly. The inflection point of the chapter is the evaluation of architects' desire to resume their command over the entire productive process of construction, thanks to new digital technologies. From this point on, we will go back and focus on construction workers, their old and new attributes, working conditions, violated rights, and the presence of migrants—in short, the dynamics of a hard productive sector that cannot be exported to the third world, like other chains of production, because it is stuck to the ground.

The chapter's point of arrival will not be just rent, but the production of value. What does the construction of complex, difficult-to-execute forms represent from the standpoint of labor value? Do brand architecture buildings, similarly to the luxury economy, seek the value of representation inherent in the treasure-form?[1] That is what we will see next.

THE CURRENTNESS OF THE "CONSTRUCTION SITE-FORM"

The relative delay of the construction site in relation to industrial sectors that adopted machines and conveyor belts seemed to be overcome with modern architecture made of concrete, steel, and glass. The ideology of progress and the machine aesthetic were adopted by modern architects who wanted to transform the archaic construction site into a modern factory. Le Corbusier, visiting the Ford factories in the 1920s, similarly to Lenin, stated: "Ford's experience, repeated in thousands of activities in the modern world, in the industrious production, teaches us a lesson. Let's accept his lesson."[2]

Attempts toward the Fordist industrialization of architecture that followed were numerous and have almost always failed owing to a lack of understanding of the specificities of this particular mode of production/domination, as well as its position in capitalist accumulation. Modernization would arrive from outside the realm of production, through the determinations of new design, intending to meet the same design criteria of industrial products. Cities, in this situation, would be partly demolished or just started from scratch in order to receive new products. However, the partial prefabrication of pieces to be assembled on-site—which has even become the hegemonic method of production—did not substantially change the productive conditions at the construction site, especially regarding the stages of production invariably performed inside the site, such as excavation, laying of foundations, erection of the structure, and plumbing and wiring. The standardization of components required in Fordist economies of scale generally resulted in inhospitable and monotonous buildings, poorly integrated into the urban fabric. The main realm for the exploration of prefabrication has been proletarian housing and industrial buildings, both influencing the direct costs of workforce reproduction and fixed capital. In the case of workers' housing blocks, often isolated from the city in housing estates, the social and urban disaster was evident.

The industrial production of architecture advocated by modernists was more publicized than practiced. Buildings did not begin to be produced like other consumer goods. This does not mean that changes in material, modulation, and the standardization of design did not occur, in addition to innovation in certain production techniques. The blind spot for the modernization of construction, however, was the result of a misunderstanding on the part of the architects—and hence their self-deception—regarding the social and economic conditions that defined architecture's place in capitalist accumulation. Architects placed excessive expectations on their design and gave it an unreasonable central role. According to the English sociologist Michael Ball, "every other agent involved in the construction process is idealized into a shadowy plasticity, prepared to do anything required of them by the designer."[3] This concealed the fact that social agents active in the production of space (capitalist builders, real-estate developers, financiers, landowners, and construction workers) were ignored by architects, along with their interests, positions, and conflicts.

This is how, forty years after he had visited the Ford factories, in the construction of the monastery of La Tourette in 1960, Le Corbusier presented yet another work of industrial aesthetics, but without the corresponding evolution of productive forces. According to the Dessin/Chantier laboratory research team, which conducted a detailed study of the monastery's construction drawings, construction diaries, letters, reports, interviews, and carefully considered its built form, unlike what was exhibited by the plasticity of its mechanical precision—making us believe in a sort of "large-scale assembly"—we are faced with an "overly messy" production, with no regularity, almost exclusively made through individual cases and adaptations. The construction work was supposedly "a permanent confusion, with drawings arriving after the execution or not even getting there, delays, disagreements among working teams, dysfunctions, crises, etc."[4]

Le Corbusier, however, knew how to impose readings of his works that suited him on his interpreters, that is, ones that matched his constructive principles. He persuaded through the power of intense plasticity, aesthetic rapture, and a type of discourse—the "rhetoric of verisimilitude"—leading us to perceive only the superficial appearance of the work. But behind the staging, there is a construction site, which, even if concealed, still writes the script, as Sérgio Ferro argues, hence the possibility of detecting meanings of built space from the history of its production.

However much modern architects insisted, the construction site looked like a space of production at odds with Fordism and even with earlier forms of Taylorist control. It therefore came to be known as "laggard" or "backward,"[5] as opposed to sectors of accelerated industrialization with high organic composition of capital.[6] Its production characteristics, relatively unmechanized and seemingly chaotic and labor-intensive, have been described as a stage to be overcome. It was a fetishized view of technology, corresponding to the notion of linear technical progress.[7] And it was a stage to be overcome, but one that found parallels with the very situation of "underdevelopment" as a mere stage to be crossed on the path of capitalist development, as was claimed by the supporters of peripheral industrialization and bourgeois revolution in the third world.[8] This is a comparison that, when viewed from a nonstageist perspective, is certainly provocative: like underdevelopment, seemingly archaic production on the construction site appears impossible to overcome, because both are coeval forms of capitalist accumulation and its uneven and combined development, as Celso Furtado has explained about Latin America.[9]

By avoiding the dualist regressive/modern labeling, as well as stageism, in the definition of the construction site (as opposed to the Fordist factory), Sérgio Ferro, Michael Ball, and Benjamin Coriat proposed their own conceptualizations based on interpretations that highlight what is unique to this form of production. Ferro, in his 1979 book *O canteiro e o desenho,* explains the productive rationality of the construction site from the standpoint of the factory-based mode of production, as described by Marx, with the particularity that "in the production of space, the factory is that which is mobile, and not its products."[10] The basis of manufacturing is the centrality of the collective laborer as a prevalent force in the production process, prior to the real subsumption of industrial machines. In capitalism, this collective laborer exists solely as such because of his or her separation and subsequent totalization into a product, within the division of labor, as commanded by capital and its intermediaries. Hence the heteronomy of the worker, not imposed by the machine but rather stemming from violence and the alienation of the worker from what he or she does, such as the geometry of the architect's drawing, and the polished surfaces that erase the trace of other builders.

Ferro's interpretation avoids stageism, as he considers that the manufacturing nature of construction is not a stage to be overcome but a "condition overdetermined" by political economy as a whole, an extraordinary field of surplus value production, in a way to counterbalance the profit rate's general downward trend. The result is both its configuration as a space for class struggle and the successive defeat of workers, and the rejection of the idea that there is some "nature" or "specificity" intrinsic to the act of building that imposes this condition. As an architect on the periphery of capitalism, Ferro goes on to recognize aspects intrinsic to underdevelopment on the construction site— and in this way, he seeks to describe the political economy of construction as an allegory of underdevelopment.

Michael Ball, in his 1988 book *Rebuilding Construction*, also rejects naming the construction sector as laggard. His main target, beyond the ideology of modern architects, is French structuralist sociology (mainly Ascher, Lacoste, Topalov, Preteceille, and Lipietz),[11] to which attributes the "backward" production of the construction site and its low organic composition[12] to an external factor: the determining power of absolute land rent over the surplus value of construction. The owner of the land would act as spoiler of the productive sector, as in the process of primitive accumulation. The rentier stranglehold over unproductive agents is what supposedly prevents the development of productive forces in this sector, without the endogenous dynamics of the latter. On the one hand, land rent and operations with land and real-estate development would be more advantageous than the immobilization of capital in new techniques and methods of production; on the other, the landowner's rent monopoly would ensure the increase in market prices, regardless of production conditions. Thus, issues of rationalization in the construction industry become secondary when compared to gains associated with rents and the behavior of financial variables. For Michael Ball, these interpretations give exaggerated centrality to the landowner; they blend production problems with surplus value distribution, are theoretically simplistic, and are empirically hard to verify.[13] This does not mean that factors associated with land ownership are not relevant in defining the productive bases of architecture, but they need to be analyzed case by case, verified according to other variables, and therefore cannot be made absolute as an unequivocal determination.

Jorge Oseki, for example, commenting on the land situation in countries or regions where there is a shortage of urbanized land (such as Hong Kong, the Netherlands, and Japan), which results in high prices and strong gains with absolute ground rent, affirmed that in those places construction did not patently lag behind—on the contrary.[14] On the other hand, the construction sector in Eastern Europe, even with state ownership during decades of barracks communism, has rapidly modernized in relation to the rest of Europe. Ferro, after stating that land rent is a "dubious and insufficient" cause for explaining the material basis and relations of production in architecture,[15] suggests that the position of French sociologists is owing to programmatic designations of the French Communist Party, which, in the 1970s, directed its criticism toward "unproductive" and "speculative" sectors sparing production, and arguing in defense of employment. Here again, a parallel could be made to the strategy for overcoming underdevelopment by combating imperialism (which would take a similarly parasitic role to land rent), in alliance with the national bourgeoisies, as advocated by Latin American communist parties aligned with Moscow.

By refusing to call it the laggard sector and to see land rent as the determining factor, Ball proposes analyzing construction based on itself, which does not mean mere immanent analysis, because we find, inside the form, its relations with the whole of the system. To avoid previous mistakes, his analysis is eminently empirical and filled with data, graphs, and tabulations regarding the sector's internal differences, its modes of productive organization and hiring, its techniques of production rationalization and rise in profits, the particularities of its labor market, its recent restructuring and articulation with other industrial sectors, and so on. He starts from the conviction that "all that can be said empirically is that building work is different from other productive activities and uses considerable amounts of labour." And he plays with metaphors by Lewis Carroll, without any displaced Darwinism, in order to compare the situation of the construction and automotive industries: "Is an elephant more technically backward than a racehorse?"[16]

A new group of French researchers in the early 1980s, linked to research institutes and not aligned with the dogmatism of the French Communist Party, opened new avenues for interpreting the construction sector. Sociologist Benjamin Coriat summarized some of the positions of the group in his 1983 paper "Construction-Site-Type Work Process and Its Rationalization."[17] As a sociologist of labor, Coriat recognizes that despite the key role of construction in capitalist accumulation, "the construction site remains one of the forms of production less well known and perhaps less understood."[18] Thus the backwardness would lie not in the construction sector, but in the research on the field. Instead of defining it as "insufficiently Taylorized" or unadaptable to Fordism, one must recognize its difference, by means of an "analysis that originates and progresses from 'site.'"[19] The naming that Coriat proposes is simply "construction site-form," as opposed to "factory-form," thus preventing the manufacturing/heavy industry polarity, which might convey a misleading impression of progressive stages.

The main features of the construction site-form are the nonrepetitiveness of tasks and extreme variability of work types, which makes establishing a stable series of Taylorized workstations highly unlikely; the partial and in most cases marginal character of standardized components in the final product, in contrast to Fordist sectors; the irregular timing of tasks, with much greater variation than at factories; the extreme difficulty of scheduling work, calling for original and specific types of management in order to cope with unpredictability; products being implemented on the ground in such a way that it is the work process itself, in its entirety, which circulates and must adapt to a different medium.

The notion of a "variable" or "variability regime" is central to defining the construction site-form. Myriam Campinos-Dubernet, a French researcher on the subject, unfolded it into external modalities, associated with the heterogeneous nature of the products and sizes of operations, and internal ones, arising from differences in the amount of work required at each stage of production during the project.[20] To this Coriat adds a distinction between spatial and temporal variables, the latter being the study of the cadence of successive and/or simultaneous operations required in the act of construction, which, in turn, differentiates it from the productive rhythms of Taylorism/Fordism. Variability is also responsible for the maintenance, even if with modifications, of a wide field of qualified activities, preventing the work from becoming as abstract as in the factory-form.

According to Coriat, the variability of the construction site-form will require flexible forms of production management and organization (versatility, teams, autonomous groups, "time blocks," etc.) in order to cope with its specificities. Interferences in the production process must acknowledge and take advantage of the limitations that perpetuate situations of variability and randomness, rather than seek to suppress them. Those are forms of production rationalization and organization that contradict the Taylorist/Fordist paradigm, while continuing to be strategies of capital to remain in command of accumulation. Hence the opposite movement, that of colonizing the construction site-form through classical manufacturing rationality, found barriers and was, in general, a failure.[21]

The final hypothesis put forward by Coriat, which will be evaluated throughout this chapter, is that "perhaps more than any other industry, the construction site-form gathers favorable internal conditions to transition to *the flexible forms of production*." And not only that, given its currentness, the construction sector should no longer be regarded as a "laggard" and "insufficiently Taylorized" sector and should start to be acknowledged within new categories, which perhaps indicate its "'exemplary' value" for the new accumulation regime, where "the construction site constitutes a privileged laboratory for experimentation."[22]

Regarding this unexpected currentness, Helen Rainbird and Gerd Syben also remind us that "the method of organizing the production process [in the construction site] has always had those elements now considered to be 'new' in manufacturing industries, as they attempt to resolve the objectives of being highly flexible and highly automated at the same time."[23] In this way, the so-called restructuring of the construction industry will actually not refer to "new methods of reorganizing the production process, but rather the extension and development of the existing ones."[24] The paradox could perhaps be summarized as follows: the production of an immovable manufactured commodity proved to be unexpectedly flexible (mobile), while the production of a mobile commodity in the Fordist industrial era became standardized and invariable (immovable).

Similarities between construction site-form and the paradigm of "flexible accumulation" are numerous, starting with the fact that architecture has often sought the unique form (standardization was marginal and restricted to certain niches), and has organized its productive forces and relations of production in order to generate individualized products.[25] Besides the similarities already mentioned by Coriat regarding its regime of variability, production in architecture has anticipated, almost involuntarily, some major managerial innovations. Stock management, for example: Because construction sites are typically small spaces, storage has always been minimized, and tools and materials have had to be used immediately. In fact, steel and concrete arrive at the time of use. In this way, even if rudimentarily, the coordination of teams and inventories already anticipated the lean production system, the just-in-time delivery of components, and the organization of teams per task.[26]

For this reason, construction-site management thoroughly consists of the coordination of material flows, equipment, and tasks, and its productivity depends on the ability not only to predict and link them, but also to accomplish this coordination in a highly unpredictable environment, given its variability, complexity, extension in time, and the influence of not-entirely-predictable factors (such as subsoil, climate, risk of accidents, and even legal and ownership status). We must add to it the instability that arises from capital domination over workers in manufacturing, with no possibility for the real subsumption of collective labor by the objectivity of the machine. Thus, unlike the certainty and predictability of Fordist/Taylorist scientific management, the construction site-form management faces the randomness and adversity of various elements and needs to understand and arrange them in order to "create order out of chaos."[27] Thus, one notices a certain precedence of the construction site-form when dealing with situations seemingly adverse to capital, and when adopting flexible forms of organization, risk, and the management of uncertainty.

The work, divided per task, performed by relatively autonomous teams, and paid according to productivity and results—called "flexible specialization" in managerial vocabulary—had provided the basis for adopting layers of subcontracting or subcontracts early on, even before the dissemination of outsourcing and bonuses in the rest of the productive sector.[28] The structure of capital favored by the construction industry—which is highly fragmented in small regional and family-owned companies and a few larger ones—has enabled smaller companies to specialize in certain services and to be subcontracted by larger ones that maintain an increasingly lean body of engineers and technicians in positions of third-party operations management. As production is decentralized, their command increases. Subcontracting, often informally, had provided a better organizational response for the variability regime as described by Coriat and Campinos-Dubernet, and for the transferring and sharing of risks, exacerbated in the construction industry by its chronic instability among a wide array of agents—a transfer that "implies a worsening of working conditions with regressive social strategies."[29]

Rather than through the introduction of automation and new technologies, which today are only applied in a few operations, the sector's increased productivity was generated largely through increased exploitation and job insecurity, subcontracting per task, thus anticipating some forms of "disaffiliation" of post-Fordist capitalism.[30] Small subcontractors have become central, no longer marginal appendages, to the manufacturing system, while participating in an increasingly unfavorable relationship between workers and their unions. Subcontracting is not only a form of risk management, but also a way to increase control and reduce costs.[31] As we shall see, subcontracted workers generally come from poorer regions (internal to each country or from abroad), are poorly paid, and are subjected to the worst health and safety conditions. They have very low participation in trade unions, they have variable schedules and salaries, a high turnover rate, and are often not covered by labor and social protection rights—all of which results in a crisis of the workers' skills at construction sites, as workers are simultaneously asked to engage in modernization and to meet new quality targets.[32]

Above all, subcontracting allows for individual negotiation and the replacement of a "wage relationship with a commercial relationship," which means, according to André Gorz, a step toward the regressive abolition of wage-earning.[33] In the post-wage society anticipated at construction sites, "companies are free to collect from a plentiful stock of all kinds of service providers those who offer the best service at the lowest price," without the limitations that, after two centuries of struggles, the labor movement managed to impose on exploitation. Thus, the "emancipatory function" fulfilled by wage earning and all it represented—the qualification of the worker as a "general social individual," a status superior to the subjection that prevailed in traditional society—disappears.[34] According to Gorz, work presents itself as "service" *(servicium, obsequium)* owed to a master, that is, the same that has already been taking place in the construction site-form, in which the work has always been understood as service to a master (be they a master builder, engineer/architect, or owner).

Parenthesis: this increase in exploitation, and in the (absolute and relative) surplus value rate, in the limits of the wage-earning explosion, is part of the dominance of the logic of finance over the economy in general—when the law of the system becomes that of capital-to-interest and no longer of labor value, as Marx predicted at the end of *Capital*. To the extent that interest is internalized in all operations as a factor in production, it anticipates the production of value in a "dictatorial" way and demands equal profitability. Financial dominance will require ever-greater levels of productivity and labor exploitation. Time begins to be controlled and accelerated by a force external to the sphere of production. As a result, processes of financial globalization and the expansion of businesses in network structures are concomitant, as François Chesnais explained, always in search of locations that combine low wages, high productivity, deregulation, and lower taxes.[35]

If the construction site-form anticipates, in its own way, the network of specialized companies, coordinated by an increasingly digitized, lean, and sophisticated nerve center (the design sector and its consultants), as we saw in the preceding chapter, it still presents a crucial difference. According to David Harvey, one of the novelties of flexible accumulation is the "growing convergence between 'third world' and advanced capitalist labour systems. Yet the rise of new and the revival of older forms of industrial organization (often dominated by new immigrant groups in large cities, such as the Filipinos, South Koreans, Vietnamese, and Taiwanese in Los Angeles, or the Bangladeshis and Indians in East London) represents rather different things in different places."[36] But we are talking about an articulated network that, in the case of architecture, given its fixity to land, cannot be exported to companies located in the third world, where the outsourcing of "redundant work" generally occurs, as in the sewing of designer clothes.[37] Thus, in civil construction, the production process cannot escape the central, first-world countries, and despite the construction surrounding it, can be seen by all passersby. Instead of exporting production, the workers are the ones who are imported. The construction site is a place of hard production that should be located in the third world, and that nonetheless remains at the center of advanced capitalism, signaling the permanence of the old working world. It is on display, with African, African American, Arab, Latin American, and Asian workers climbing scaffolding, bolting and welding parts, pouring concrete slabs—the periphery in the center, "an island of underdevelopment in a society that in some aspects intends to be postindustrial," as Riboulet put it.[38]

This displacement of the construction site—which looks like an "out-of-place" (sub)world of work—allows, simultaneously, for the strategies of outsourcing and precarization adopted at its most extreme level to be replicated in other sectors. This is how the currentness of the construction site-form presents itself as perverse, despite the discourse of apologists. For although it suddenly became one of the "vanguards" of new production management, it is equally the "vanguard of the disintegration" of the working world.

German sociologist Ulrich Beck described welfare in ruins and the regressive transformations of the new working world based on traditionally penurious and predatory work forms in Brazil, calling them *brazilianization*.[39] Beck's position is not ambiguous at all. It describes Brazil as the "positive paradigm" of the *Brave New World of Work,* "a unique laboratory, in which our certainties fall apart." The Brazilian dualization of the labor market, dating back to slavery and to our eternally unfinished formation,[40] would take us back to the status of a "country of the future." According to Paulo Arantes, "we are the genuine prototype of the 'risk society' on its way," and "once again skipping stages, we find ourselves at the forefront—that is, the forefront for 'overcoming' the full-time work regime of the Western world."[41] Similarly, one could say that we are witnessing the working world "becoming a construction site," maintaining the duality between those who command and produce information and those who execute subordinate and redundant work organized in layers of subcontractors, thus anticipating the fractures of the wage-earning work system.

But the analogy should be viewed with due caution because it is not about affirming that the supposedly laggard construction site has become modern in a twist of history. The construction site, of course, did not serve as a model for the new post-Fordist Japanese organizational practices, born mainly from internal changes in the automotive industry and its relationship with aspects of Japanese culture.[42] The permanence of manufacturing production on the construction site, the fixity of its product, and the slow turnover of capital stock are limits that prevent the construction site-form from becoming an example, even regarding the paradigm of flexibility, for increasingly automated and accelerated sectors (accompanying and promoting the reduction of turnaround time in consumption), whose industrial processes are much different.[43]

There are significant similarities and convergences between the construction site-form and the factory-form regarding flexible accumulation, however, in contrast to what occurred in the Fordist paradigm. Perhaps it would be more accurate to affirm the existence of "elective affinities," rather than any causal or exemplary relationship. Such affinities allow for speeding up the changes in architecture's productive forces, because current industrial managerial practices are more compatible with the construction site-form. Convergence allows for the theme of construction's industrialization to come back to the stage, but with new assumptions: it is no longer conditioned by serialization and standardization, but is open to custom-made prefabrication of unique parts— favored by the new "continuous flow" of digital information among multidimensional design models, machines, and robots that can produce complex forms with high variability. The introduction of these innovations, as we shall see, is often surprising, and for this very reason, it also fulfills an ideological function, as it helps to hide, with a high-tech veil, the maintenance and even the deepening of some of the traditional forms of production/domination on the construction site, which remain at its foundation.

ROBOT-MASON

Bricklaying is ancient work and has hardly changed over time. Fordist prefabrication of cladding components was never able to automate the execution of traditional masonry, and sought to replace it with various types of modular and standardized panels, whether light or heavy. Flexible automation allows the execution of a mason's movements through robotics. The robot as the "noble object and key object" of the Third Industrial Revolution, in Coriat's expression, is capable of "learning" complex moving actions, with the "ability to pick up materials, parts, tools, or specialized devices and submit them to programmed actions," which allows it to execute long and complex sequences of movements of a worker or a mason.[44]

In this extreme example that we will discuss, the current limitations of automation to replace skilled human labor will be verified, similarly to what we have done with regard to the automation of forms in design when analyzing Peter Eisenman's methodology and discourse. Recently, however, the "attack on the subject" occurs at the construction site, without the mason playing the central role in its dissolution, as in the case of the architect who mobilized the computer to partially automate the morphogenesis of his or her designs. The divergent practical and political consequences of the two forms of automation will be discussed at the end of this section.

Before meeting R-O-B, the robot-mason, and seeing how and why it replaces masons, we need to review the gestures and "choreography" of the ancient activity of bricklaying. Until recently, bricklaying was a prerogative of human motor skills that had not been "stolen" by capital and turned into dead labor, with the exception of its elimination by means of replacement parts. We will go through four brief descriptions of the bricklaying action. The first is by the Egyptian architect Hassan Fathy on ancient techniques of Nubian masons to build vaults with bricks; the second description, given by Sérgio Ferro, is a materialist and psychoanalytical description on the alienation of a bricklayer named "Rô"; the third is an account by Frederick Winslow Taylor based on a study conducted by his assistant, Frank Gilbreth, on the duration of the bricklayer's gestures; and finally, the fourth description I give based on a personal account of the work of Valdeci da Silva Matos, or "Lelê," the best bricklayer with whom I have ever worked.

Hassan Fathy observes: "The masons laid a couple of planks across the side walls, close to the end wall, got up on them, took up handfuls of mud, and roughly outlined an arch by plastering the mud onto the end wall. They used no measure or instrument, but by eye alone traced a perfect parabola, with its ends upon the side walls. Then, with the adze, they trimmed the mud plaster to give it a sharper outline. Next, one at each side, they began to lay the bricks. The first brick was stood on its end on the side wall, the grooved face flat against the mud plaster of the end wall, and hammered well into this plaster. Then the mason took some mud and against the foot of this brick made a little wedge-shaped packing, so that the next course would lean slightly towards the end wall instead of standing up straight. In order to break the line of the joints between the bricks the second course started with a half-brick, on the top end of which stood a whole brick. If the joints are in a straight line, the strength of the vault is reduced and it may collapse. The mason now put in more mud packing against this second course, so that the third course would incline even more acutely from the vertical. In this way the two masons gradually built the inclined courses out, each one rising a little higher round the outline of the arch, till the two curved lines of brick met at the top . . . Thus the whole vault could be built straight out in the air with no support or centering, with no instrument, with no drawn plan; there were just two masons standing on a plank and a boy underneath tossing up the bricks, which the masons caught dexterously in the air, then casually placed on the mud and tapped home with their adzes. It was so unbelievably simple. They worked rapidly and unconcernedly, with never a thought that what they were doing was quite a remarkable work of engineering, for these masons were working according to the laws of statics and the science of the resistance of materials with extraordinary intuitive understanding. Earth bricks cannot take bending and sheering; so the vault is made in the shape of a parabola conforming with the shape of the bending moment diagrams, thus eliminating all bending and allowing the material to work only under compression."[45]

In Sérgio Ferro's description: "Early on, on the construction site— before the beginning of working hours, there was the distribution of tasks. Befitting anyone, we suppose, who builds a wall: predetermined dimensions, positions, and technique. All working materials are gathered—

mortar, bricks, wire, plumb line, shovel, scoop, trowel, etc.—and the operation begins. Elementary motion schemes: hold, rotate, raise, spread, collect, etc. Gestures demonstrate the wisdom of a path already heavily trodden. Soon, the monotony no longer requires more than sinusoid attention. On the hands, the viscosity of mortar, brittle resistance of the brick, the scrape of sand grains; in the ears, rough-wet ambiguous sounds, beats of adjustments; on the body, repeated movements, almost rhythmic, variations in weight, familiar gestures. Little by little, pleasure is transferred, while a furtive 'perversion' escapes, in the heat of reencounter. The distance of the representations lets censorship sleep, thinking of something else. Through the arm, mute vibrations come in: no word has yet tried to name a loss that has installed itself while naming. Soon the overflow, the excess, as misplaced lust. From time to time, a step back for assessment, the correction; the head tilts, looking in a cozy repose grateful for having done it correctly: the object of pleasure almost has a body of its own. Beneath the ludic shell, from far away, childhood songs arise, or associated phrases. At the end of the day, the master concludes and takes stock: he simply appropriates the work (thank you, Rô). Something has gone, who knows what. The next day, it would be better if the songs were war songs, commenting on the taste for loss: aggressive drives may be more productive. If the sunny whistle succeeds the frowny face, maybe the wall moves faster. The master grunts. In the underfed body, tiredness, the hand burned by cement, the resected lung announcing silicosis, earn an almost tender regard: those are the only present signs of what was lost. But even so, at some point of the day, the friction of the shovel against a joint, or a well-nestled brick, or the shameless way the mortar swells under the beats, at some point of the day, it is sure, something else has beckoned. Maybe will come back tomorrow."[46]

Taylor describes Gilbreth's studies of the rationalization of time and motion in the bricklayer's work as follows: Gilbreth "experimented with every minute element which in any way affects the speed and the tiring of the bricklayer. He developed the exact position which each of the feet of the bricklayer should occupy with relation to the wall, the mortar box, and the pile of bricks, and so made it unnecessary for him to take a step or two toward the pile of bricks and back again each time a brick is laid. He studied the best height for the mortar box and brick pile, and then designed a scaffold, with a table on it, upon which all of the materials are placed, so as to keep the bricks, the mortar, the man, and the wall in their proper relative positions . . . Think of the waste of effort that has gone on through all these years, with each bricklayer lowering his body, weighing, say, 150 pounds, down two feet and raising it up again every time a brick (weighing about 5 pounds) is laid in the wall! And this each bricklayer did about one thousand times a day. As a result of further study, after the bricks are unloaded from the cars, and before bringing them to the bricklayer, they are carefully sorted by a laborer, and placed with their best edge up on a simple wooden frame, constructed so as to enable him to take hold of each brick in the quickest time and in the most advantageous position . . . We have all been used to seeing bricklayers tap each brick after it is placed on its bed of mortar several times with the end of the handle of the trowel so as to secure the right thickness for the joint. Mr. Gilbreth found that by tempering the mortar just right, the bricks could be readily bedded to the proper depth by a downward pressure of the hand with which they are laid. He insisted that his mortar mixers should give special attention to tempering the mortar, and so save the time consumed in tapping the brick. Through all of this minute study of the motions to be made by the bricklayer in laying bricks under standard conditions, Mr. Gilbreth has reduced his movements from eighteen motions per brick to five, and even in one case to as low as two motions per brick."[47]

Lelê is a man about fifty years old with blue eyes, a white mustache, and always wears a cap—he refuses to wear a helmet. He has been doing masonry work at *mutirões,* or collective self-construction, in social movements for almost twenty years. He says he likes to "work without a boss." Secure in the quality of his craft, he does not accept the subordination to those who depreciate his work, nor the intermediation of contractors who benefit over him. Sometimes he takes jobs on conventional labor contracts but ends up dissatisfied and goes back to the *mutirões,* where he is usually hired at a lower rate than on the market. Lelê often works with his brother, Nenê, forming one of the most beloved working duos. They can read floor plans and are excellent first-course layers, thus freeing other less skilled masons from this type of work. As is apparent from those joint efforts, they like to work with ceramic building blocks. Besides considering the ceramic block beautiful, its size (usually 39 × 19 cm) increases working efficiency over solid bricks. Hence, Lelê ended up developing his technique especially for this type of block. After the first course, the walls start growing from the "headers," the edge blocks, on which a little wooden U-shaped jig with two nails to fasten the level line fits, which, when stretched, guides the placement of the remaining intermediate blocks. The level is always checked at each header block with the help of an instrument consisting of a rope with a metal weight hanging and a wooden spacer on the other end so that the faces are lined up. The level of the headers is also verified with special care in the first course, and then at intermediate stages, with the use of a small transparent hose filled with water. The mortar, prepared by a helper, is always checked, stirred with a trowel until it gets to the point and consistency of the "good for handling" and "softness." Lelê likes the mortar to be made with a mixture of fine and medium sand so as to not get too rough. To spread the mortar on the top of the blocks, and because they are hollow, he uses what he calls a "palette," which consists of two slats the width of the mortar box, nailed, which he fills in the exact amount to reach the edge of the blocks, without the mortar falling into the holes. Then he covers the edges of all blocks already laid on the bottom course over which he will lay the new blocks. It is time to hold each block in his hand, and with the trowel spread the grout mortar on its side. The block is positioned with the hand, and then tapped with the handle of the trowel, which is considered essential for precise alignment. Then Lelê proceeds to the next block. When the height of the masonry requires a scaffold, he and his brother, with the aid of a helper, assemble the planks of the scaffolding in front of the masonry through its entire length, because the headers should remain accessible when marking the work, and the mason needs to move from side to side. Wood pieces and easels are checked to ensure safety. The mortar box and a few blocks are positioned on the scaffolding planks, which the helper supplies as necessary. The mortar that oozes out of the blocks must be cleaned from time to time with a dry foam sponge. Exposed blocks require the mortar to be raked, so that the blocks stand out and the mortar is lowered slightly. For this he uses the steel ruler and gently pushes the mortar in, removing excesses. Masonry by Lelê and Nenê is the most highly praised at the construction site. Although they also teach new masons how to lay those kinds of blocks, the craft is not learned as fast as one might imagine. The rhythmic coordination, at the same time precise and agile, is only achieved with much practice.

Let us now go to Switzerland, where R-O-B resides. As Ruy Gama recalls, this was the country in which Mary Shelley wrote the story of Dr. Frankenstein and his monster, made up of pieces of corpses into which life was imprinted, to which he adds, "Switzerland is not present in the story only as the background; there are other Swiss things in the monster. Machine mounted with parts from various sources, which brings it closer to watchmaking mechanisms of the automatons, it is also an artificial being, reminding us of the ideas of another Swiss-like Dr. Frankenstein, Paracelsus (1493–1541), according to whom it was possible to create a motherless 'homunculus,' from sperm only."[48]

Those who enter the Department of Architecture at the Swiss Federal Institute of Technology (ETH) in Zurich find a small glass room, climatized and lit, in the middle of an industrial-type shed, where one can read the acronym *d-fab-arch (Architecture and Digital Fabrication)* written on the facade. This is where R-O-B, the robot-mason, lives. The R-O-B is fastened to a rail about ten meters long in which it slides forward and backward when building walls. As we will see, R-O-B also travels in a container, and will stroll round New York City streets, building walls. Its trainers are professors Tobias Bonwetsch, Fabio Gramazio, and Matthias Kohler, the last two of whom are authors of the book *Digital Materiality in Architecture.*

R-O-B is an industrial six-axis robot, widely used in the automotive industry, whose "hand" can reach any parametric point in an area of 3 × 3 × 8 meters. This hand can be equipped with different tools to perform various actions with chosen materials. Its programming is transferred directly from the three-dimensional modeling software used by students, in a continuous flow of information. Gramazio, Kohler, and their students have been working with the robot since 2006, initially handling ceramic bricks, and then wood, plaster, concrete, and polystyrene plates. The first and most significant experience was the building of "the informed wall," an exercise in which the students were challenged to imagine how to lay a brick wall whose position and bonding made its execution impossible for a human being. The target was not to repeat existing constructive possibilities, but to achieve a technical and aesthetic result made possible only through digital manufacturing. Not

by chance, what was chosen was the most ancient and widespread architectural element: the brick. Students began the activity by manipulating
conventional bricks, searching for different possibilities of bonding,
verifying their level of stability and constructive difficulty. Next, with
the aid of digital design software they designed a 3 × 2 meter wall, geometrically ruled and with ornamental accessories. The information was
then communicated through algorithms to R-O-B, which was programmed to build the wall.[49]

R-O-B slides along the rail looking for the best position to execute
the wall on top of a wooden base. It moves its arm and holds the brick
with its mechanical claw, and turns it upwards. From a tube fastened to
its arm, a line of glue is projected. The robot moves its hand in a way
that the fast-drying glue is placed only in the area where the brick will
make contact with the other brick to which it must adhere. The hand
again rotates the brick with the glue facing down. It slides to the optimum
point for laying the brick, positioning it according to the coordinates
it has received. Precision is millimetric, plumb, level, and alignment,
automatic. There is no dropping of mortar or glue, thus eliminating the
need for raking and cleaning. The robot can position each block in any
desired spatial coordinate without any additional effort that would be
required from a bricklayer. Each block is laid in twenty seconds. A good
mason would take twice as long to build a conventional wall with the
aid of a helper. The finished wall is then removed from the room in
which the robot is located with the help of a forklift.

R-O-B's first commercial use was building the ceramic brick panels
for the envelope of a building that would house the fermentation and
tasting area at a Swiss winery. Architects Bearth and Desplazes contracted the *d-fab-arch* team to develop an ornamental brick facade that
simultaneously allows for ventilation and lighting through its openings in
the interior of the fermentation room.[50] The panels had to be embedded
in a structural grid of concrete columns and beams. From this, Gramazio and Kohler had the (somewhat literal) idea of throwing virtual
balls inside this structural crate as if they were grapes in a basket. Balls
of various diameters were "thrown" using a three-dimensional modeling
program that simulated their fall through gravity, until they were "pack-
aged" in the virtual basket. They were then projected onto the facades,
where the visual effect was attempted by rotating the position of the

bricks. The result is also three-dimensional, because the panel comprises the wavelike distribution of the blocks over a concrete base wider than the brick. The panels were executed by the robot over a concrete base and transported in a truck to the construction site, where they were lifted by a crane, positioned, and manually adhered to the frame.

Each small shift in the pieces' positioning produces effects with the reflection of sunlight, resulting in a panel of differentiated lighting that changes throughout the day and according to the movement of the observer. Smooth and rounded forms were thus obtained from the hard, rectangular component of brick. The textured effect of light and shadow is not new, of course, but the precision with which it was designed and executed confers its uniqueness. The end result is disconcerting: the use of brick and its disposition in organic forms that once meant the worker's freedom of motion at the construction site now stand for mechanical precision, a technical paragon, for there is no trace of human labor in the accuracy with which the pieces were arranged. There is thus a semiotic inversion between signifier and signified. With robotics, the most ancestral movements of craftsmanship, such as bricklaying, can not only be reproduced, but also taken to a limit that exceeds human motor capacity.

R-O-B was presented at the Venice Biennale of Architecture in 2008. In Venice, it executed one hundred meters of winding and oscillating walls with complex bonding, impossible for the human hand to execute, like a "cyber Gaudí." The robot thus became among the greatest attractions in the world's leading architecture biennial. It "steals the show right at the entrance of the Swiss Pavilion, and standing there, seeming to welcome those who came firsthand to see its masterpiece."[51] It "humanizes" itself while performing a task that could not have been done by the human hand.[52] The following year, it was time for the robot to travel to New York. It embarked in its container and was parked on a truck trailer on Pike Street, in Manhattan.[53] The container itself used for transport serves as a shelter for the robot when working outdoors in public streets, because two of its faces are mobile and when displaced by pneumatic arms, they form a covering that protects it from the sun and the rain. In the following days, R-O-B, closely watched by a small crowd, built a twenty-two-meter-long wall with several spiral loops that could be repeated endlessly as fractals. The initiative was the first test of the action of the robot outside the protected context of sheds, indicating its application in construction.

According to the *d-fab-arch* team, R-O-B differs from other robot-masons previously developed[54] because it "was not designed to mimic existing construction processes, but rather to serve as stimulus for innovation, not only in efficiency and cost, but also in favoring the achievement of new building components, both in performance and in aesthetic appearance."[55] The cost of these robots—about 200 to 250 thousand euros—makes their use in conventional executions prohibitive. Their viability lies precisely in the production of nonstandardized complex elements, at the time a demand restricted to brand architecture in its pursuit of the "rent of form." As the Swiss architects say, "the highest value added by digital manufacturing, above all, is of an aesthetic nature."[56]

Exposed bricks have always been one of the main indices, or refuges, of the skill of the construction worker. Its various and apparent apparatuses demand skilled labor, and therefore its presence is a sign of both the existence of know-how and the labor power that corresponds to it. The disappearance of this skilled labor's meaning and its replacement by the robot-mason cannot be celebrated as mere progress of productive forces without noting here a new episode of class struggle on the construction site, even if the Swiss architects who spearhead it do not realize this. They do not; nonetheless they carry it out.

Masons were, by the late nineteenth and early twentieth centuries, one of the most important categories of revolutionary organized labor. Workers' know-how and power were associated, and not casually, because the period architecture of exposed bricks was commanded, to a large extent, from within the construction site. As Ferro states, "brickwork masonry denotes effectiveness in the practice and skills gathered, in the worker's know-how," for here lies the inclination of capital to destroy those skills.[57] In his text "O concreto como arma" (Concrete as weapon), he points out how concrete is a "material that partially owes its existence and success to the fact that it indirectly ruins the (political) strength of the know-how of masons and carpenters at the end of the nineteenth century."[58]

A powerful metaphor for social change is self-contained in the mason's work, because it is the best symbol of the builder, the city, and the revolution itself, as Vinicius de Moraes expressed in his poem

The R-O-B installed at the ETH Zurich. It can be transported by truck inside a special container and complete tasks on the construction site. Copyright Gramazio Kohler Research, ETH Zurich.

"O operário em construção" (The worker in construction). When building space, the mason would have, literally in his hands, the skill needed to build a new society. As the poet said, if he learns to say "no," rejecting the exploitation to which he is subjected, he could then "build himself" as subject of social change.

The robot-builder is thus not just a gadget. Depending on its future application, it can have several consequences for the organization of work and for the automation of architecture. Given its high costs, however, widespread reproduction at construction sites is unlikely, substituting the subcontracting of bricklayers. It seems more reasonable that it will remain restricted to educational applications, and to the prefabrication of special parts for brand architecture. But even then, the political and symbolic consequences may be relevant.

In university laboratories, the robot-builder could become the "architect's best friend," executing his or her wishes perfectly and immediately, without mistakes or complaints, which a worker would not. The robot favors the increase of the drawing's command over the construction site, because it removes the difficulty and resistance of execution given by laborers' working conditions. It is a dream world of the architect, where there is no obstacle for the execution of his most extravagant designs. The pedagogical invisibility of the construction worker, almost always the rule in the architect's training, is now fetishized by the presence of the robot. The "digital-otherness," as Kostas Terzidis would have it, replaces real otherness.[59] The architect, as capital's middleman, no longer has to meet his or her other, the manual laborer, the construction worker, so he or she can command the entire construction process without obstacles, resistances, or strikes.

There is an essential difference between the automation of forms in architectural design and the automation of the mason's skilled labor. In the first case, even in a "metaphysical" discourse, the architect controls the operations and the form-related choices that he or she has based on more or less random computer manipulations. The machine is "at his/her service" and does not replace the architect, except in a controlled manner for specific tasks in which the designer has the last word. As Marcos Dantas suggests, "hardly ever, the greater the evolution of 'artificial intelligence,' will creative activities stop being essentially carried out by living labor, unlike other activities, which tend to be increasingly delegated to dead labor."[60] From the standpoint of the mason who executes his apparatus or builds brick vaults, the robot divides the worker into two halves, which will no longer belong to him. The ability to intervene is once again transferred to the intellectual work beyond the construction site, to the architect who designs without the experience of handling material and his or her motor memory (which evokes knowledge and pleasure, as we saw in the "ballet" of the Nubian masons of Rô or Lelê), but now with the help of digital tools that enhance abstract creativity based on geometric games and random combinations. Moreover, the sequence of complex movements, now cut off from that memory and its very creativity, can be decoded by algorithms for the robot to execute.

Here, as in the case of digital design tools, we are not talking about denying technological advances and their eventually liberating potentialities, capable of technically solving the problem of scarcity. It is not the case of attacking the robot-mason with wooden clogs in Luddite sabotage. Recognizing the age-old craft knowledge of masons and the way it was fought against does not mean adopting a technophobic stance. As Ferro states, "the likely evolution of the separated draftsman and the builder begins with its denial, a denial that will be the genesis of the new manifestation of the builder at a higher level (and not a regression to the mythical figure of the craftsman in a still-abstract unity between the doing and the thinking). Impossible to apprehend ahead of time: only at its formation it will present what it will be."[61]

What is at stake is comprehension of the meaning and form of technological innovation in capitalism and how it could be changed in a different context toward an emancipatory practice for all involved in the act of building. If there is no way to develop a socialist technology outside of socialism, there are initiatives closer to the interests of the majority being tested at present. An example is the public factories for fabricating hospitals and schools in Brazil, coordinated by the architect Joaquim Filgueiras Lima, or Lelê.[62] In them, technological innovation is developed in a joint act by designers and workers, in one single collective of builders, indicating various possibilities for technological development in architectural production. The end points are already many: schools, hospitals, kindergartens, and urban infrastructure facilities (slope retention and stream canalization plates, bus stops and terminals, and pedestrian walkways). The means of production are various as well: public factories, some of them managed as cooperatives, in which designers and workers operate jointly. The results achieved are not only of great quality, but they also express other working relations and the appropriation of productive forces.

Like a Brechtian tale, the story of R-O-B precisely disarms the "naturalness" with which we usually face technological progress. It presents the challenge of imagining how high technology can penetrate the construction industry not as a new form of domination of intellectual work over manual labor, but appropriated by the collective of workers as a means of strengthening their practices. In order to do so, it is necessary to overcome the temptation of technological progressivism, which endorses each and every development of the productive forces as intrinsically positive, whether by systemic ideology or orthodox Marxism. It is an eminently political task to identify counterhegemonic social subjects, capable of "incorporating class content into the process of redesigning" technology, "with values and interests different from those of capital."[63]

CONTINUOUS FLOW

R-O-B's experience is relevant, as is Eisenman's, for they clarify the extreme boundaries and limits of the metamorphoses of building praxis in the digital age. But now, let's go back to our main character, Frank Gehry's firm, which is not only an innovation agent in the field of digital design but is also one of the groups most directly involved with the introduction of digital automation on construction sites, and whose applications have been most widely spread in complex projects that explore the "rent of form." Not only did this transformation of productive forces occur in the architecture office, but it was also prefabrication and on the construction site that made the deformed structures of starchitecture feasible.

In addition to its design innovations, the construction of the Guggenheim Bilbao was also an inflection point in the production process. This was the first major instance of a prefabricated building in the flexible paradigm, with thousands of single, tailor-made pieces assembled on-site. No demand for serialization and standardization had restricted the industrialization of most of the components. According to Javier

Cantalejo, one of the architects responsible for the overseeing construction, "80 percent of the constructive systems and a good proportion of the materials employed were innovative," which forced his team to "reinvent architecture manuals."[64] The work at Bilbao also benefited from its industrial context—the Basque country is the center of Spain's naval and aviation industries—which by providing technology, equipment, and workers made some of these heterodox initiatives possible.[65]

Innovation in this and other projects we will mention occurred without major investments in fixed capital, because the programmable machines used in flexible production allow for the execution of a wide variety of actions on raw materials themselves, with no need to invest in molds, cutting tools, and industrial parts. They also allow each new action to be different from the previous one, through reprogramming only, at no extra cost. Thus, demands for standardization and serialization to achieve gains are no longer determinative in the production process. Prefabricated components are no longer, as was the case in the era of Fordism, an a priori catalog of parts to which designers must remain subordinate, either modulating their design accordingly or assuming an aesthetic of uniform serialized components. In this way, the architect resumes his or her command and precedence: it is his or her design that instructs the new nonstandardized industrial production, not the opposite.

As we saw in the preceding chapter, the programming of digital design models of the CATIA or BIM type prepares information for direct transfer to prefabrication machines and for assembly instructions on the construction site, largely removing the need for conventional representation on paper (section, plan, and elevation). This transfer of information reduces intermediaries and avoids the possibility of various misunderstandings, thus accelerating the transfer from design to production. The passing of instructions directly from the designer's computer to machines and workers in heavy industry is commonplace and has occurred for decades. In the case of architecture, however, the transfer of design data from the architecture firm to manufacturers or the construction site has always taken the form of boards, boxes, or rolls of printed paper. The idea of "continuous flow" in architecture, between design and production, or a digital continuum, in Kolarevic's term, dates from the early 1990s.

In turn, complex forms generated as a part of the digital project, and qualified in BIM, find enormous difficulties in being transposed to conventional two-dimensional representations. Nevertheless, it is often what needs to happen, says Dennis Shelden, from Gehry's team, because manufacturers of the parts, external designers, and construction companies are not always technologically prepared to receive the continuous flow of three-dimensional parametric information. In such cases, the BIM model is converted to simplified descriptions in conventional CAD, requiring partial redesign work, board by board, then updated separately and in parallel to the multidimensional model. These are the drawings that are sent to the construction site to guide various jobs, which are plotted at full 1:1 scale when mockups are needed at actual size, or for the craft execution of special parts.

The first stage of continuous flow occurs between designers and component manufacturers, even before it reaches the construction site. The quest for novelty that drives the "rent of form," as we have seen, stimulates not only the development of different designs, but also the great variability of each piece that composes them. Digital design and flexible production allow for both unique designs and unique pieces. For each design, a different piece at one-to-one scale is achieved only through recent industrial manufacturing with programmable machines allowing for the execution of various operations to produce unique pieces. These are CNC (computer numerically controlled) machines, specialized high-precision equipment, whose novelty is not only mechanical, but also with regard to the application of numerical methods to the programming of the machine's movements.[66] Such machines' cutting system can be laser- or waterjet–based.

In the production of components for architecture, CNC machines have been utilized in three main ways: cutting parts of any shape in flat sheets of different materials; arching tubular or flat pieces in one direction in a large variety of sequential rays; or even executing molds to cast complex double-curvature pieces, carving in materials such as polystyrene into which liquid material such as concrete or acrylic is then poured. Programmable machines also allow for prototypes of parts of the adopted constructive system to be easily checked, not aiming at serial production, but to analyze constructive details, finishings, fastening, and to test resistance.

Gehry's office tried these three modalities of nonstandardized prefabrication in several design projects. A CNC machine, designed to cut stones in various formats, was installed at the Guggenheim Bilbao construction site. Its main purpose was to cut the pieces of the sculptural tower that marks the entrance to the city at La Salve Bridge, whose complex and curved volumes demanded maximum effort from the assemblers to join heavy flat pieces to achieve the effect of a smooth curvature.[67] Most of the irregular surfaces of Gehry's buildings are cut in CNC—sometimes far from the construction site, as in the case of Bilbao's titanium panels, which were made in Italy from plates manufactured in the United States using Australian ore. This allowed, for example, the surface of the Experience Music Project (EMP) building in Seattle to be composed of twenty-one thousand distinct plates,[68] favoring the smooth and continuous visual effect thanks to the better adaptation of each piece to its curvature (as indicated by Gaussian analysis of the design's critical points in the surface's evolution). For a two-dimensional machine-cut piece to be molded in the desired curvature for assembly, the material must allow the required flexibility, as the cut is made from the unfolding of a three-dimensional design into two-dimensional coordinates. Only in this way can a flat plate acquire the curved shape needed for assembly and precise fitting with the surrounding pieces. This transformation of three-dimensional surface into two-dimensional surface to be then returned to three-dimensionality is extremely difficult to achieve manually without the help of a computer in the representation and in the instructions for cutting. For assembly, specialized workers are required, many of whom come from the shipping industry.

The curved structural ribs, similar to ship hulls or aircraft fairings, which support the covering skins, were also made through numerically controlled cutting. The cores of the curved beams were cut one by one out of sheet metal, with obvious wasted material from the resulting leftovers. The continuous and narrow plates of the upper and lower table that compose the beam are first bent in a different machine, and calendered to acquire the shape of the core's edge to which it will be welded. This technique was first used in the Seattle project, whose skin is extremely complex and could not use the more conventional solution adopted in the Bilbao and Disney Concert Hall projects, which led Gehry's team to assume (and change) the design and shipbuilding technique.

CNC machines were essential to make the glazed roof of the DG Bank in Berlin feasible, as was also the case with the toroidal roof designed by Foster + Partners for the British Museum. Jorg Schlaich, who had been invited by Gehry to engineer the roof of the German bank, tried to modulate the evolution of the curvature so that it could be composed of equal triangles, and then all connectors and pieces of glass could be standardized. But Gehry's team wanted to release the form from such constraint, which could only happen because of the CNC machine that allowed all connection nodes to be cut one by one at different angulations, along with the 1,500 pieces of glass. Foster did the same in the deformation of the British Museum's toroidal roof, flattening it slightly, which resulted in 1,566 connectors, 4,878 metal bars, and 3,312 pieces of glass, all different from each other and assembled on the construction site.[69]

Another variant of the use of the CNC by Gehry's team took place in the construction of concrete walls of complex forms and double curvatures for the Neuer Zollhoft Tower's wavy design, in Düsseldorf. Using CATIA software, the computer made a negative image of each piece in order to give each individual mold different parametric coordinates. Starting from a solid block of polystyrene (Styrofoam), the CNC machine cut the cavities of the molds one by one. The polystyrene was then removed from the cutting area and taken to the concrete pouring area in which it received steel reinforcement, and then liquid concrete was poured into it. After which the final finishing process was done manually using trowels. After being removed from the mold, the cured concrete slab was then transported to the construction site, and the polystyrene was recycled for reuse.

In addition to concrete, molds were also used for curved glass. A critical point for the execution of construction work in Bilbao was the installation of flat glass panes onto the irregular structures of the huge central atrium. On the facade, major assembly and sealing problems required complicated solutions.[70] In the later design for Café Condé Nast, in New York, Gehry's team tried using double-curvature laminated glass, executed individually.

Construction of the Guggenheim Museum Bilbao, designed by Frank Gehry.
Photograph by Wilfried Wang. Courtesy of the School of Architecture Visual
Resources Collection, the University of Texas at Austin.

Prefabrication of panels for construction of Neuer Zollhoft in Düsseldorf, designed by Frank Gehry, 1998–99. Courtesy of Gehry Partners, LLP.

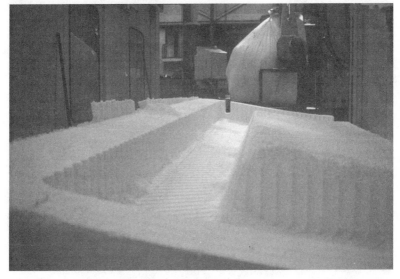

All these thousands of unique factory-made pieces arrive, at some point, at the construction site to be assembled like a huge puzzle. Executing such a puzzle from drawings and written instructions is unworkable. Accordingly, in coordination with derricks and cranes, other digital devices are used on-site to position the parts. The BIM system favors the temporal planning of the construction site supply flow. Runtimes and the transport of pieces to the construction site are informed by BIM, which establishes a dynamic schedule for ordering parts and delivering them at the precise time, optimizing the just-in-time system already used in construction inventory management. This planning can be combined with traditional time management systems, such as PERT, a legacy of Fordism.[71]

Construction of Neuer Zollhoft in Düsseldorf, designed by Frank Gehry, 1998–99. Copyright PERI GmbH. Courtesy of PERI Formwork Systems.

Construction of Neuer Zollhoft in Düsseldorf, designed by Frank Gehry, 1998–99. Courtesy of Gehry Partners, LLP.

Neuer Zollhoft in Düsseldorf, designed by Frank Gehry, 1998–99. Photograph by Rick Ligthelm, Creative Commons CC by 2.0.

Each component arrives on-site with a bar code, which is read by a hand scanner. In the bar code, the exact positional coordinates of the piece with its adjacent intersections are provided. The information is fed into computers at the construction site and into the laser positioning systems of parts through "total station" screening machines typically used by surveyors or in CATIA stations of the aeronautical industry.[72] The piece is usually hoisted by a crane, and assemblers on scaffolding or on mobile platforms lifted by crane receive the fitting orientation, then position and secure the piece in place. With this, complex works such as the Bilbao museum could be executed without a need for measuring tape or any other traditional instruments for measuring plumb, level, or alignment.[73]

The flexible prefabrication system has been adopted not only by Frank Gehry's office, but also, and increasingly, by the group of starchitects who seek to associate mechanical precision with the possibility of executing unique forms. Gehry and his team appear, once again, as innovating pioneers and key players in this transition. This type of ongoing prefabrication seems to be the most favorable to the construction industry's regime of variability—allowing for the convergence of flexible accumulation and architectural production, while also providing the material basis for the expected gains from the "rent of form." In this way, and more than in other sectors, the logic of flexibility and of increasing command is brought to paroxysm. Thus, there is an (ir)rationality inherent in the luxury economy, from high fashion to jewelry: a problem that we will deal with at the end of this chapter.

DIGITAL MASTER BUILDER

The continuous flow of information from architectural design to factories and construction sites, and the corresponding reconfiguration of relations between design and production is accompanied by an ideology of its own. Architect Branko Kolarevic, a Harvard graduate and an important ideologist of architecture in the digital age coined the term "information master-builder" to designate the architect's possibly new condition of full command over the construction process.[74] Kolarevic argued that architects have progressively lost their direct power over construction decisions to other agents such as engineers, builders, developers, and materials manufacturers, thereby becoming almost irrelevant figures, masters only of the production of "special effects."

In the United States, for example, architects are currently forbidden to bear legal responsibility for construction supervision, because of codes that regulate professional practice. According to an American Institute of Architects (AIA) statement: "the architect will not have control over or charge of and will not be responsible for the construction means, methods, techniques, sequences or procedures."[75] The full exit of the architect from the construction site, which could mean greater autonomy to dedicate fully to design conception, ended up resulting in a technical downgrade, loss of professional prestige, and progressive marginalization.

Michael Ball suggests that one of the reasons for this growing loss of importance occurring since the 1960s—after the war, architects had unprecedented power during the reconstruction and in the housing boom that followed—was probably the profession's fragmentation into many small semiartisanal architecture offices, which have proved inefficient, from the standpoint of their clients' interests, in coordinating design and construction and in planning costs, delivery times, and results in a realistic and competent way. The same has occurred in the public sector, with successive failures in urban planning and housing provision. With that, along with a disseminated "catalogue of building disasters," the profession "failed miserably."[76] In the 1980s, architects were seen as "misguided or grandiose amateurs incapable of managing the complexities of the building process." The world of construction has changed in those years and the architect lost his or her status as "supreme coordinators" (to entrust the architect with the exercise of that function was in fact considered foolhardy) and has come to be seen as an archaic professional, requested only to solve problems of taste. With the growing complexity of construction and the expansion of subcontracting—which had increased fragmentation and unpredictability in construction— "architects had neither the means nor the will to impose the necessary organizational discipline on such trends."[77]

By then, the solution to this impasse was being discussed at the Royal Institute of British Architecture (RIBA). In an article published in the RIBA journal, the two English Lords Esher and Llewelyn-Davies asserted that if architects do not develop new integrated construction management skills, they "will find themselves sooner than they expected on the fringes of decision-making rather than at the center, acting as stylists for other people's products."[78]

The "digital revolution" in the construction industry, which allowed for the concentration of information in a single unified data model capable of managing and coordinating almost all design and construction processes, appeared to architects as their chance to maintain their jobs. Whoever controls the management of information will lead the entire process, as was already known by Hal 9000, the computer of the second Odyssey—this time in space, in Stanley Kubrick's *2001: A Space Odyssey*. According to Kolarevic, the digital age opens "unprecedented opportunities for the architects to regain the authority they once had over the building process, not only in design, but also in construction."[79]

Favored by new digital technologies, the continuous flow between model, manufacture, and assembly, under design's command, would allow the redefinition of the relationship between architects, engineers, manufacturers, and contractors, headed by the former. According to Kolarevic and other apologists, only the architect could promote the unity between them all, in the figure of the new master builder—a builder with full control over all decisions in the construction process whose heyday was the Renaissance. The architect demiurge of the digital age must associate his or her knowledge of the craft of production with the newly refined techniques of digital design and, above all, he or she has to take on the skills of manager, capable of innovating in one of the most important areas of business: the construction industry and the real-estate circuit of capital reproduction. If this is reached, says Chris Luebkeman, the director of Ove Arup Associates, the engineering megacompany that also controls many innovations in architecture, we "have almost achieved the 'holy grail' of a new kind of mastering."[80]

The unified digital design model, as initially developed by Gehry's team up until it reached its commercial form with BIM, allowed for his team to resume the role of main producer and coordinator of information between the various players in the design and production process. In recognition of the leadership Gehry and his closest collaborators have assumed in all design and construction stages, one could designate them as the "ideal type" of new "digital master builder."[81] Gehry's background

and training as an artisan-architect, who not only handles matter physically in models and sculptures, but also at the construction site—as in
the several experimental reconstructions of his home in Santa Monica—
give him an affinity with the constructive process that overflows from
digital creation, in which he is otherwise more of a spectator of his collaborators' work. Given his broad training and predigital background,
this comparison with the old image of the architect as the master builder
does not sound implausible.

"No pretty pictures," said Jim Glymph, Gehry's partner; the digital modeling that the firm searches for is that which allows for a direct
connection between the designer and the manufacturer erecting the
buildings. "It's the old image of the architect as master builder," which
permits the "control to come back where it belongs, in the hands of the
architect from beginning to end," Glymph says.[82] Gehry's team is trying
to build a new type of production process management, which would
eliminate the major construction companies—"if they get into the business, we fall out"—in order to deal directly with manufacturers and
subcontractors. "That's how we did it in Bilbao and Prague," he asserts.[83]

According to Michael Ball, in the 1980s English architects tried the
same through what they called the Alternative Method of Management
(AMM).[84] By means of this method, main construction companies
were set aside and the architects took over the managerial control of
subcontractors. This was possible inasmuch as the construction companies themselves were increasingly becoming managers of other subcontractors, rather than actually hiring workers. However, the weak
position of the architects at the time vis-a-vis the construction companies prevented their plans of seizing power from succeeding. At that
time, English architects "failed to put themselves at the top of the pyramid of construction management."[85] However, their chance was renewed
in the 1990s, thanks to the strengthening of design projects through new
digital tools. As Gehry and his team signaled, architectural firms that
were prepared for such could try to replace construction companies, for
it is the programmers of digital models who accumulate all manufacturing information, including planning and costs. Thus, the architect
should be prepared to directly command, as the manager, the chain of
subcontracting manufacturers and assemblers, and in this way to remove
some of the layers of intermediaries that separate design from building.

Communicating that which one wants to build directly to the builders, as Jim Glymph stated and the Englishmen proposed in their AMM, is also a means toward achieving greater efficiency and economy, and accelerating the pace of innovation in a historically conservative sector. David Gann summarizes this conservatism as the result of the fragmentation of the production process, the separation between design and production and its own economic rationality, which makes builders more interested in perfecting their management processes as a means of expanding their earnings than in introducing technological innovations. When an innovation occurs, its dissemination is always slow. What collaborates with this "locked system," according to Gann, is the growing specialization, the codes that govern practice, the construction of standardized procedures and norms, and the defense of traditional practices, such as the defense of employment by unions.[86] As Sérgio Ferro has already said, there is an unusual "common interest" between capitalists and workers, mainly semiskilled employees, in order to keep the conservative levels as a means of self-preservation, in order to protect their own social reproduction. However, "the interests that add up have different weights, according to their very position in the production process—the interest of the worker is basically nondecisive."[87]

Under such conditions, the regaining of power by the architect favors the accelerated pace of innovation, as we have seen in the history of our main character, Frank Gehry. From David Gann's viewpoint, the role of architects as "catalysts for change" is central to breaking the "locked system," refractory to technical innovations. Their initiative, however, should transcend purely form-related experiments, to derive from these, through the help of the new digital tools, a reordering of the whole process of production. The continuous flow between design and production would permit a strategic "alliance" among the architects, now renewed, the computer industry, and the factories equipped with programmable machines and robots, relegating to the construction companies the simple role of assemblers of millimeter-detailed preprogrammed and pre-executed pieces.

This possible reunion of design and execution favors the illusion of restoration of the "lost unity" between design and construction, as desired by Kolarevic. For him, the master builder is the builder of

Gothic cathedrals who used to work at construction sites as a member of craft guilds. However, this is a historical mistake, as it does not fit the architect invigorated by the full control of information through powerful digital design models. The heyday of the master builder was the Italian Renaissance, when architects guided the entire construction process, from inside out, through transformations on various levels: from representational drawing and coding, to the organization of production processes, from the invention of new tools and mechanisms, to the improvement of materials and their use, and, thanks to all this and combatting strikes, they obtained the full direction over all workers at the construction site.[88] This is the master builder to whom architects might refer for inspiration in regaining their power, and not the medieval craftsmen. This is the dream of Stephen Kieran and James Timberlake, for example, two architects awarded the AIA Gold Medal for having proposed the resumption of this ideology, inspired by the example of Filippo Brunelleschi.[89]

Digital models could mean a unity between design and production only when the same group designs, builds, and collectively appropriates the results of its work. In this case, the programming of digital models should mainly be directed toward the development of horizontal mechanisms of cooperation, in which designer-builders would engage in a democratic dialogue, in an integrated and coordinated, yet decentralized, manner. There is no unity between the drawing and the construction site if there is no convergence, once again, between intellectual and manual labor inside the same group of people, and preferably, in each of its members. In this way, self-management between the drawing and the construction site could never be only digital, because it involves construction as its concrete, complementary, and inseparable moment.

The paradigm of the "digital master builder," in contrast, concentrates power and knowledge on the intellectual work, rather than distributing them, and it is for this very reason that the architect can imagine himself or herself climbing again to the top of the pyramid of workers that he or she intends to control. As Ferro ironically points out, "whenever there is a 'master'—in Hegel, in the university, or at the construction site—there is a 'slave.'"[90]

Actually, there is a broadening of the distance between the poles of design and the construction site. The drawing gathers more and more knowledge and power, and not only that. Be it Gehry designing as a sculptor of physical matter, or Eisenman of virtual (or metaphysical) matter, the process of creation is increasingly closer to the imaginary, "free" logic of the arts. The forms these architects create are transcribed during construction through high-precision industry software, with many parts made by machines, arriving at the construction site ready for absolutely accurate assembly. As we shall see next, this operation—a sort of download to reality—is much more difficult than the one described in the preceding section. The millimetric precision of complex parts produces an "insane" assembly game, "a nightmare," in the world of the builders—we are dealing with an irrational accuracy for architecture, which leaves no room for the adjustments and minor corrections that are needed in construction work. The knowledge and the skill of the construction workers, the basis of their power, is once again depreciated (and the crafts, suppressed) by capitalist technological innovation.[91] If, at one extreme, the starchitect searches for the new limits of free creation—or autonomy—the worker on the construction site is reduced to an automaton—maximum heteronomy. This is not an army of R-O-Bs, but rather an army of migrant and informal workers being called to close ranks.

HYBRID CONSTRUCTION SITE

Construction companies have tended to reduce their directly hired staff and started managing an army of subcontractors with the goal of reducing costs—on Bilbao's construction site, for example, there were only fifty such staff.[92] Increased productivity is obtained through improving the techniques of coordination of flows between crews at the site and suppliers of materials and components, allied with payment only per task performed—and not per hours worked—as a way of transferring risk to all agents involved. "Subcontractors and independent operatives are forced to produce more for less," and their multiplication on the construction site promotes a "lack of continuity between tasks," "the most significant cause of delay and idle time."[93] This has represented a worsening of working conditions and remuneration, as the "transfer of risks" occurs in one direction only: from capital to labor. The result is what Michael Ball and others have called a *skill crisis* in the industry, and its corresponding loss of speed and quality.[94]

As it erodes work, the deepening of subcontracting chains promotes a reverse productivity crisis. Consequently, managerial innovations find themselves in the face of a paradox. In the United States, for example, says Jim Glymph, while "overall productivity in the economy has been going up because of the impact of technology and different business practices, it has dropped by 15% in the construction industry."[95] It seems to be a no-win situation, because it is precisely the low pay of construction workers associated with workforce "layers of casualization" that discourages investment in machinery and equipment aimed at sparing labor. The imbalance in the capital–labor ratio inhibits the replacement of living labor by dead labor, as has happened in other industries, thus slowing and minimizing the impacts of digital transformation in the construction industry, regardless of what innovation agents intend.

The novelties of the digital continuum here described are often no more than superficial skins, even in Gehry's work, and do not even take place in the work of most other starchitects, including that carried out in Europe, as we shall see. Dennis Shelden, from Gehry's team, recognizes that CNC machines are set in motion only if the artisanal method is not cheaper—after all, even in Gehry's firm, "the most important driven force in decision making behind the firm's design development phase is the *project budget control*."[96] According to him, only some solutions are more economical with prefabrication, while others—involving combinations of materials, sizes, and forms—require hiring qualified workers to complete them. Increasingly scarce in the construction industry, these workers might be recruited from other industries such as shipbuilding and metallurgy. Even mountaineers can be mobilized to assemble structures at great height.

Prior to its being widespread in the construction industry, information modeling added additional costs that often undermined gains in productivity. In addition to expenses with software, there are costs with the programmers at these workstations who are highly skilled and well paid. The amount of information needed to program a CNC machine is much greater and more expensive to run than with conventional manufacturing. Moreover, because few suppliers of building components are equipped with the latest technology and programmable machines, they charge more for it, obtaining additional profit when compared with conventional companies.

The result is that, under current conditions, the development of design and construction through continuous flows and CNC manufacturing is almost always more costly than traditional methods. Only special designs that promise additional gains through the "rent of form" can mobilize this new technology on a larger scale, inasmuch as it enables novel combinations of forms and materials, as we saw in R-O-B's case. Even in such cases, prefabricated parts of complex and nonstandardized forms might be adopted on the surface of the building in order to produce the intended visual effect, while the remainder of construction is completed conventionally.

This superficial application of the layer of technological innovation over a conventional structure is exemplified in a recent Frank Gehry design project in New York: "New York by Gehry" (formerly the Beekman Tower). The seventy-six-story skyscraper, located near the Brooklyn Bridge, almost had its height cut in half during the 2008 crisis and one of its undulating facades eliminated, to reduce costs. The concrete structure and production process were absolutely traditional, while the CNC prefabrication was centered on elements of the main facade only, seeking to keep a portion of the visual effect that could assure the Gehry "wow factor."

Large-scale production using programmable machines, even within the paradigm of flexible production, finds limits in architecture. CNC machines and robots are used in other industrial sectors not only as means of suppressing highly skilled labor, but to obtain the high-precision components required for the mechanical performance of their products. This is how pieces cut by numerical control or welded by robots enable gains in performance and safety in airplanes, ships, and automobiles. In construction, this maximum precision, millimetric or micrometric, is not necessary for the proper performance of a building. Its use obviously implies additional costs.

To erect a building as if it were a ship or an airplane represents a mismatch between the applied technique and the resulting function. It is a technology transfer of paradoxes and inconsistencies. Ships and planes, ultimately, have archetypal forms shaped by the dynamic determinations of physics. In this sense, they tend toward standardization, with minor variations between models. In the architecture we are reviewing, this same technology is used to obtain maximum variation between projects, demanding similar variability for parts and processes. Moreover, because each building is unique—a prototype made into final product—even the prefabricated components cannot guarantee high performance, given that they are being tested for the first time. It is also a mix of technologies, materials, and production processes that favors the occurrence of mismatches between components—see, for example, the mismatch between base and superstructure (in the literal sense) in architecture: the difference between work with land and foundations, which are relatively inaccurate, and the desire to implement, on this basis, a superstructure of great precision, designed and cut as airplane parts.

Design projects like the Stata Center, conceived by Gehry for the Massachusetts Institute of Technology (MIT), have resulted in many problems of this kind. The Boston technological institute sued the architect over flaws in the design. The building, planned to be a "geek palace for some of the brightest minds on the planet," has become a "leaky tenement." According to MIT, which spent $1.5 million on repairs, "poor drainage almost immediately led to cracks in the outdoor amphitheater, snow and ice fell off the irregular angles of the walls and blocked emergency exits, and mold sprouted in the exterior bricks."[97]

Labor market conditions and the average minimum wage in the construction industry of each country are also important elements when determining the advancement of prefabrication. In one of Gehry's most interesting projects, dubbed the Dancing House (or Fred and Ginger)—an office building carefully inserted in a corner in front of the Vltava River in Prague—prefabrication was minimal. The building was approved by referendum, with a majority of 58 percent, and considered by Gehry a victory for democracy in a country formerly integrated in the communist bloc. The building information electronic modeling was executed in a similar manner to his other projects, prepared to communicate directly with CNC machines. The idea was to execute the entire steel structure, the cut of the glass, and the curved concrete plates in factories, as in the Düsseldorf project. But according to Jim Glymph, who participated in the project, "Czech labor rates were so low that we wound up simply templating directly from the computer to craftsmen,

"New York by Gehry" (formerly the Beekman Tower), designed by Frank Gehry, 2006–11. A reinforced concrete structure is lined with elements prefabricated in CNC machines. Courtesy of Gehry Partners, LLP.

who would build wood forms and then ultimately pour concrete and complete the walls."[98] As one can deduce from the executed work, the molds were complex, with soft and varied curves, undulating levels on the facade, and window openings at nonmatching heights.

In such cases, in which CNC machines are replaced by highly qualified labor, the design reaches the hands of artisans on a full 1:1 scale, as in the Middle Ages.[99] Manual production of elements of complex forms requires full-scale templates, similar to cutting fabric for clothes making, in such a way that irregular curvatures are executed accurately. On the site, these parts are still subjected to minor adjustments, similarly to tailoring. In the design of a high-tech home in Switzerland, the Chesa Futura (Home of the Future), another toroid by Foster, an all-glued-laminated timber structure was covered with timber shingles. The shingles were cut one by one with an ax by an eighty-year-old craftsman and nailed to the structure manually by the rest of his family.[100]

Craftsmanship is also required for the assembly at construction sites. The metal surfaces of several of Gehry's projects required hiring specialized workers from the shipbuilding industry for their assembly: in Bilbao, in the DG Bank, and in the EMP in Seattle, for example. These workers were responsible for the three-dimensional application of the plates on the structures, which arrived flat at the construction site. Undulations, joints, finishes, and minor adjustments required workers trained in the production of surfaces such as ship hulls. In the Guggenheim's construction work, all the titanium plates in the confluence between planes, the "closure pieces," were manually cut and applied one by one.[101]

In the projects we have examined, the recurring appeal to state-of-the-art prefabrication, and to the work of craftspeople, and sometimes to both, is a sign that the production process, when compared to modern architecture, has broadened toward both extremes: automation and craftsmanship. On one side, the machinofacture, automation with numerical control machines and robots that enable 1:1 customized manufacturing, and, on the other, old craftsmen with their instruments, manufacturing complex parts from 1:1 templates. Such a construction site can be considered more technologically hybrid than the site of previous phases; in this way, flexibility arises from this broadening of productive and form-related possibilities.

Chesa Futura in St. Moritz, Switzerland, designed by Foster + Partners, 2000–2004. The timber shingles are hand cut. Photographs courtesy of and copyright Foster + Partners.

The worker-assembler, the one who is closer to abstract labor on the construction site, is midway between these extremes. Contrary to what is claimed by the dominant discursive formulation of the automated construction site operating like an aircraft factory, these workers are put to the test in the most difficult assembly situations. The complexity and novelty of built forms, and the use of certain materials associated with unforeseen situations—part of their daily work at the construction site—make it a particularly arduous task. In Bilbao, for example, there were numerous "difficult zones to be solved" by assemblers, because the secondary curved structures over which the closure parts were applied "produced complicated geometric problems of relationship and connections between the parts, which further aggravated control over the joints in order to achieve building tightness," says the architect responsible for the exterior cladding.[102] Assembly of the main steel structure was another challenge for assemblers. Despite advanced prefabrication having reduced the problem with isolated pieces, the structure, when erected, was not stable, making assembly work laborious. The architect in charge of the task observes that "everything is perfect when the work is finished, but until then nothing was stable."[103] According to him, other "extremely difficult" elements to be executed were the sculptural tower beside La Salve Bridge, and the roof over the terrace of the museum's central atrium, facing the reflecting pool. This covering is a high marquise, shaped as a cap flap, supported by a single pillar. Gehry seems to acknowledge the builders' efforts: "I love my clients, and I love designing buildings with them, but my favorite part of it is the construction process, and the craftspeople like you and your team that come in and make it all happen."[104]

Eisenman's megaproject in Santiago de Compostela was a festival of difficulties with the assembly of its tailor-made pieces. The American architect and journalist Danny Forster, producer of the *Build It Bigger* series, personally accompanied several work teams at the City of Culture construction site, and could show in a direct way, step by step, the enormous complexity to build it: "the building is crazy, every single piece is different. I had no idea that architecture could be so dangerous—who designed this?"[105] The prefabricated parts had to all be hoisted and positioned at a certain height, but local weather conditions were critical, with daily rain and strong winds. Some pieces broke apart during transportation or arrived with the wrong measurements; with this, the assembly puzzle was kept incomplete, sometimes paralyzing a whole workforce. When a piece that had problems arrived back at the site, after days of waiting, the workers could return to their positions for a specific installation, which resulted in newly wasted time. The sloped concrete hit inclinations up to 60 percent and needed to be made and remade several times until a solution was found on the construction site (for it was not foreseen by the architect), "more lost time and wasted money." Forster, dumbfounded, claims that "never before, buildings with such features have been built, and now, they are building six at the same time!" The workers at the site do not understand the logic behind the design—"What did the architect want with this?" and "Is he a madman or a genius?"[106] is the question heard over and over again in the site. The most "insane" aspect of the work, he says, is the stone roof, the great undulating surfaces that simulate mountains. The quartzite stone plates are heavy and need to be carefully aligned on the ceiling. The reporter describes the sensation of lying inside the metal structure that supports the stones: "it is a terribly uncomfortable job for its weird positioning."[107] In just one of Eisenman's mountains, thirty thousand stone panels are used, which requires the manual adjustment of 120,000

The City of Culture of Galicia in Santiago de Compostela, designed by Eisenman Architects, 1999–2011. Photograph by Eladio Anxo Fernández Manso, Creative Commons CC-BY 2.0.

screws. Their function is purely decorative, because the drainage system is installed under the stones and will not be crossed on foot by future visitors.

Conventional construction sites without any prefabrication are equally present in signature works. The Casa da Música, in the city of Porto, designed by Rem Koolhaas and the Office for Metropolitan Architecture (OMA), is one such example. According to the Order of Architects,[108] and the testimony of the architect Jorge Carvalho, manager of the local office in which the design was developed in conjunction with OMA,[109] the execution of the building was "completely handmade" and had to face a number of challenges. As we saw in the execution of Eisenman's walls, for example, given the inclination of the concrete curtain walls and the threat of collapsing, an expensive and laborious shoring system was required, besides the additional risks to which the workers were subjected when building and hoisting the concrete framework.

There was no concern about prefabrication, not even of the elevators, also custom-made, copper-coated, and with higher ceilings. Even industrially sourced materials, such as the metal decking and the perforated sheets hiding mechanical equipment and lighting, were individually cut. In the case of the perforated sheets, each panel was measured and subdivided into equal sections, and the sheets were cut one by one, without constraints standardizing the pieces' width. Almost all elements were cut and executed on the construction site or by craftsmen in workshops, and the measurements were carefully taken on-site, like a tailor taking his or her client's measurements. The visuals of building with high-tech-looking elements, as at Le Corbusier's La Tourette, do not correspond to the productive forces that gave rise to them. But behind it, labor, even if suffocated, can be seen.

MIGRATIONS AND VIOLATIONS

When architects design works with complex forms and develop innovative techniques, little attention is usually given to the working conditions at the construction site.[110] In simulations of sophisticated multidimensional digital design models, rarely are studies conducted about the degree of difficulty in their execution, worker ergonomics, risks of injury, or acute toxicity. In most cases, when construction phases are being planned, only the physical organization of the construction site is examined: things such as access and storage of materials, the positioning of support buildings, the location of cranes, details of formwork, and so on. Technical and formal innovations, to architects, are normally dissociated from other innovations in order to reduce work hardships and difficulties on the construction site. As the award-winning architect Jacques Herzog stated, "we have nothing to do with the organization of the construction site, neither in China nor anyplace else in the world."[111]

The assembly of pieces at the construction site, as we have already mentioned, involves several challenges. The aid of the laser-tracking engine, contrary to what it might seem, is an additional complicating element, given its demand for millimetric accuracy. An article by *New York Times* journalist Alex Marshall, "How to Make a Frank Gehry Building," based on the testimony of laborers who worked in the construction of his buildings, describes some of these challenges: "the workers

Construction of the Casa da Música in Porto, designed by OMA, 1999–2005.
Copyright PERI GmbH. Photographs courtesy PERI Formwork Systems.

cannot rely on experience or intuition to get it right; they must do what the machine tells them. Each piece fits into imaginary dotted lines in space, dictated by the CATIA coordinates." Not a single mistake is allowed; otherwise the other pieces would not fit at the end of the chain. Given the precision of the CNC cuts, the smallest imperfection could compromise the entire set. In a conventional structure, an error of a few centimeters can be corrected by the team executing the masonry, and no one will notice the difference. But in Gehry's buildings, with their spirals and curves in space, centimeters at a given point might turn into meters down the road. As a site engineer affirms, "the old adage is, you measure twice and cut once" does not apply to a building like this, because "here, you measure a dozen times."[112] The consequence is an increase in both time and costs. The square meter of university buildings designed by Gehry costs double the price of conventional buildings, according to Alex Marshall. A young worker in charge of the assembly said, "It's a nightmare! Two mills out at the first joint, and you're 20 millimeters out at the other end! A nightmare!"[113]

The complexity and irregularity of the forms turn workers hostage to instruments of technical precision, and they end up unable to use their knowledge to make decisions during construction. At the same time, they are placed in absolutely terrible working conditions, hanging from cranes or balancing on scaffolding at great height, needing to fit parts millimeter by millimeter in windy conditions, rain, or the scorching sun. The structures of Koolhaas' mega-building for the central Chinese television network, CCTV, had to be connected during night shifts because sun incidence caused the structure to expand irregularly throughout the day, thus interfering with the millimetric adjustment of its fittings.[114] The Allianz Arena in Munich designed by the duo Herzog & de Meuron demanded alpinists to assemble its metal roofing over the playing field,[115] and the Beijing National Stadium, or Bird's Nest, involved very complicated work to hoist thousands of unique, extremely heavy and irregular pieces to their precise fit, and all of it against the clock. The work of Eisenman in Galicia required the adjustment of tens of thousands of screws in its roofing, millimeter by millimeter, with workers crawling backward in the extremely limited space of the support structure.[116] Renzo Piano has obliged workers of the IRCAM (Institut de Recherche et Coordination Acoustique/Musique) to sand bricks one by one in order to achieve the project's desired pinpoint accuracy.[117] Workers who assembled the framework at the Casa da Música in Porto had to work in dizzying positions, tucking their boots in the small gaps between the rebar to keep their balance.[118] The number of examples of disregard for the worker is endless, but these are stories that are not usually told in texts and magazines.

The submission of the worker's body to the most extreme and unhealthy demands is accompanied in many countries by an increasingly foreign composition of the workforce in the construction industry. Many of these projects are executed by significant contingents of migrant workers subjected to precarious living conditions, legal uncertainty, and few labor guarantees, which, as we shall see, contribute to a reduction in the social reproduction of labor costs and to a lowering of the wages in this sector as a whole. The real-estate sector recognizes that "illegal immigrants play an important role in the construction labor market," for without them, buildings "wouldn't be built on time or on budget." Michael Fink, from the Leewood Real Estate Group, explains that "if (construction workers who are here illegally) are removed from the workforce, the construction business will suffer tremendously."[119]

As we saw at the beginning of this chapter, the construction site is a real, hard form of economic production that cannot be exported to the third world (now called the Global South), so it is the underdeveloped world, in the form of migrant workers, often illegal, that is imported to construction sites in the rich countries that lead global capitalism. These workers are mobilized at the end of construction subcontracting chains, hired by smaller companies more difficult to supervise, or else, hired as self-employed workers, with no employment obligations.

While writing this book, no specific migrant data was found in the works we are analyzing. In Ianna Andréadis's *Chantier ouvert au public,* one of the few books dedicated to understanding starchitecture's construction sites, specifically the Quai Branly Museum by Jean Nouvel, the physiognomy of photographed workers is revealing.[120] In the list of workers who released their images located at the end of the book, one can see that the vast majority of about one hundred names listed includes Arabs (a dozen Mohammeds, also Hassan, Arbib, Irfan, Ali . . .), Africans (N'zembo, N'Songo, Mamadou, Miloud, Niakaté . . .), Portuguese or Brazilian (Gonçalves Silva, Dos Santos, Barroso, several Joaquins and Antonios). In the construction of the Allianz Arena in Munich, there were workers from twenty different countries, mostly from Eastern Europe.[121] In the Casa da Música, similarly to the Portuguese construction industry, there were Romanian, Ukrainian, Brazilian, and African migrants. At the time, Jacques Herzog said about architects like himself: "it is not within our power to change the conditions for migrant workers, nor is it our responsibility."[122]

In the United States, one-third of construction workers are not native, and of those, it is estimated that 40 percent are undocumented.[123] In Europe, the data is similar—a situation that increased with the creation of the common European labor market.[124] Gains for employers are obvious. According to information provided by construction unions in New York, for example, a skilled worker, such as a carpenter, receives forty dollars an hour, plus benefits. A young Irish immigrant in the same working position would receive twenty to twenty-five dollars an hour, while a Brazilian worker would receive between fifteen and twenty dollars, with no benefits (in Brazil, in turn, his or her hour is worth about five dollars). These workers are pressured not to unionize and, afraid of losing their jobs or being threatened by organized crime, end up isolated.[125] Similar fear, however, is disseminated among all workers, and not just migrants. The result is that, at the time of writing, only 16 percent of U.S. construction workers were unionized, and strikes in the sector were very rare.[126]

The number of accidents and deaths in construction remain high. In the United States, one in every five workplace deaths occurs at construction sites, three times more than the average of other productive sectors.[127] In 2005, in the United States, 1,186 construction workers died at work,[128] twice the average number of annual deaths for the U.S. military during the Iraq occupation.[129] According to American unions, the Division of Construction Inspections, commonly known as the Building Department, cannot respond to the problem. There are not enough inspectors, and an annual salary of thirty-five thousand dollars is low for encouraging the recruitment of people ready-and-willing to inspect such high-risk situations. With the absence of adequate inspections and penalties for offenders, construction companies cut investments in safety and accident prevention and try hiring workers for the lowest possible values.[130]

The U.S. health-care reform passed by the Obama administration, for example, suffered great opposition from the construction industry. In a document written by the AGC (Associated General Contractors of America), they requested that Congress vote against the reform, saying that compulsory health insurance for employees would excessively burden the sector, because insurance for workers in hazardous conditions is costly. Construction companies also criticized a new law that eliminated the advantages of small contractors, as if they were not part of the subcontracting chains of big construction companies. In the name of guaranteeing jobs and overcoming the U.S. recession, construction companies therefore railed against the health-care reform.[131] It is worth remembering that, in previous years, the construction sector had benefited from the U.S. speculative housing bubble and was the nerve center of the 2008 global crisis.

In Europe, similar to what happens in the United States, migrant labor in the construction industry is not exactly a novelty, but it operates on a different cycle with specific traits. Until the 1980s, migrant workers in the construction industry came from former colonies (mainly in Africa and the Middle East), or from peripheral countries in Europe, such as Portugal, Greece, and Turkey—usually low-skilled laborers coming from rural areas. From the early 1990s on, there was a new cycle of migrants in the construction sector, coming mainly from countries of the former socialist bloc: a process that accelerated as some of these countries joined the common European market.

In *Le Monde diplomatique* in 2002, Hervé Dieux comments on the traits of these new migrants who occupy the building industry in hopes of better jobs. They are characterized as "disciplined" and "highly qualified," many of them endowed with university degrees ("they are doctors, engineers, technicians"), a legacy of the communist regime and its policies of access to education. In search of better living conditions, they access the labor market in other European countries through the door of the construction industry.[132]

A study on migrant labor in Britain found that this gap in education promotes a reverse stigmatization: "one factor may be the difference in education level where many of the migrants were working below their education and skill level and may therefore have little in common with others doing the same job. 'How can we expect to integrate someone with a diploma in astrophysics with a bricklayer?' In some instances migrants did themselves voice that concern—for example, a Polish philosophy graduate who complained about the lack of intellectualism among British construction workers. Others, however, suggested a problem in the attitude of British workers towards migrant labor. A Bulgarian construction worker told us: 'They simply have us as a different category of people. The English do not have a great respect for us. We are just labor and we are no longer needed if the market is oversupplied."[133]

An English recruitment agency for Eastern European workers for the construction industry advertises on its Web site as follows: "Are you looking for experienced construction tradesmen? Need carpenters, bricklayers, painters, plasterers, joiners and welders? Can't find workers locally? Why not to take an advantage of the new European labor market? Eastern European construction workers are commonly known for their hard work, dedication to the employer and work excellence. We offer you highly skilled workers from various building professions. Our candidates have developed their skills from the construction work experience in their home countries and while working abroad. We can provide you with the highly skilled Lithuanian, Latvian, Polish, Slovakian, and Hungarian building and construction workers. Construction tradesmen from Eastern Europe are a real opportunity to achieve higher productivity at lower cost."[134]

The adoption of migrant labor in general, and particularly from the low-cost Eastern European skilled migration cycle, is a strategy to increase the rate of surplus value. Western European countries benefit from their professional qualification and training in discipline, provided by the former socialist bloc, and they freely appropriate the "past work" this workforce contains. In turn, contrary to what one might expect regarding the costs of reproduction of these qualified workers, in their new conditions and new country their costs are low, because migrants endure poor conditions related to housing and food. The result is skilled labor at low cost: for capital, it is as good as it gets.

Tenements, similar to those described by Engels in the nineteenth century, are once again profitable activities for landlords who rent rooms to foreign tenants. Many times "there are ten to 11 people in flats with only one bathroom," says a Bulgarian construction worker.[135] Subleasing becomes an alternative for migrant workers to maximize their incomes and accept wages not compatible with the social reproduction costs of an English worker. Thus, besides promoting gains for their employers, migrants favor the rentier businesses of vacancy lessors in tenements and recruitment agencies.

Migrant labor's degree of fragility, associated with low rates of unionization, represents a huge imbalance in the capital–labor relation, favoring predatory accumulation. Nonetheless, they are not the only ones to be penalized by this. In varying degrees, this situation extends to all construction workers. Failure to follow work safety conditions, low inspection rates, and high numbers of deaths and accidents, besides the usual increase in working hours, are examples of how the construction industry is one of the most violent, exploitative, and predatory areas of the workforce. And that is why it constitutes one of the most important "surplus value reserves," intensively exploited by capital, and whose earnings are transferred to other sectors of the economy, as Ferro explained.

Starchitecture projects outside rich countries also take advantage of these poor working conditions in even more critical situations. Havens of spectacular architecture and their construction sites are analyzed in three reports by Human Rights Watch (HRW). One reports on the working conditions at Beijing construction sites, including the Olympic projects; two others report on migrant workers in the construction industry in the United Arab Emirates (Dubai and Abu Dhabi). Some of the reports' recommendations are directed at the works of renowned architects, in which they warn these architects (in vain?) about the type of working conditions they are promoting.

Migrants who work in the construction industry in Beijing are mainly Chinese who come from the rural interior to try their luck in the big cities. This constitutes a phenomenon of migration within national borders, such as what occurred in Brazil in the decades of accelerated growth. The "invisible army" of workers on Beijing's construction sites is estimated at two million people.[136] They suffer from different types of exploitation, in addition to restrictions on organizing. The most common situations spotted in the report are wage arrears and defaults, poor housing and food, lack of applied safety measures and workplace accident prevention, and threats hindering unionization and strikes. Migrants are subjected to extra precarity, such as lack of access to public services and free medical care, even in case of accidents. This is because, according to Chinese law, only local workers with household registration in Beijing have rights to these services and guarantees.[137]

According to the HRW report, local law prohibits independent unions, and wage negotiations outside the All-China Federation of Trade Unions. The official union does not accept migrants, thus preventing their representation even in this instance. Bureaucracy stalls labor claims. Protests and strikes are suppressed by the police, and contractor henchmen arrest or threaten demonstrators; exploitation is systemic and the amalgam among entrepreneurs, the Communist Party, and the official union prevents workers from defending their rights and most basic needs. However, the *Mingongs,* as these internal migrants are called, remain nationalist and proud of their work[138]—perhaps similar to Brazilian *candangos,* the name given to workers who migrated to build Brasília, who felt they were participating in the construction of a new country that, however, did not reserve a place for them, neither in the city nor in politics.

Researchers from Human Rights Watch attempted to investigate the construction sites of the Olympic projects, but "access to such sites is strictly controlled, making on-site research impossible." According to the researchers, there is no reason to believe that in these construction sites the situation differed from that elsewhere in Beijing. The purpose of the report, of course, was not to influence the Chinese government to take measures that favor workers, but to attract international attention to conditions under which the "Chinese miracle" occurs and how China's new and shiny skylines are produced. It is in this way that the "spectators at the 2008 Olympic Games in Beijing should be made aware that the venues in which they are watching the Games may have been built by workers who were mistreated, never paid or paid late for their labors, or faced dangerous and unsanitary conditions, with tragic consequences for some. Spectators should also know that the International Olympics Committee has never made serious efforts to ensure more humane treatment for such workers."[139] Neither did the architects, as Herzog had already confirmed.

Pressed in an interview to justify his "partnership" with the Chinese government to build one of its most emblematic buildings, the CCTV state television networks building, Koolhaas says: "it's wrong to condemn China simply as a dictatorship. The country has come an enormously

Construction workers at the Bird's Nest, Beijing, designed by Herzog & de Meuron, 2003–8. Photograph by Iwan Baan.

Construction workers at the CCTV Tower, Beijing, designed by OMA, 2003–12. Photograph by Iwan Baan.

Construction workers at the CCTV Tower, Beijing, designed by OMA, 2003–12.
Photograph by Iwan Baan.

long way in recent years and made great progress. Within a very short time, a wholly underdeveloped economic system has been reformed, and along with that a lot of rights have developed, for example, the right to own property."[140] A symptomatic response, after all, this is the only right that really matters for capital to ensure continuity of Western (material and symbolic) investments in China.

The situation in the United Arab Emirates, the most eye-catching showcase of contemporary architecture and a paradigmatic enclave of the new rentier economy, as Mike Davis described it, is even worse.[141] Foreigners make up 95 percent of the Emirati workforce, with 2.7 million migrants.[142] The construction industry is one of their main destinations, with migrants coming mainly from poor and rural areas of India, Bangladesh, Pakistan, and Sri Lanka. Their average monthly salary is $175 (there is no minimum wage in the Emirates), in a country where the per capita income is $2,100 per month. These workers are recruited in their countries of origin by worker trafficking companies, which charge between two thousand and four thousand dollars for transferring them to a construction site in the Emirates. This debt is paid by raffling all of the workers' personal savings in their country of origin, or, over the years, already on the construction sites, at extortionate interest rates. With visa and employment agreement in hand, the migrants have their passports illegally retained by the construction company that receives them in the Emirates. According to HRW, the remuneration stipulated in the contract was always lower than what was promised in their country of origin, often by 50 percent. Working hours ranged from ten to twelve hours under the blazing sun, averaging 38 degrees Celsius during peak working hours, causing dehydration, sunstroke, and other diseases. At the time of writing, there was no reliable data on deaths and accidents during construction. While the government stated that thirty-four workers died on construction sites in 2004, an independent survey indicated 264, again according to HRW.

Migrant workers are housed in 1,033 "labor camps," or worker concentration camps, fenced and monitored, composed of prefabricated housing, in which bunk beds are the only furnishings. The bathrooms are awful, and commonly lack water. There is no free medical assistance or insurance for accidents—thus workers must pay any health expenditure from their own remuneration. It is not possible to file labor claims, there are no independent lawyers to defend workers' interests, and the government does not recognize any human-rights organization. There are only forty-eight labor inspectors, who, according to interviewed workers, were never seen on the construction site. Unionization is discouraged and the right to strike is prohibited by law. The worker does not even have the right to change jobs or companies, in this case, under penalty of deportation. The result is that when there are strikes and protests, they are violent and wild, destroying administrative offices, burning cars, and pillaging machines and work vehicles.[143] Repression is tough, with tens of thousands of workers imprisoned and awaiting deportation, according to the HRW report in 2009.

"There is persistent violation of workers' rights," which characterizes it as a "forced labor" system, says the report.[144] As Marx explained, without legal and moral limits to restrain it, capital has the natural urge to "suck the workforce disproportionately," up to the limit of its "premature exhaustion and death."[145] The United Arab Emirates is a borderline case of this "greed for surplus value," which we are describing throughout this chapter. And such extreme cases always teach us about what is latent in the remaining cases, because in them everything is explicit.

The United Arab Emirates, as described by Mike Davis, is governed by a sheik who is both the emir and the CEO of large undertakings, including oil and real estate, in a system of transfusion of rents and surplus values that involves investment funds and international millionaires. Thus, political and economic powers are unified under a single command, in a true "apotheosis of the neo-liberal values of contemporary capitalism: a society that might have been designed by the Economics Department of the University of Chicago."[146] And they have achieved what was just a dream for American conservatives: "an oasis of free enterprise without income taxes, trade unions, and opposition parties (there are no elections)," fueled by the flow of oil revenues—at that time, on the rise. That's why Davis calls this place a "paradise"—obviously an "evil paradise."[147]

It is this very machine for crushing workers involved in the production of the artificial island of Saadiyat in Abu Dhabi, the "Island of Happiness." Designs by Frank Gehry (Guggenheim branch), Jean Nouvel (Louvre branch), Norman Foster (Sheikh Zayed Museum, affiliated with the British Museum), Zaha Hadid (Performing Arts Center),

Tadao Ando (Maritime Museum), Rafael Viñoly (New York University branch), in addition to hotels, golf courses, and high-end luxury residences, are there. The Human Rights Watch team communicated with all of these institutions and architectural firms regarding the inhumane working conditions that were going to be adopted in their projects, with the goal of having them take measures to avoid these conditions. The commitment requested by HRW was to assure the "domestic and international public that your project will not be tainted by the prevalent practices of migrant worker abuse."[148] From the institutions involved, only the French Museums Agency took some initiative, after several meetings with HRW, in order to press their local partners to comply with international labor conventions. However, according to the HRW report, there was neither formalization of that provision in contracts with the construction companies nor penalties for noncompliance. Gehry and Nouvel were the only architects to answer HRW, but as a formality.

Koolhaas also has projects in Dubai: "We're planning something serious and adult there, a district that will be as urban as possible. In Dubai, everyone goes by car, even from one building to the next. Where we're building, you can walk, there'll be a metro, we're mixing homes and offices." And he continues: "The job is actually very abstract, because we don't know how society is going to develop there, who's going to live and work there, or what needs the area has to satisfy."[149] After all, it is not a city, but an equally abstract speculative production, still without buyers, a ghost town hoping that capital flows will guarantee its rentiers gains. Meanwhile, the same migrants and semienslaved workers, in another form of "abstract labor" value production, will erect the new city. The architect is concerned about not knowing who the residents (who do not exist) will be, but ignores the conditions of the workers, who exist and will build the architect's city. They are beings of the (social) underground that no one wants to see.

Thus, the lightness of new architectural forms is far from hovering in the air. With the welfare crisis of the 1970s, new wealth could freely settle in the old unfettered extraction machine of absolute surplus value, working tirelessly to increase accumulation and counteract the falling rate of profit in sectors that dispense with living labor. And the more the various forms of rentism lead to a perverse redistribution of social profit, appropriating considerable slices without taking into account the real

Construction workers in Dubai, 2006. Photograph by Abbas/Magnum Photos.

dimensions of production, the more is required of the productive sectors to expand the exploitation—and the construction industry is one of its most prosperous frontiers.

THE VALUE OF DIFFICULT FORM

The works of starchitecture we are analyzing here are special commodities and must be evaluated as such while we investigate their production of value. They are buildings that symbolically represent a certain power, whether it be administrative, civic, religious, or corporate, and that are made to order by governments or companies. In other words, they are not exactly real-estate market products, they are not directly "for sale," despite the fact that they are often part of strategies of the very "cities for sale,"[150] or strategies of the valuation of brands. Their use value is one of representation and distinction, as "symbolic capital," in Pierre Bourdieu's expression.

Unlike other commodities, the projects we are analyzing are almost always built to be removed from real-estate circulation. Private orders for starchitecture are associated with strengthening corporate brands more than with the real-estate market. The spectacular and unique forms of the buildings are acquired at high prices to merge with the values of the brands they promote—be it designer clothing such as Prada, cars such as BMW, banks such as the DG Bank, or wineries such as Marqués de Riscal. In these cases, the identity between the building and the brand is nontransferable, meaning that it cannot be sold to third parties under the penalty of weakening its corporate value, both symbolically and financially. In other words, these projects do not constitute conventional real-estate gains derived from buying and selling real estate, but arise from strategies of strengthening governments and corporations and the "transcendental" values of their brands.

Within this topic, however, our goal is to understand how the production of value occurs in these buildings, and therefore leave the issue of rent provisionally in the background. Stating that the return on invested capital occurs in these buildings mainly through rent and not through exchange value does not mean that they lack labor value. As we have seen in this chapter, the amount of labor employed is far superior to any other commonplace building that could fulfill that same function.

From the point of view of the construction companies that execute the projects and are paid for it, they value their capital according to the law of value—thus they are commodities, strictly speaking. But there is a specificity to the production of labor value in these works of difficult execution and unique forms. Conventional public orders, however, such as schools, hospitals, and housing, generally ensure that buildings are fairly standardized and have their construction cost calculated per square meter. The relative homogeneity of those works allows them to be easily measured. The average socially necessary labor time to execute each task is estimated based on public and market charts that detail labor times, values, and the composition of materials per service. It is possible to obtain an average value for each type of square meter built (classrooms, sports fields, bathrooms, dining rooms, clinics, surgical centers, etc.).

In addition, the works we are analyzing, even if they appear to be part of public services, are generally investments of public–private partnerships, aimed at obtaining combined symbolic and economic gains. As we saw in the first chapter, these are investments made in a context of competition among cities, in which public actions are based on their financial return, following business logic. These works are executed because they favor the advance of the local economy, attract investors and tourists, and foment an increase in revenues, in a virtuous market cycle, as the World Bank would hope.[151]

It is precisely in order to attract worldwide attention that such works need to be extravagant and even sumptuous. The opportunity for additional gains for construction companies is derived there. The extraordinary capital profits that construction of these projects generate lie exactly in the difficult execution of their complex and novel forms, in which each construction site configures novelties: constructive systems used in unorthodox ways, profusion of unique pieces, new materials or traditional materials employed in an unusual manner, difficulties in prefabrication and assembly, the need of skilled workers for artisanal services, and complex shoring.

The results, on the other hand, are not only decisive gains, but also difficulties in calculating and measuring the work needed. In a context of high variability regarding technical and formal innovations, as well as the often imponderable risks of the construction activity, there is a "lack of mechanisms to quantify 'socially necessary labor,'"[152] which can already be perceived in the difficulty of dealing with the "heterogeneous and incommensurable temporalities" of the processes of creating forms—in our case, the forms conceived at architecture firms—in the new economy.

Works such as those we are analyzing repeatedly suffer from "disproportion" at all levels, including "disproportion of value."[153] Labor time is no longer the measure of all things, as Marx predicted in the *Grundrisse*: "As soon as labor in the direct form has ceased to be the great well-spring of wealth, labor time ceases and must cease to be its measure."[154] Disproportion is a sign that anticipates the crisis in capitalism; it is the "crisis as potency," as Jorge Grespan explains, because "the loss of reference of self-valorization leads to 'overproduction,' that is, production in excess."[155]

The forms of disproportion we are witnessing are associated with the predominance of financial and rentier valorization over the logic of production—that is "capital's ambition to become the 'subject' of valorization and measurement."[156] Productive forces are geared to respond to requests not inherent to production, but rather external to it, of the order of rent and interest. In our case, it is the limitless search to expand the "rent of the form" through extravagances of all kinds that exacerbate this disproportion.

Construction companies take advantage of this situation. Financial imbalances are recurrent in such works. The multiplication of initial budgets is notorious. The Casa da Música in the city of Porto was budgeted at less than half the final cost.[157] The City of Culture, in Santiago de Compostela, cost more than five times the estimated budget, which led to a Parliamentary Commission of Inquiry to investigate the facts.[158] The same has happened with the Christian de Porzamparc's Cidade das Artes (former Cidade da Música) project in Rio de Janeiro.[159] Examples would be innumerable, with rare exceptions, as seems to have been the case of the Guggenheim Bilbao.[160]

Construction companies justify the cost increase as a result of construction difficulties and procedures not provided for in the contract. Architects do not provide enough detail with regard to the construction phases, nor do they anticipate all of the pertinent difficulties involved in the execution, so they repeatedly miscalculate budgets. For governments, in turn, these underbudgeted works can be more easily approved by the legislative body; otherwise, they would not even be included in the budget, let alone be brought to completion.

The case of the construction work for Peter Eisenman's City of Culture in Galicia is exemplary. It was budgeted at 108 million euros by his office, and the values reached 475 million. Given this financial imbalance, an audit and a parliamentary commission of inquiry were set up.[161] A detailed report by the auditors of the Consello de Contas of the Galician Administration presents problematic points in work management, including deficiency in the contracts (which do not follow public law); the hiring of companies whose owners or partners occupy senior positions in the Xunta de Galicia; a fivefold increase in construction costs; the high cost of maintenance of the order of fifty million euros per year, which must be shouldered by the government.[162] The president of Spain at the time, the socialist Carlos Zapatero, temporarily halted work and there is suspicion of illicit enrichment by the Galician secretary of culture.[163] Eisenman received 13.9 million euros for the design and his remuneration was a percentage (13 percent) of the work's final cost; this means it could be multiplied. The quartzite rock roofing, which required extraordinary assembly work, was one of the main targets of the inquiry commission. The order of fifty thousand square meters has depleted the quartzite quarries of the region. Project and budget calculations did not properly assess the potential of deposits. The bidding for the supply of stones was won by a company whose owner is a local mayor and politician of the PP (Popular Party), Antonio Campo, with a six-million-euro contract.[164] The quarry from which the stone was extracted did not have a mining license. The entrepreneur/mayor then subcontracted other companies that invaded, with their machines, environmentally protected areas.[165] The stone cover was finished with the import of twenty thousand square meters of quartzite from Brazil.[166]

Eisenman's promise, however, was the promise of an economic project: "we build our works with very low budgets and keep the quality. We do not employ expensive materials," and he continued, mocking Gehry: "The only titanium I use is that which the dentist put in my mouth. Taxpayers won't have to pay for expensive materials."[167] Zeal that did not prove to be true. In the same lecture, however, Eisenman recognizes that architecture media works are part of a risky policy: "Conservative politicians are willing to take more risks than those on the left, who, wanting to keep the cities intact, hinder progress. All my clients are conservative politicians who want to take risks." In this case, risks related to the most expensive work in progress in Europe at the time are shared with all citizens, including those in the poorest province of Spain. Investigations led by the commission of inquiry resulted in the project being shut down in 2013, including the suspension of the buildings that would house the Opera House and the International Arts Center.

It could be that such cases of corruption occur in other conventional public works, but the decisive element is that the associated legal battles are over the construction complications and difficulties imposed by the projects themselves. For this reason, some architects have been taken to court: Eisenman, in this case, and Christian de Portzamparc, for his work in Rio de Janeiro.[168]

In the private sector, such imbalances are inadmissible because they are directly shouldered by entrepreneurs. Frank Gehry's firm developed a system of budgets, because they worked for many private clients, including real-estate developers, who would not accept the situation verified in public works. His project in New York (the Beekman Tower) is an example of this, with forty floors previously in the design almost removed owing to the crisis. His team was under pressure for the construction to remain within the expected budget, for "Gehry's ornate design could burn the developer if it leads to cost overruns."[169] For Gehry's team, this was also a marketing opportunity to demonstrate the efficiency of the company's software in the real-estate sector.

Profits that construction companies obtain from works of starchitecture cannot survive only on the basis of overbillings and shenanigans, of course. There is additional profit derived from the difficult form that cannot be minimized or covered over by scandals of misuse of public resources. Buildings of complex and unorthodox forms that are difficult to build interest construction companies because they provide a generous mass of value. There is a large amount of work deposited in the complex and often random structures of this architecture.

In the construction phase, the law of value, even maddened by its unruliness, continues to command rationality. In this moment, the builder wants to take the opportunity to circumvent the law of value and obtain additional gains from the difficult form. The entrepreneur, in turn, cannot accept such incommensurability, and presses the architects and builders to again find ways to measure this value, using advanced software and regaining control over production schedules. The entrepreneur presses for control because he or she buys the work of the builder as a commodity and is not willing to pay a premium for it. The entrepreneur, in turn, whether public, private, or in a public–private "partnership," wants to monopolize the gains resulting from the construction of that singular work. It is a speculative operation: it is about an investment in the construction of an eye-catching artifact that will function like a "brand" hoping to grab a larger share of surplus value than that justified by the investment.

We are dealing with the dislocation between price and value that occurs with rare works, such as works of art and luxury products. This dislocation produces the entrepreneur's additional gain in the form of monopoly rent, which David Harvey has named the "rent of art" and the "art of rent," as we saw in the first chapter.[170] The rarity of the "treasure-form" dislocates the price from a direct relationship with the amount of work needed, binding it to the buyer's desire.[171] This rarity is not only one of scarce natural resources, but can also be voluntarily produced: this is what occurs, for example, in the fine arts, from the ideology of the genius to market manipulation.

In the case of the prominent works of architecture we are analyzing here, the treasure effect is the result of their unique forms; but it also stems from the very concentration of an enormous mass of labor (unlike painting pictures, for example). It is a treasure-form not dissociated from the volume of labor contained in it, and in this sense, again it moves toward value. In it, the rarity of the unique form, and the disproportionate amount of labor put up to execute it, are combined—to the limits of technique, matter, and human skills.

What Sérgio Ferro explains about the "bourgeois mansion" can be applied, to a large extent, to our "building-treasure": "its ostentatious aspect collaborates with its treasure function, because ostentation is basically the exposure of unused, yet concentrated labor. Treasure, in any form, has its value determined by the hours of average social work put into it. The sumptuary object is dense and rich in coagulated work . . . from this also comes the horror of any mass-produced object, which almost always indicates low unit cost, when compared to handicraft objects. Bold and far-fetched forms, difficult coatings, specialty window frames, etc. are the proof of craft production, with high expenditure of labor force, and therefore, valuable."[172]

Treasure on display, in the buildings' forms, in artworks, or in luxury objects, acquires the function of capital in this act of exhibitionism. It may function as spectacle, promote tourism, or attract investments. The entrepreneur presents its capital to the public, dormant in the treasure-form. Similar to the Egyptian pyramids, here we visit the gold, the mountain of accumulated labor. This visitation generates the "rent of form," a pilgrimage paid to observe the miracle of technique, aesthetics, and human labor accumulation. At the same time, the building houses new treasures in its interior: works of art, orchestras, libraries, fashion shows, pop stars, cuisine, multimillion-dollar sports teams, or luxury suites.

The prevalence of the treasure-form can be seen as the opposite of what the project of modern architecture intends, while simultaneously being the archetype of the most profitable forms of current economy: the art market and luxury production. Rem Koolhaas, justifying his boutique designs for Prada, praises luxury as follows: "luxury is *wasted* space," it is the "empty" space; it is also the unique form, it is "fascination with rarity."[173] That is, the exact opposite of the will for mass production and for an exact and functional form, which prevailed during the heroic period of modern architecture.

Luxury ideology refuses standardization and serialization, the exact and functional space, thus assuming "aristocratic" values, in the sense of appearing "nonmercantile" and "antibusiness." Hence, such luxury spaces are the opposite of shopping malls—which are, according to Koolhaas, the most complete expression of the type of consumer society that gathers in contemporary "generic cities"—to "resemble spaces of museums, which, in turn, paradoxically, are increasingly being used for consumption."[174]

If, however, luxury seems to restore the "auratic" value inherent to artwork, it is equally inserted in consumer society. The values it conveys, far beyond the aristocratic imaginary, so to speak, materialize as capital profits and rents. One cannot forget that "luxury is an industry," as Gilles Lipovetsky has said, and it is increasingly becoming a highly profitable business niche led by marketing.[175] Not coincidentally, Koolhaas is one of the architects who most successfully uses marketing (of his own firm).

In this way, if associated with forms of rent in the symbolic economy, the crystallization of labor in treasure-form is not archaic. The "treasure-houses" of starchitecture—museums or designer shops—are large-scale jewelry works, and the value concentrated in them is synonymous with the "social power" of their owners. It is the disproportionate amount of labor deposited there, in the limit of its own excess, which confers treasure-value to these buildings. Disproportionate, if we consider that the same use of each building could be accommodated with a much lower expenditure of work.

Therefore, the architecture of the difficult form is a huge dissipation of work in the form of symbolic and material concentration of power and wealth. Its outcome is simultaneously admirable and degrading, surprising and infamous. In a more egalitarian society, this dissipation-concentration would not make sense until the most basic needs are adequately resolved and met. However, according to Lipovetsky, for the time being "it is useless to try to moralize luxury" because it "is an absolute need for representation, arising from an unequal social order."[176]

It is no coincidence that, for concentrating and dissipating work in the juggling of the difficult form, the proliferation of building-treasures has occurred over the neoliberal decades. This was a simultaneous indication of the workers' defeat and of a huge capital surplus—a partially fictitious abundance, as the global crisis of 2008 demonstrated (and the successive cancellation or postponement of dozens of sumptuous works by starchitects). We will come back to this issue in the Conclusion.

CONCLUSION
THE NEXT FRONTIERS

DISTRIBUTION OF MEDALS

When Norman Foster, coming from Switzerland, arrived at his office on the shores of the Thames, in the early 2000s, he took a walk to check the current projects in progress. The most representative drawings of each project were hung on boards with magnets, and nearby tables were cleared to display the models. A small crowd remained attentive to the minimal gestures and words of the eminent architect. Foster circulated with an entourage taking notes of his comments on designs that caught his eye—to the disappointment of several teams, he passed the majority of the boards. His opinions were followed right away, sometimes redirecting entire weeks of development work. Contentment or dissatisfaction was immediately detectable in the architect's physiognomy. "Foster is a celebrity in his own firm," said Caio Faggin, one of the firm's employees at the time. "Most of the architects who work there have never talked to him."[1] At the end of his stroll, Foster sat at his enormous round table in front of the Thames, surrounded by his main partners, arranged like the "knights of the round table."[2]

The irony of the medieval metaphor is not accidental. In 1990, (Sir) Foster was knighted by the queen, and in 1999 he was decorated with the honorary title of Baron (Lord). In that same year he received the Pritzker Prize. In honor of the services rendered to the international glory of English architecture, and in reference to the location of his office on the banks of the London river, he was named Lord Foster of Thames Bank. Besides the nobility's investiture, Foster is the only one among renowned architects to boast all four of the most important architecture medals (Pritzker, RIBA, AIA, and Mies). As of 2010, eight of his well-known peers did not exceed three medals: Frank Gehry, Rem Koolhaas, Renzo Piano, Rafael Moneo, Tadao Ando, Álvaro Siza, Richard Meier, and I. M. Pei.

The Pritzker award jury, in Foster's biography, notes that he has the "biographical material of which great novels and film stories are made. He was born into a working class family in a suburb of Manchester, England in 1935, where the odds of his making a career in a profession were highly unlikely . . . Since his first commission thirty-five years ago, he has won worldwide acclaim for his modernist buildings, including his profession's highest honors." The jury continues that Foster was awarded the Pritzker for his "continuing process of discovery, inspiration, invention and innovation . . . [and] steadfast devotion to the principles of architecture as an art form." In his words of thanks, Foster recalls that it was in his formative period at Yale that his Manchester mentality had changed: "America gave me a sense of confidence, freedom, and self-discovery."[3]

At the age of seventy-four, Foster had accumulated prestige and fortune, not only with projects and prizes, but also through selling 85 percent of his stake in the firm to a group of investors for 350 million pounds, as we saw in the first chapter. In order to not pay the taxes and fees resulting from the transaction in England, Foster took up residence in Saint-Moritz, Switzerland, where he received the sum. With part of the dividends, he bought a castle in the Alps (the Château de Vincy). The default on the English public coffers became a scandal.[4] In 2008, the architect was pressured to resign from the House of Lords. He was included in a list of nobles accused of tax evasion who should be stripped of their investiture, according to a constitutional reform aimed at reforming the House. In 2010, he and four other evaders resigned from the House of Lords, but were allowed to retain their titles of nobility.[5]

In 2009, with the global crisis, Foster + Partners dismissed four hundred employees and closed the year with a loss of eighteen million pounds. The architect, however, received a salary of five hundred thousand pounds (six hundred thousand dollars) for his occasional presence in the office. The company's chief executive received a total of 1.7 million pounds (two million dollars) in wages and bonuses, 40 percent higher than the previous year, even with the effects of the crisis and the accounting losses.[6] The discrepancy between top-level compensation and the company's overall situation was similar to what happened with the international banking scandal in the midst of the crisis, with executives being rewarded million-dollar bonuses as companies and their creditors racked up losses.

Apart from the financial scandals, Foster's prestige continued to fall following the receipt of the Pritzker and the title of Lord. The workload of his firm, and its aggressive media policy, still guarantees him the position of one of the most published architects in specialized magazines to this day. However, his small participation in design in the face of the scale of production results in a disconnection between authorship and the brand's name, as we saw in the first chapter. Almost none of his firm's design projects are his creation, with his supervision over only a portion of the production. However, as the company's showman, he continued to make presentations to clients and juries, receiving briefings on the designs to which he barely contributed. With his commercial turnaround and business growth, "Foster's brand lost prestige among architects, while maintaining it with investors in Dubai, for example," says Brazilian architect and former Foster + Partners employee Martin Corullon.[7]

The same can be said for Frank Gehry, not only because of the large number of projects managed by his office, but also because of the repetition of certain design procedures and formal schemes. Its apogee was concomitant with Foster's, and his exhaustion seems to result from the saturation of his metalized and irregular surfaces. His three top medals were prior to 2000. When he won the Pritzker Prize in 1989, Gehry had recently won the competition for the Walt Disney Concert Hall. At that time, he was decorated for his "highly refined, sophisticated, and aesthetically adventurous work that emphasizes the art of architecture." Ada Louise Huxtable, in her essay presenting Gehry, emphasizes that he pursued "the union of art and architecture as his highest task," to the point of finally "turning the practical into lyrical, and architecture into art."[8] Gehry thanked her in the same key, extolling "the moment of truth, the composition of elements, the selection of forms, scale, materials, colors, finally, all the same issues facing painters and sculptors. Architecture is surely an art, and those who practice the art of architecture are surely architects."[9]

The jury and the award winners' speeches and justifications reaffirm the artistic status of architecture and, more than that, the understanding of architecture as Great Art. It is no coincidence that the world's main architecture prize, which recognizes the subtleties of the profession, has this conventional and conservative view of the practice. It is this alibi that dispenses with more objective criteria, because juries make choices on merit according to judgments of taste. When judgment criteria are restricted to artistic ones, other dimensions of architecture are forgotten or are allowed to atrophy. After all, questions such as these could be posed: Does award-winning architecture present good solutions to urban problems? How adequately do its buildings respond to users' needs? Are the construction sites respectful of workers' rights? How correctly do its techniques address structural problems and material requirements? Do the projects favor public spaces and the democratic use of the city? Are its budgets economical and balanced? Are environmental issues incorporated into design decisions? In sum, is the public interest and social welfare strengthened by this architecture?

But this is an unreasonable demand to make, of course, precisely because this type of decorative professional hero mimics the ideology of artistic genius as a form of architecture's social and political emptying. The heterogeneity of the production process and the goals of art and architecture cannot be ignored. Prizes and patronage, however, advocate for the convergence of both as a way to reaffirm their elitist and antisocial version of the discipline.

Prioritizing judgments of taste is the best way to cover up the fact that the social production of space in an unequal society occurs on a terrain of social struggles, and architecture is part of them. When prizes are awarded to private architecture offices that work for the representatives of power and money, the dominant economic and cultural regime is reinforced. Architects involved with public policies (and not just government works of symbolic and monumental value) are not usually awarded medals. As of this writing, no black architects have been awarded the Pritzker Prize. Zaha Hadid was the only woman individually decorated by the Pritzker jury (Kazuyo Sejima was awarded with Ryūe Nishizawa), among the dozens of men awarded the top four prizes. Privatization, racism, and sexism are explicit and need not be disguised.

There is no doubt that the emphatic reaffirmation of architecture as Great Art barely masks vested class interests. But it has the great advantage of expressing such interests in the plane of high culture, while at the same time consuming public funds with sumptuous works. The architects most capable of transforming hard, material domination into soft, symbolic hegemony are rewarded. Only great architecture is capable of such alchemy, as Jacques Herzog states in his award speech: turning the heavy architectural materiality into immaterial values.[10]

The world of the stars is like that: some decay, others ascend, like Herzog himself. With different forms and techniques, they play a similar role: designing new symbols of power and money, and making forms that generate rent as financial assets. As we saw in the first chapter, Herzog is one of the experts in this matter. Customers view awards like the curves of the stock market. The well informed seek to hire the stars at their maximum brightness, before they fade. In a competition restricted to four international names already awarded the Pritzker to build the new Dance Hall of São Paulo, João Sayad, the secretary of culture, reported that Jacques Herzog and Pierre de Meuron were chosen because "they excited us, they were the youngest and respect their clients, their design projects always differ from each other, today they are on the crest of the wave."[11]

Global outsiders, who have appeared from time to time in the Pritzker, such as Sverre Fehn, Paulo Mendes da Rocha, Peter Zumthor, and Eduardo Souto de Moura, are perhaps the exceptions that confirm the rule. They are more sober professionals, with an operation generally restricted to their places of origin, working in almost artisanal workshops, unlike the global machines of spectacular projects. Even though they are professionals who do not like much fuss, their architecture nevertheless does not fail to be equally formalistic, albeit in a minimalist and erudite expression. In the cases of Zumthor and Fehn, their works are contextual and sensorial readings of the social experience in villages of rich countries, such as Switzerland and Norway. The Portuguese Souto de Moura, less media savvy than Siza, designs within a Miesian matrix, with neutral volumes integrated into the landscape, having dared to vary colors and shapes in the design of the museum dedicated to the painter Paula Rêgo, in Cascais. Mendes da Rocha, working in a globally recognized and unequal country such as Brazil, has a discourse less centered on the poetics of the building and more on the production of territory, of America as the place of a civilizing utopia yet to be built—which is the dubious track on which runs something that could be called Brazilian ideology. However, in spite of his unpublished urban plans and humanistic discourse, Mendes da Rocha's work is mainly recognized by the production of isolated buildings of great symbolic value, such as museums, designer stores, sports buildings, and bourgeois houses, and not accidentally, almost all of them were built in elite areas of the richest and most unequal megalopolis in Latin America, São Paulo. In this way, if these architects are exceptions in relation to more media-savvy and global professionals, they can be assimilated by awards that praise the architecture's form, which is still presented as eminently artistic.

Three Japanese firms won the Pritzker Prize after the 2008 global crash, which portended a crisis for the architecture of spectacle. Since awarding Zumthor in 2009, the Pritzker jury has been looking for a post-era-of-excess architecture. Although they maintain a sober architectural style, SANAA (2010) and Toyo Ito (2013) still follow the profile of the media-savvy architects of museums, large corporations, and designer stores. Shigeru Ban (2014), in turn, represents another, more experimental wing in Japanese architecture, using spatial structures, trellises, and paraboloids in wood, bamboo, steel, and even cardboard. Ban is a producer of three-dimensional shapes that combine new technologies and craft knowledge. Not surprisingly, a year later, in 2015, the German architect Frei Otto was honored, mainly with works from the 1960s and the 1970s. He was perhaps the greatest master of innovative structural systems, tensile structures, and gridshells. In 2016, the Pritzker jury gave the most commented-on prize of the decade to the Chilean Alejandro Aravena for his affordable "evolutionary" houses, a theme to which we will return.

The award parties are not just moments of dreams without shadows. The real world seems to want to appear, like a nightmare, in the sometimes-hesitant speeches of award winners—perhaps embarrassed by medals of merit awarded in an increasingly devastated "planet of slums."[12] At the end of the speeches, it is not uncommon to hear it hinted that there are larger tasks that architecture is not fulfilling. Foster comments on how shocked he was at the misery and lack of sanitation in the suburbs of Mexico City; Jean Nouvel mentions Rio's favelas and the industrial ruin of the Ruhr; Rogers talks about environmental tragedies and conflicts that mainly affect the poor; Siza recalls that once architecture had intended to respond to the needs of the masses. Koolhaas, in turn, makes a surprisingly dry and lucid speech. He does not pour out sweet words of reverence, pride, and gratitude, as others ritually do. He recognizes that, fifty years ago, the architectural scene was not so much defined by values of the unique, the individual, the genius. In the postwar period, he says, there was an architectural world, a movement to think about the city and broader themes. Now, only unique identities, signatures, and the most senseless client requests, made with "daring ambitions and expensive trajectories," are those "we architects support whole heartedly." Architects have supposedly abandoned any discourse on "territorial organization, no discourse about settlement or human co-existence. At best our work brilliantly explores and exploits a series of unique conditions." It is in this way that the contemporary architect preserves his or her "political innocence . . . in a post ideological era"—requested to enhance the domain, without phraseological detours, of abstract wealth. Koolhaas concludes by stating that "Unless we break our dependency on the real and recognized architecture as a way of thinking about all issues, from the most political to the most practical, liberate ourselves from eternity to speculate about compelling and immediate new issues, such as poverty, the disappearance of nature, architecture will maybe not make two-thousand-fifty."[13]

But medals cannot be expected to produce critical awareness and a transformation of practice, precisely in those rewarded for having done what the system could best hope for. Perhaps medals bring some discomfort, some doubt, as Nouvel says, perhaps the unpleasant feeling that something is not right. But the medals sparkle to state the opposite: that everything is still going well. Our immortals are decorated less for what they have done so far than for what they have brilliantly not done. The award to Chilean Alejandro Aravena, in 2016 seems to show that the "social" dimension has finally been acknowledged by the system of values and higher decorations of the privileged architectural circle.

END OF THE ERA OF EXCESS?

The architecture of liquefied forms, structural contortions, and sceno-graphic juggling that we have seen and analyzed in its various dimensions throughout this book is one of the most unmistakable signs of the world's current uncontrolled course. Its deformity and visual instability are plastic and technical evidence of the disproportional characteristics of capitalist accumulation aggravated by financial dominance. As we have seen, complex forms and difficult execution not only visually express capital's intent of self-valorization, but are also themselves commodities not easily calculable from the point of view of socially necessary labor. They are works in which value and price are disconnected, and where the dominance of circulation defines its rentier and speculative character. In them, the dynamics of senseless capital valorization manifest through an unrestrained search for dissociation from its foundation: labor value.

It is no coincidence that the quest for maximum rent assumes command of the whole process, condemning productive forces to the creation of unique objects, like single pieces, rather than mass production. The profusion of works that assume this treasure-form is both a demand of monopoly rent and the reflection of an absolute surplus of overaccumulated capital that does not meet the objective conditions for its valorization through living labor. The flow of this capital is transferred to other less traditional investments, such as the real-estate sector, which in the last decades has become a real backing for speculative credit operations.

Architecture in the digital-financial age, which contradictorily seeks to deny its weight and the weight of work, and to tectonically reach the magical world of immaterial valorization, is the anticipation of the very crisis of power. According to Fredric Jameson, architecture becomes inflated as a "balloon," both in plasticity and in its remuneration, through rent and credit.[14] Following the logic of financial capital in the compulsive search for self-valorization inherent to this architecture, self-centered like a speculative monad, it is possible to perceive the functioning of a moneymaking machine at the expense of the cities in which it has landed. In it, excess production appears as the very production of excess.

If the disproportionate growth of fictitious capital in relation to real assets was the omen of a major crisis, architecture in the neoliberal decades (since the 1980s) was also a symptom of speculative excess and the concentration of capital. Cities and corporations, by means of promotional investments, sought to sustain a part of their growth through their peculiar ability to attract surplus capital from across the globe. Such investments, as we have said, not only signaled the welfare crisis but were also part of a distributive conflict over social wealth, in which workers always lost. At the same time that the project of full employment was collapsing and social assistance programs were being dismantled and partially privatized, policies of spectacle and "cultural animation" proliferated.

With the exponential income growth of the social strata at the top of the pyramid, and the average wage remaining drastically stagnant,[15] the concentration of power and wealth became widespread, further deepening social polarization. The dizzying growth of credit and patterns of corporate and household debt was brutal in this period, especially in the United States. Loans were not only created to stimulate consumption of superfluous goods, as Martine Bulard explains, but they were also largely used to increase spending on health, education, and housing.[16] That is, the formation of the subprime market that was at the epicenter of the crisis was the result of speculative and aggressive policies of credit supply, a lack of housing policies, the weaknesses of the health and education systems, and the private nature of social security. American and European workers, though the latter to a lesser extent, were pushed into the credit "solution" as part of the breakdown of welfare policies.[17]

Thus, backing part of the expansion of credit was, not by chance, the mortgaged real estate of these working families. Defaulting on loans because of predatory mortgages and the instability of the new world of work, the assets of these families began to be taken over by creditors, at the same moment in which their prices fell precipitously. The result of the crisis and its effect of contamination through financial securities are well known, but little has been said of the commitment in their estates that these families accumulated through work for generations, which turned into smoke. These workers were not rescued like the banks were. At best, they have been mobilized through government jobs programs of limited duration.

With public resources being drained to bail out the financial system, superfluous or speculative projects also began to be canceled. Investors held positions and yet withdrew their chips from the falling real-estate sector. For municipalities and governments, multiplying complex buildings around the culture of excess often became unrealistic (even if it represented an increase in the aggregate demand, from a Keynesian point of view). Since the end of 2008, numerous major projects already commissioned from starchitects have been canceled.[18] The rentier paradise of the United Arab Emirates, a patriarchal dictatorship based on semislave labor, where starchitects search for megalomaniac orders, called for a moratorium after reducing 50 percent of the value of their properties, as was widely reported.[19] Even so, in January 2010 it inaugurated the largest empty skyscraper in the world, built by the rentier euphoria of the previous decade. The Burj Dubai is emblematic of an era of capital abundance and its search for spectacular forms that seems to have been suspended—at least temporarily, as this abundance is based on the price of oil.

As Frank Gehry said in an interview in 2010: "The times of excess are over. Waste is over and this challenge has to be faced. I don't know if this is good or bad, but it's reality. We have to save energy and money."[20] Nicolai Ouroussoff, then the *New York Times* architecture critic, wrote that it is the "melancholic end of an era," and predicted: "The movement of expansion of new art museums, concert halls, and drama centers that, in the last decades, has transformed cities across the country is officially closed. Money is gone—and who knows when it will be back."[21] Across the Atlantic, a columnist from the *Guardian*, Jonathan Glancey, asked the same question: "Has the era of ostentation come to an end?" adding that "the noughties were bound up with financial speculation and rampant consumerism; architecture inevitably followed suit," and citing Mies van der Rohe's declaration that architecture is "the will of an epoch translated into space" (or steel and titanium . . .).[22]

The global crisis of 2008, therefore, allows us to review the set of phenomena we are analyzing in a new historical perspective, because the financial meltdown affected this architecture on two ends: that of the money, and that of the symbolism it carries. "Excess" and "waste" are not the most desirable qualities for production shaken by the new wave of scarcity. Sobriety and moderation may be once again requested by clients, and even rewarded, as was the case for Zumthor, who won the Pritzker Prize in 2009, immediately after the crisis.

If the aesthetics of speculative delusion was inadequate following the 2008 financial crisis, when the discourse of austerity began to impose itself, new digital design technologies could be adopted with a different approach, that is, for maximum accuracy and economy in the planning of projects. This was the challenge Gehry faced with New York by Gehry (formerly Beekman Tower), as Gehry's digital design program was being tested extensively and thoroughly in order to avoid waste and excess.

New emerging agendas dispute the sequence in a cycle that appears to have come to an end, or is at least provisionally suspended. In addition to the merely moralistic and simplifying critiques of the forms of excess and conspicuous consumption, the agendas that seem to decidedly advance are those of green architecture and "social" architecture. These are the two new frontiers, not only regarding authorship, teaching, exhibitions, and awards; they are also the new frontiers of business.

THE GREEN FRONTIER AND THE MASDAR PARADIGM

With the impact of the crisis, the agenda of sustainable architecture that had emerged strongly in the past decade was verging on hegemonic, even among starchitects. As Gehry states (or laments), the inevitable path seems to be "to make green architecture, everything needs to be green now."[23] This architecture can also be mobilized in favor of brand, distinction, and the ostensive innovation that draws these exceptional architects.

But starchitects know that, unlike the production of iconic buildings and unique shapes, green architecture is not their privilege, and for a time was not even their concern. On the contrary, for decades, sustainable architecture was associated with local territories, climates, and cultures and maintained by anonymous builders and "barefoot architects."[24] More recently, the agenda of "environmental planning" or "ecological landscape planning" has begun to form part of public policies.[25] There are already many professionals engaged in these practices, and architecture's star system is coming late to the subject—to a large extent, pushed by the crisis—in search of its "differential."

Unlike the architecture of the "rent of form," whose self-referential tendency is similar to fictitious capital's pursuit of disproportionate self-valorization, the green agenda faces real problems, such as the phenomena of imbalance between societies and the environment that have led to climate change and its disastrous effects. Research into alternatives in this field is therefore not only necessary, but also urgent. However, the way to interpret the problem, formulate proposals, and implement practices is the subject of controversy and dispute among scientists, governments, and activists, as well as between socialists and liberals.[26]

Many progressive authors have been striving to unify environmental issues with those of social justice, formulating the ecological problem in materialistic terms—the so-called green–red alliance, which gave rise to the ecosocialist movement. Among the main contributors to this agenda are David Harvey, John Bellamy Foster, Jean-Marie Harribey, Michael Löwy, and Naomi Klein. The common diagnosis of these authors is that capitalist valorization has a predatory character and its productive forces are advancing by degrading labor power and nature equally toward a catastrophic turning point. Accordingly, Marxists should revise their often uncritical positions on the consequences of technological progress, and ecologists should recognize that real preservation of the planet will only be possible in anticapitalist frameworks, with the implosion of the gigantic grinding machine of work and nature.

On the other hand, the dominant ideology (a mosaic of ideas of the dominant classes) and its repetitive discourse of "sustainable development" promise to reconcile capitalist progress with environmental preservation. This would be something like a "green capitalism" that turns the recovery of that which it structurally degrades into business in a feedback cycle. In it, nature is valued monetarily (although it has no intrinsic economic value) and is priced in a mercantile way, that is, through the acquisition of the commodity-form.[27] Environmental economics has become a discipline that tries to "reintroduce in traditional economic calculations the social costs engendered by environmental degradation," while turning the valorization of environmental goods into a form of capital valorization.[28] This is how nature goes from a negative externality to becoming a new and increasingly promising business (from carbon credits to new energies). And it is not only about building the preservation market, but also a "(de)contamination market," through the sale of pollution permits, as the World Bank recommends and the Kyoto Protocol proposes.[29] Therefore, it is not difficult to recognize that the concept of sustainability in capitalism is paradoxical, to say the least; it is a system based on the constant production of all kinds of inequalities—including an unequal distribution of entropy, spreading hot and cold societies across the globe, making it also not so difficult to guess which of these thermodynamic poles feeds the other.

In architecture, this new branch of business has grown enormously. A significant portion of the field's productive forces is beginning to address this emerging market, whether in the production of new advanced performance software, the accreditation of sustainability medals, or in the development of new materials and construction techniques. These projects receive designations, such as green certificates, which guarantee additional exclusive rent, but whose principles differ from the "rent of form." It is possible to consider that this architecture, less based on its unique and appealing form and more in exhibiting the effectiveness of its performance (although they are not necessarily exclusive), eventually revives some of the modern precepts, among them the mass production of certain prefabricated products (such as solar panels, green roofs, vertical gardens, water reuse systems, and effluent treatment). Therefore, the replication of solutions, rather than the obsession with novelty, might be seen as favorable to business and beneficial to well-placed agents, to capture new dividends such as: green material producers, eco-professionals, the software industry, universities with specialized courses, financing lines exclusive for academic research, magazines and publishers that focus on the subject. In this sense, what we are seeing is a reconfiguration of the architectural field, going from the "rent of form" to new forms of rent, such as "green rent."

China, whose rapid growth has largely replicated the Western world's unsustainable pattern of consumption and urbanization, aims to lead the ecological turn and its associated businesses—even though its cities are considered the most polluted in the world. Architect Steven Holl, one of the starchitects surfing the green wave—still with a flashy and exuberant design style—designed the Linked-Hybrid project in Beijing, a large mixed-use complex following some of the precepts of sustainable urbanism. The 2010 World Expo in Shanghai is an example of China's intended leadership with the green agenda—despite its predominantly "dirty" growth to date. With its theme "Better City, Better Life," the Chinese megaevent attracted architects and urbanists from around the world to show China's leading role in the technological achievements associated with sustainable urban development. Chinese initiatives, however, go far beyond the Expo and already motivate what Thomas Friedman has called a "technological race similar to the military-space race" that the United States and the USSR fought for decades.[30]

Starchitects, in their own way, are positioning themselves in this new territory of projects and businesses. Norman Foster, who has invested in green building since 2007, designed a model city called Masdar. This was the most important work of his firm, to which he paid special attention.[31] This work, although more on the urban scale than on the scale of the building (the so-called green building), might synthesize the terms in which starchitects' green turn may occur. In 2009, Foster said: "In Abu Dhabi, for example, right now we're building the first CO_2 town therein the world, Masdar, for 90,000 inhabitants. The people in charge are enormously shrewd. They are not waiting for the oil to run

Foster + Partners project for Masdar City in Abu Dhabi. Photograph courtesy of and copyright Foster + Partners.

out; they are beginning now to plan for a future without oil. Just imagine, the city is to be ready in 2018. That's about as if we wanted to settle on the moon in ten years."[32]

Masdar, located in a deserted area next to Abu Dhabi International Airport, is in fact an almost lunar setting, like a space station. Its relation to natural space is sui generis because the desert is a seemingly poor and simple ecosystem, a situation distinct from a majority of cities, mainly in the so-called third world. In this sense, this experience is extremely limited from the point of view of problems related to environmental planning in critical and complex situations associated with real urban settlements. Complexity, once again, folds over on itself, in an artificial separation from the truly complicated and conflicting structures of the truly existing society and city.[33]

Not by chance, the artificial city presents itself completely walled off, like a monad, in fact a fortress—supposedly only to protect itself from the arid climate. The physical and symbolic circumscription of the experience reveals its artificial character, as it is a fundamental part of its marketing and mediatic visualization. After all, the modus operandi of brand architecture remains dominant, and the incorporation of a green agenda is perceived as a "brand repositioning" strategy.

For Masdar, the stated goal of Foster's team is to combine some of the breakthroughs of green high technology with local and traditional, ancestrally ecological, construction practices that were being lost. As the architect says, "the main thing that's important with this project is to learn as much as possible from local building tradition."[34] The density of the built mass of the Arab city, with the set of internal courtyards and narrow streets, as well as natural exhaust and ventilation solutions, is much smarter than the glazed towers of the new Abu Dhabi and its sprawling suburbs simulating the American pattern of urbanization. Foster's design proposed state-of-the-art materials such as new windows that work as solar batteries and produce energy, as well as monorails for circulation (cars remain outside, as in Venice). The city was intended to be self-sufficient in water and energy, fully capable of treating and recycling its own garbage, and surviving without fossil fuels.

This valorization of the knowledge of local populations about their territories, climates, and materials is still a paradoxical phenomenon. On one hand, when the high-tech-brand architect goes on to scour older techniques for recognizing greater environmental efficiency, it is a sign that all the paraphernalia of Western technological progress alone is not enough to solve the problem. An instrumental reason forever directed by the demand to dominate nature (both external and internal) by violently abstracting qualities and values of use sooner or later turns against itself, converting the metabolic exchange between society and nature into a vicious circle of mutual destruction. Foster's gesture is thus a forced acknowledgment that the ambiguous opportunity afforded by many of the "breakthroughs" in civil construction—with intensive use of materials such as steel, cement, glass, aluminum, plastics, and petroleum-derived chemicals—is environmentally unsustainable.

On the other hand, the use of traditional knowledge in architecture reproduces, in its own way, other commercial uses by transnational corporations regarding the biodiversity of territories (also called "biopiracy").[35] Foster's firm, fueled by investment funds, is remunerated for the replication of age-old local techniques. Moreover, the city is not designed to shelter the populations that still hold this constructive knowledge—let alone the migrant and semienslaved workers who are erecting it—because the Masdar fortress is destined for the "creative class" of global agents of green innovation. The city already has a Research Institute (the Masdar Institute of Science and Technology was opened in 2010, with consulting from MIT), together with the headquarters of the Abu Dhabi Energy Company and the International Renewable Energy Agency (IRENA), thus becoming a center of production for new ideas in the fields of bioenergy and clean technologies—a veritable green-businesses theme park.

The initial value of the investment, at the time of writing, was estimated at twenty-two billion dollars. Ironically, the sustainable city is sponsored by precisely the same oil revenues, dictatorial government, and investment funds responsible for replacing local construction cultures with a real-estate machine based on the Western model of skyscrapers and cars, of a new Abu Dhabi erected by semislave migrant labor.[36] Added to these patrons is Credit Suisse, and the interest in innovation and green marketing of the German company Siemens, among others.

The 2008 crisis also affected the "clean-tech" city because of its high construction and operation costs. Only 5 percent of the planned city was erected, deadlines were postponed to 2030, and the zero carbon target was changed to a 50 percent reduction in emissions. As recently as 2016, a few dozen people lived in Masdar, now a candidate to become a "green ghost town."[37] It is a sign that green technology must be associated not with large mammoth works for city (and starchitect) marketing, but directed toward the real needs of people in existing urban centers with intelligent low-cost solutions.

THE SOCIAL FRONTIER AND THE ELEMENTAL PARADIGM

Another frontier that has begun to be explored by the star system, following the cycle of speculative financialization, is what can be called the "new social concern" with unequal urbanization. In the years after the 2008 global crisis, the social returned under a new guise. If, on the one hand, it is a reaction to neoliberal excesses, it is also its fruit, either for the millions who have deepened in misery and now need new policies and rescue strategies (with "innovative design," preferably) or because architectural ideology is increasingly impervious to any political position in which the "social" might have a socialist or anticapitalist connotation. The architects of the jet set, whenever possible, openly declare themselves "postutopian" and above any ideology.

In 2016, Pritzker Prize jurors attested to the rise of the Chilean architect Alejandro Aravena and his group Elemental, and their intent to consecrate a "new field" of professional performance. In the award announcement, the jury states: Aravena "gives the profession of architect a *new* dimension . . . The role of the architect is *now* being challenged to serve greater social and humanitarian needs . . . Aravena has *pioneered* a collaborative practice . . . This *innovative approach,* called 'incremental housing,' allows for social housing to be built on more expensive land closer to economic opportunity and gives residents a sense of accomplishment and personal investment."[38] It was also the first time the Pritzker was awarded to an architect mainly for his production of social interest.[39]

In 2016, the challenges posed to architecture by unequal urbanization are in fact "new" only to the "Pritzker world" and its constellation of stars, whose elitist view of the profession and alienation from the real world are notorious. The Elemental paradigm brings interesting questions to the debate and introduces a theme that has been neglected in previous decades into the mainstream liberal agenda of architecture, in schools, exhibitions, prizes, and the media.

In the research I carried out in 2010 on the most-published design themes in global architecture magazines, I verified and measured the contents of the journals *Arquitectura Viva, Architectural Record,* and *GA Document* (totaling more than three thousand pages of content analyzed), over the course of five years (2005–9). Social housing projects accounted for only 0.6 percent of all material, as detailed in Table 1. Even adding projects and works destined to improve life conditions in cities and the social reproduction of the workforce (which includes schools, hospitals, parks, and collective housing) accounted only for 6.8 percent. In contrast, architecture associated with the promotion of symbolic capital and its "rent of form," reiterating the vocation of the profession as producer of monuments and buildings with strong visual impact, occupied 84.2 percent of the pages of three of the most important global architecture magazines in those five years.

From the point of view of the location of the projects and works published in these magazines, there is a vast hegemony of the Europe–North America axis (totaling 79.5 percent of the pages). The so-called Global South (Africa, Latin America, and Asia), a part of the planet that houses most of the world's population and where architecture and urbanism pose urgent questions, accounted for only 6 percent of the pages of those three magazines, as shown in Table 2.

I did not conduct this research again after 2010, but the 2016 Pritzker Prize, awarded to the Chilean architect Aravena, as well as his curatorship at the 2016 Venice Architecture Biennale, one of the main global architecture exhibitions, are signs that the privileged circle of architecture is being forced to recognize the importance, even the urgency, of tackling social, environmental, and housing problems. These are the fruits of an accelerated and uneven urbanization especially in the Global South, and the result of the real-estate crisis in the Global North, in addition to the natural catastrophes of the past. Finally, it is necessary to turn to seemingly prosaic questions, those of the material reproduction of life and the survival of large populations.

As I mentioned, the "new theme" for the Pritzker jury and for starchitecture is nothing new for the rest of the world's inhabitants. We

Table 1. Types of designs published in the magazines *Arquitectura Viva, Architectural Record,* and *GA Document**

Type	Number of articles on the subject	Percentage of total articles surveyed	Number of pages	Percentage of total pages surveyed
Importance of symbolic capital	**713**	**76.5**	**2533**	**84.2**
Cultural buildings	293	31.4	1165	38.7
Corporate and commercial buildings	135	14.5	423	14.1
Single-family dwellings	81	8.7	157	5.2
Higher-education buildings	48	5.2	227	7.6
Stadiums and sports buildings	47	5.0	126	4.2
Government buildings	45	4.8	215	7.2
Hotels and tourist complexes	31	3.3	119	3.9
Ephemeral buildings and exhibitions	17	1.8	66	2.2
Religious buildings	16	1.7	35	1.2
Infrastructures and productive fixed capital	**99**	**10.6**	**250**	**8.3**
Urban infrastructure	58	6.2	166	5.5
Reurbanizations	29	3.1	61	2.0
Technological development	10	1.1	19	0.6
Industrial buildings	2	0.2	4	0.1
Social reproduction of the workforce	**99**	**10.6**	**203**	**6.8**
School buildings (basic education)	16	1.7	57	1.9
Multifamily housing	41	4.4	68	2.3
Parks and squares	23	2.5	29	1.0
Health buildings	12	1.3	32	1.1
Social housing	7	0.8	17	0.6
Others	**20**	**2.1**	**23**	**0.8**
Multiple uses	14	1.5	9	0.3
Nonidentifiable	6	0.6	14	0.5

* Based on twelve issues of each magazine, between 2005 and 2009, totaling thirty-six issues.

Table 2. Location of the works and projects published in the magazines
Arquitectura Viva, Architectural Record, and *GA Document**

Region	Number of articles	Percentage of total articles surveyed	Number of pages	Percentage of total pages surveyed
Western Europe	549	50.7	1584	48.7
United States and Canada	328	30.3	1001	30.8
China	47	4.3	199	6.1
Japan	33	3.0	157	4.8
Asia (without China and Japan)	30	2.8	92	2.8
Latin America	30	2.8	91	2.8
Middle East	27	2.5	57	1.7
Eastern Europe	23	2.1	54	1.7
Africa	14	1.3	14	0.4
Oceania	2	0.2	4	0.1

* Based on twelve issues of each magazine, between 2005 and 2009, totaling thirty-six issues.
Pages can include projects and works of more than one region.

need not recall the European history of addressing the "housing question," with nineteenth-century reformers (such as Owen and Fourier),
then in the 1920s with the German Siedlungs, the Viennese Hofs, and
the second CIAM meeting (in Frankfurt in 1929 with the theme of
the minimum housing unit—*Existenzminimum*), not to mention all the
socialist and social-democratic policies of housing provision and subsidized social rent for the working-class that were implemented in the
following decades. In the Global South (formerly the third world or
underdeveloped world), housing projects designed by local architects
and implemented through public policies specific for workers' dwellings
have existed since at least the 1930s, and, more broadly after the Second
World War, when large housing complexes started being built—many
of them disastrous, but others extraordinary and little known by the
international public.

The worldwide critique of functionalism and the international
style, from the 1950s to the 1960s, which includes its large housing
projects (that also proliferated in Europe and the postwar United States),

drives the search for evolutionary, participatory alternative solutions appropriated by the users, recognizing constructive popular knowledge, and dialogue with local contexts and actors. In that same period, with the emergence of third worldism and the social and independence revolutions, there was a rediscovery and new involvement of architects from the Global North with problems of precarious housing and accelerated urbanization in the Global South. The International Union of Architects congress, held in 1963 in Havana, which was then in Che's and Fidel's revolutionary Cuba, was a milestone in the dialogue among architects from around the world on topics such as the Urban Reform agenda and the challenge of mass housing production in a highly unequal country, devastated by a dictatorship that had turned the country into a farm, brothel, and casino for the United States. Three years later, Fernando Belaúnde, a moderate leftist architect who had assumed the presidency of Peru, held an international design contest for evolutionary social housing in Lima: the PREVI initiative—including architects James Stirling, Aldo van Eyck, and Christopher Alexander, among others. In 1968, the Uruguayan National Housing Law was approved, and in 1970 the Uruguayan Federation of Housing for Mutual Assistance (FUCAVAN) was founded, both of which were landmarks of a new type of housing policy in Latin America based on self-management, collective property, and associativism. In 1969–70, the book by the Egyptian architect Hassan Fathy, *Architecture for the Poor*, a best-seller and landmark in the debate on the engagement of architects in learning ancestral and popular techniques, materials, and knowledge, was published in English and French. In the following years, forced by the new practices and social struggles of the *pobladores* (squatters/settlers) and the *favelados* ("slum" dwellers), the World Bank renewed its housing agenda and proposed the qualification (and no longer the removal) of the precarious settlements. In 1976, the United Nations held the first Habitat conference, and the theme gained prominence among architects and schools of architecture. That same year, the English architect John F. C. Turner, after having spent time in the *barriadas* ("slums") of Latin America, published his most famous book advocating for the production of housing by users: *Housing by People: Towards Autonomy in Building Environments*.

The ideology of autonomy and the valorization of popular knowledge, on the one hand, and the reformist policies of human rights of the first NGOs and multilateral organizations (not coincidentally Turner became a consultant to the World Bank), on the other, were part of a complex context surrounding the emergence of the third world, its post-colonial agenda, and accelerated industrialization. At the same time, because Chile was already the advanced laboratory of neoliberal policies for the Global South, public policies based on market precepts were tested to serve the poorest: housing size and location according to payment capacity of each beneficiary, private provision of housing, progressive housing, and urbanized lots that depended on workers' effort to complete the projects were used as a way to reduce state expenses. This policy of "sites and services," "embryo houses," or "half-houses," complemented by "self-help," proliferated in Latin America in the late 1970s and 1980s, the same period in which many countries (including the three largest—Brazil, Mexico, and Argentina) declared insolvency and were extorted by the IMF for "structural adjustment" of their economies and payment of creditors. This drained public resources destined for social policies (including housing) in order to pay off debts with international investors. This in turn created the need for workers to contribute labor and their own savings for housing, in the absence of public policies to address the problem.[40]

Prior to awarding the Pritzker to Aravena, the hegemonic circulatory system of architectural ideas and practices had already held exhibitions and awarded "social" projects with less repercussion than Aravena's. In general, they were projects designed to theatricalize technical and urban solutions, from infrastructure to landscaping, through colorful facades and structural juggling, resulting in impactful images for the media (a small "Wow!" factor, aiming at prizes rather than at meeting the needs of the population). These projects function in the World Bank's logic of "best practices," and the propaganda of governments, politicians, and architects (not always transparently hired), resulting in works that received resources well above the average of other housing projects. Several of them fulfilled the mission of a marketing facade, working to hide the remainder of a poor housing policy (but highly profitable to their promoters), covering up the forgotten favelas alongside award-winning works or even situations of forced eviction and population removal.

We must highlight, however, the series of exhibits at the influential Museum of Modern Art (MoMA) following the 2008 crisis that exposed the problem of mass housing and its new configurations, including in the United States itself, with the explosion of the housing bubble, predatory mortgages, sub-prime loans, and foreclosures. In 2010, MoMA held an exhibition titled "Small Scale, Big Change: New Architectures of Social Engagement," curated by Andres Lepik, proposing the hypothesis that after the 2008 global crisis, stellar architecture of iconic buildings became unsustainable—and even ceased to be profitable—and calling, therefore, for the return to the local, the community scale, by re-sewing the social fabric after the speculative real-estate tsunami. In 2014, MoMA brought back the "Small Scale" hypothesis, but with greater programmatic ambitions. The exhibition "Uneven Growth: Tactical Urbanisms for Expanding Megacities," organized by Pedro Gadanho, was more than an exhibition; it intended to be a collaborative platform to register innovative design practices in urgent contexts, which require inventiveness and collaboration. The actions, some sponsored by public policies, generally transient and with strong visual appeal, adopted the name "tactical urbanism." In a postcrisis context of continuing losses for the working class, with no horizon of reconstruction for universalist and public-welfare policies, the "tactical" became a euphemism for the urban do-it-your-selfers—preferably with architects or designers as artists-mediators, agents of creative solutions, to face the global problems of an uneven urbanization on the microscale.

The multiplication of field trips, workshops, studios, or whatever name is given to advanced units in North American and European universities visiting the third-world metropolis, with "local partners" for projects in the favelas, is symptomatic. Although we cannot criticize the sensitivity (and even sympathy) of the students living in more affluent (but no less conflictive) societies regarding the relations of poverty, inequality, and precariousness of housing conditions in the Global South, it is also an internal/external mission to study design, policy, and business tools in cities of the Global South. The projects resulting from these favela studios do not resemble the housing policies of (even weakened) welfare states; rather, they somehow reproduce precariousness. The motto seems to be to reaffirm that the survival strategies of the poor are already part of the solution, with architects complementing them with their global vision and innovative design (whose visual and virtual tools are extensively practiced in the northern schools). On the other hand, global design companies, which in the future will hire some of these students, are breaking new ground in the management of public policies and actions, and in the execution of projects and works in peripheral metropolises. There is a growing internationalization within these companies, which requires staff consultants and technicians with know-how in the "favela-based design" and in the legal, environmental, and social complexity of the metropolises of the Global South.

The missions of foreign students also favor other business strategies in higher education. Private universities in powerful countries are increasingly penetrating peripheral education markets, with branches that are anchored in the possibility of acting on local problems with instruments, methodologies, and ideologies imported from dominant matrices and think tanks. Free and public universities are being dismantled globally, with rare exceptions, and pushed toward private funding, partnerships, or even succumbing and making room for global private universities.

The soup of social architecture thickens with the proliferation of NGOs engaged in philanthropy, social marketing, and research on miracle solutions to low-income housing during the neoliberal decades. In Latin America, the NGO that had the most spectacular and continent-wide growth was from Chile, founded in 1997, called Techo para mi país (A roof for my country), with its volunteer practices for the provision of housing. It enrolls university students to collect funds at traffic lights, schools, families, and workplaces, and to devote free days to build temporary wooden houses for families at risk of or in catastrophic situations. This philanthropic initiative received awards from the United Nations, the Inter-American Development Bank (IDB), and various governments. In some places, its enormous expansion adopted practices similar to those of a religious sect, until 2011 when it formally established cooperation with the Society of Jesus. In Chile, in recent years, a radical movement of secondary students (the "Pinguinos") supported Techo in adopting more informed and politicized positions on direct action and the fight for the right to the city, which impacts its international actions.

The system of celebrities who stimulate the field of architecture, the "social" interpreted and imagined through the lens of the star system, still demands the demiurgic action of the architect, more benevolent, maybe, but always authorial. The Pritzker and the Venice Architecture

Biennale, delivered in the same year to Alejandro Aravena, who also teaches at Harvard's Graduate School of Design, is a partner of the David Rockefeller Center, and was a juror for the Pritzker Prize in the six preceding editions, are important signs that, in addition to the green frontier, the social trench is increasing in importance in the constellation of contemporary architecture stars, and that its leader has already been appointed. According to the jury's award: "Aravena is leading a new generation of architects that has a holistic understanding of the built environment and has clearly demonstrated the ability to connect social responsibility, economic demands, design of human habitat and the city."[41] Locally, in Chile, besides being a beloved national celebrity (to the point of being seen as the country's informal ambassador), we find the more material bases of his rise: strategic support, societal support, and orders for buildings by oil and cellulose companies (his patron, Angelini, has the second-largest fortune in Latin America), as well as noncompetitive initiatives and commissions by the national government (which he continues to receive, even though his former partner, the minister of housing, Andrés Iacobelli, also a Chilean student at Harvard, was removed from office for corruption and passing privileged information to the real-estate market).

The award given to Aravena, at the age of forty-eight the youngest architect to win the Pritzker, aroused passion and hatred as none other had: would he be the bearer of a new architecture, socially engaged with real-world problems, with design quality and economic pragmatism, or an upstart who harnessed his connections with Harvard, Pritzker, Chilean entrepreneurs, and the government to sell his image as the socially concerned young promise that the world of starchitecture had been looking for since the crisis of the era of the spectacle and financial abundance?[42]

Brazilian critic Guilherme Wisnik puts it this way: "His personal appearance and professional attitude, combining a fashionable elegance with an intelligently self-promotional air, can be seen as antagonistic signs to the political position that social architecture should embody. Would this beloved son of the Chilean elite, well connected to powerful American institutions such as Harvard University, David Rockefeller Center, and the Pritzker family, be just surfing the social wave that emerged after the 2008 financial crisis?"[43]

Aravena constructed a narrative for his meteoric rise from the Global South, conquering a network of influential allies until he managed to convince his peers that the system needed someone like him, from the real world, thinking about problems that affect millions of people. He left the Harvard classroom, returned to Chile, and turned a good design idea into something concrete, through local partners, a private oil company, and a government that accepts innovations, provided they do not question the rules of the game.

Aravena arrived at Harvard in 2000, with no knowledge of the housing problem, the favelas in Latin America, or any involvement with social movements (in fact, he boasts of being an outsider in the subject). He began dedicating his classes at the Graduate School of Design studios to think on how to produce, with the given variables, a better-quality architecture to be implemented by housing policies in Latin America. He addressed complex housing issues and urban precariousness primarily as an articulation between financial availability and design quality. Citing some references and covering up others, he came up with a one-half incremental house proposal—a product to be tested. With the support of entrepreneurs and the government, he established the Elemental Company and executed its first project, the now-famous Quinta Monroy, in Iquique, with the cost of $7,500 per housing unit.

With an increase in public subsidies to more than double the initial value and a strategy of obtaining international partners through the promotion of contests of ideas (winners did not carry out their own projects but partnered with Elemental in theirs), design projects began to multiply based on the same assumption. If the financing that the government provides for affordable housing is not enough to allow for good housing, let us make half a dwelling and leave an empty space for later expansion with self-construction. Everyone knew this idea was not new (except for the Pritzker jury), though Aravena did propose a solution with a design intelligence that improves in later projects.[44]

Aiming at higher-density housing so that resources should be enough to purchase land in better locations, Elemental does not propose tall buildings, but houses one on top of the other, the upper one being a duplex. The firm uses low-cost concrete blocks and structures molded on location, with no industrialization, including the making of stairs and guardrails with timber used on the construction site. Inside, the house is hollow and has light partitions. One of the walls of the semi-detached house is structural masonry, and the other is enclosed by a thin membrane, awaiting its rupture to expand in the lateral empty area. The household, crammed into the small space of twenty-five square meters, breaks the membrane and gives rise to the hollow area left by the architect as a strategy of survival. In a combination of precariousness and inventiveness, this allows the gray-standard modules to contrast with new multicolored fillings of heterogeneous materials and openings.

The low-tech "open-platform" model works; its expansion seems uncomplicated, and the results produce an interesting hybrid texture combining scholarly design with favela self-construction elements and state public action with popular resilience tactics. The tattooed skins of contemporary architecture, discussed in the first chapter, return here as an expression of an economy of means, and not as luxury artifice à la Herzog & de Meuron. There is no doubt that there is projective intelligence in Quinta Monroy, as well as ideological positioning. In subsequent projects, with additional resources, the installations and finishes of the houses were improved, and the roof, a strategic structural element, was constructed from one end of the row of houses to the other, leaving the empty stretch of the expansion sheltered from rain and sun.

The existence of design merits cannot conceal indirect questions presumed or not made evident by the Elemental model. The mediatic aura of the award-winning solution "looks away from real problems."[45] The good design of the incremental house can be a false problem in the face of the articulation of other factors. I suggest five questions for debate on the Elemental paradigm:

1. The naturalization of the lack of resources in peripheral governments to guarantee housing as a basic right, and abdicate any housing solution comparable to those already given by the welfare state model (although it is currently undermined), or the cooperative and self-managing production that has achieved such good results on the Continent—as well as larger units than those produced by private companies. Do we accept that half of a house is the solution for a half-citizen, or for a citizenship cut in half?[46]

2. The naturalization of the right to housing as being identical to the right to property. That is, that the provision of access to housing must be fulfilled exclusively through individual private ownership

(including family financing and indebtedness). Social welfare or social-ist policies were able to distinguish housing rights from property rights: it is possible to live paying subsidized rent without owning a commodity-house—increasingly expensive if well located and of high quality. Indeed, this is a way to de-mercantilize the built environment, or at least to counteract the processes of speculative real-estate valuation. However, the ideology of the "dream of homeownership" or the "home ownership society," which is American above all but has also flourished in South American dictatorships, have both linked housing rights to individual private property. In peripheral countries, this is still advocated by pro-gressive groups, given the precariousness of social security and public services (the house functioning as personal savings). Thus, the "owned house" appears as the only alternative for complying with the right to housing. It was up to the World Bank and the IMF, through neoliberal adjustment policies, to attack any alternative to the public provision of housing and social housing rent, even requesting the privatization of what was already public.

3. As a result of this second point: the Elemental paradigm not only naturalizes the "owned house" but also states the goal of promot-ing real-estate valuation for its dwellings. If conventional low-income housing projects do not result in real-estate valuation like those of higher-income classes, good design, good location, and the possibility of expansion by households would allow them to participate in real-estate gains like any other. In addition, the commodity-house would also serve as small initial capital for household indebtedness and entre-preneurship (with the progress of mortgage and payroll loan markets), according to the neoliberal economist Hernando de Soto (repeatedly cited by Elemental, adviser to President Alberto Fujimori, and the World Bank). It is necessary to include in the model the variable of scarcity: urban land is a finite good and its progressive valorization (as seen in Europe) ends up preventing new housing projects and even middle-class rent, producing a new wave of urban exodus to new suburbs. The more we move forward within the logic of commodity production over a scarce common good (urban land) and a fundamental human right (housing), the more the inequalities will amplify, rather than the reverse.

4. The naturalization of the productivist model, which tends to build more and more new dwellings, expands the urban footprint at an

unsustainable rate. Despite Elemental's discourse in favor of good locations, several of its projects are located in peripheral terrain. The incessant machine of businesses with land and new home construction is
interested in the real-estate sector and in the landowners, but not in the
citizens in general. There is evident scarcity of policies and financing
for dwelling improvement, both for homes already built by workers
and for housing projects already built by the state (that is the problem
of "*los con techo*" [the ones with a roof], as they say in Chile).[47] This is,
in fact, the missing incremental policy. In addition, in several countries
and cities in Latin America, the number of vacant properties is higher
than the housing deficit. But the real-estate growth machine needs to
continue delivering new houses, even if they are half-finished.

5. The last point is the true lack of innovative urban qualities in
Elemental designs. They are, in the end, much like traditional housing
projects, even if with better-designed units. They function as gated
communities for the poor. There is no connection with the surrounding
environment, no mixed use, no room for a more diverse and active
urban life, or for the complexity of the urban fabric. They remain isolated housing ghettos, rows of semidetached houses that do not enhance
the public nature of the city. Latin American studies and critiques are
repeated, showing that the main problem to be faced is not just the
deficit of housing units but, above all, the deficit of urban qualities, or,
simply put, a deficit of the city and, indirectly, a deficit of citizenship.

Aravena, however, is the best that the liberal and elitist world of
architecture can produce. He wants to improve the housing product but
remains within the same logic; it is an innovation of a pro-real-estate,
land, and builder system. In this sense, he is an enfant-not-too-terrible.
He is a hero of the poor, invented by the rich, and therefore a hero
under control. He does not attack the system, but recycles it.

The Chilean architect displayed his services in the curatorship
of the Venice Biennale in 2016 *(Reporting from the Front),* covering in
the exhibition, with no apparent reason, on the one hand, the same
list of hyperawarded architects, and, on the other, bringing (seemingly
random) news from the uneven urbanization front in the Global South
and North, shaken by the financial–real-estate crisis, unemployment,
and social abandonment. On the one side, there were eleven firms that
had already been awarded the Pritzker: Foster, Rogers, Tadao Ando,

Piano, Herzog & de Meuron, Wang Shu, SANAA, Souto de Moura, Shigeru Ban, Zumthor, and—awarded the Golden Lion in Venice for lifetime achievement—Paulo Mendes da Rocha (who, in Brazil, never came to the fore), besides young and avid European architects in search of global prizes. On the other side, architects who work in situations of extreme poverty, refugee camps, the Occupy Movement, and out-raged movements, in ungovernable metropolises, who are developing very low-cost technologies. Although some of the stars are more sensi-tive to real problems affecting the population, the exhibition did not favor a possible dialogue between these extremes, only a juxtaposition. It would have been bolder if the exhibition had in fact brought to the select public of Venice, in a critical, articulated, and informed way, news of the hottest and most complex frontiers of contemporary architecture and urbanism, making no concessions to invite the same happy few. The way it was set up turned it into a true dance of winners and losers, conducted by its curator. Does the social agenda win by coming into play? Undoubtedly, because prior to that, the miserable and indigent were not invited: architecture of social concern was by no means on the agenda of the professional elite. But who wins, above all, is Aravena, promoted as the main representative of the dark side of the globe in architecture's stellar party.

Behind the cloud of mediatic smoke, there is a lot to discover and new fields of action for those who seek transformative practices in the social production of architecture. In Latin America, besides the PREVI model, the most radical and influential production of the last fifty years can be seen on the other side of the continent, in Uruguay. In 1968, thanks to popular mobilization, the National Housing Law started to encourage and finance social, cooperative, and nonprofit modes of pro-duction. With the law, the Federation of Housing Cooperatives for Mutual Assistance (FUCVAM) was created, supported by architects of the Uruguayan Cooperative Center (CCU) and of the Federation itself to carry out fabulous housing projects in and around Montevideo.[48] Coming from another political, associative, and self-managing matrix, they promoted innovation at all levels: integration of the world of work with that of everyday life (trade unions promoted entrepreneurship, and, more recently, they embraced other modalities, with immigrants and the unemployed); insertion of projects into the urban fabric; adoption of collective property; mixed-use structures (whenever possible housing was associated with leisure, education, and commercial areas); technological innovation, including light ceramic precast; sometimes adopting progressive housing that grows toward the empty interior of a complete structure; diversity of typologies (each according to its needs); the possibility of changing units over time (some families grow while others decrease in number of dwellers); self-managing production on the construction site, without capitalist companies, through cooperatives, mutual aid, and small family businesses—and all of which is supported by a stable public policy that has survived, including through the military regime (thanks to FUCVAM's permanent struggle), and that accounted in certain periods for more than 50 percent of the country's housing production.

With the redemocratization of Latin America in the 1980s after the cycle of dictatorships, the cooperative model of FUCVAM multiplied across the continent and important experiences have arisen from it (each one with its own specific traits), mainly in Buenos Aires (the most relevant was Movimiento de Ocupantes y Inquilinos [Occupiers and Tenants Movement], with the most beautiful retrofits of factories turned into affordable housing),[49] São Paulo (the famous self-managed *mutirões* of the União dos Movimentos de Moradia [Union of Housing Movements] and its technical advisory services),[50] and Caracas (the Camps of Pioneers and the self-managing aspect of Gran Misión Vivienda [Great Housing Mission]).[51] Hundreds of other initiatives not directly influenced by FUCVAM should be better known by the international public interested in the theme: various generations of favela urbanization design projects, rehabilitation of "slums," forced resettlements, and environmental and risk area recoveries. The housing and precarious settlements issue in the Global South is very complex and mobilizes a series of initiatives, more or less successful (generally less, unfortunately), which need to work in a connected way. There is no single or elemental solution, if you will forgive the pun.

While the privileged circle of architects displays and rewards those from their restricted field who dare to set foot in the shadowy territory of the "Planet of Slums," in Mike Davis's expression, a planet that had not yet been illuminated by the stars of architecture's financial constellation, whose system of decorations and self-indulgences was unable to influence real practices. Housing production policies in Chile, Brazil, and Mexico, for example, follow the same logic of large-scale production of housing projects, endowed with peripheral and mono-functional conditions—small dwellings that are mainly of interest to builders and their commercial logic. The price of urban land in these countries soared above inflation and wages, and governments have renounced any policy of control, regulation, and democratization of access to land other than through market laws. The half-house may soon become a one-third house, and so on.

The most influential architects, however, usually do not openly criticize these initiatives, or they just stick to the form and not to the neoliberal content of the programs. Although they have come to recognize the severity of the crisis and the increase in unemployment and inequality, more vehement action regarding the production of the built environment does not seem to arouse the least bit of interest among jet-set architects. To question the concentration of wealth and property, the allocation of public funds, the unequal positioning of classes in cities, or to request guaranteed forms of real democratization of access to land and common goods, or the fulfillment of basic citizens' rights, regardless of their debt capacity, are flags that no one awarded by the system dares to raise.

How the architects who have so far dominated the field will reposition their brands in the face of the new frontiers yet to be explored is still unclear. The inability of almost all of the Pritzker Prize winners to speak, speculatively or intellectually, with the real world "front" at the 2016 Venice Biennale is a symptom that they were not interested or prepared to confront the adverse, complex, and vulnerable contexts of unequal global urbanization. In this redefinition of agendas and dominant values, one thing is certain, they will do everything to preserve their positions of exception, while a new generation will seize the moment and try to ascend to the heavens. Meanwhile, ongoing global crises see increasing poverty and precariousness for hundreds of millions of individuals, stuck in environmental and social catastrophes on a "Planet of Slums," accompanied by accelerated urbanization that is seemingly beyond rescue, not just on the periphery of capitalism. A dark planet, which no star illuminates.

NOTES

INTRODUCTION

1. Term used in *Sketches of Frank Gehry* (2005), a documentary by Sydney Pollack.

2. I adopt the term "the rent of form" in reference to the concept of "differential land rent" as formulated by Karl Marx in *Capital: A Critique of Political Economy*, volume 3 (1887). The concept of land rent, especially for urban land, has since been updated by several authors. I highlight the interpretation of David Harvey in his book *Limits to Capital* and another important article by the same author ("The Art of Rent: Globalization, Monopoly and the Commodification of Culture"), which introduces new possibilities for interpreting the concept of rent for art and culture, building on Marx's initial formulation.

1. THE FORMS OF RENT

1. Interview with the author. The other statements by Nelson Kon, if not mentioned in notes, are from the same interview.

2. Julius Shulman, *Photographing Architecture and Interiors* (New York: Whitney Library of Design, 1962), 2.

3. Ibid., 5.

4. Interview with the author. The other statements by Leonardo Finotti in this topic are from the same interview.

5. Luis Fernández-Galiano, "Papel fotográfico: imagens que constroem a arquitetura," *Projeto* (July 1994): 81.

6. Fernando Freitas Fuão, "Papel do papel: as folhas da arquitetura e a arquitetura mesma," *Projeto* (July 1994): 84.

7. Ibid.

8. Interview with Eduardo Costa and Sonia Gouveia, "Nelson Kon, uma fotografia de arquitetura brasileira," *Pós Magazine,* no. 24 (December 2008): 16.

9. Robert Elwall, *Building with Light: An International History of Architectural Photography* (London: Merrel, 2004), 195.

10. Interview with Eduardo Costa and Sonia Gouveia, "Nelson Kon, uma fotografia de arquitetura brasileira," 20.

11. Ibid., 19.

12. I am grateful for the comment of photographer Gal Oppido, who warned me that a critical view of contemporary architecture could not disregard the role of photography.

13. Elwall, *Building with Light.*

14. As Beatriz Plaza reminds us, in "The Guggenheim-Bilbao Museum Effect: A Reply to María V. Gómez's Reflective Images: The Case of Urban Regeneration in Glasgow and Bilbao," *International Journal of Urban and Regional Research,* no. 23 (1999); and also Anna Klingmann, in *Brandscapes: Architecture in the Experience Economy* (Cambridge: MIT Press, 2007), 243.

15. Fredric Jameson, *Postmodernism, or, The Cultural Logic of Late Capitalism* (Durham, N.C.: Duke University Press, 1991), 99.

16. In the Norman Foster's firm there is a "visualization team" that oversees all projects.

17. In an interview with the author.

18. Denis Moreau, "La petite fabrique d'effets spéciaux: artefactory au générique," *L'Architecture d'Aujourd'hui,* no. 354 (2004): 72–75.

19. Afterword by Éric Alliez, in *Imagem máquina: a era das tecnologias do virtual* (São Paulo: Editora 34, 1993), 267.

20. This phenomenon is not new and occurred at other moments and in other historical contexts. The historian Fernando Novais, for example, explains the colonial regime of Portuguese America as a dominance of the circulation of the production, because the slave trade was the determining element in defining the economy, including in the sphere of production.

21. Guy Debord, *Society of the Spectacle* (New York: Zone Books, 1995), 24.

22. Ibid., 32.

23. Ibid., 12.

24. Quoted in Carlos Vainer, "Pátria, empresa e mercadoría: notas sobre a estratégia discursiva do Planejamento Estratégico Urbano," in Otília Arantes,

Erminia Maricato, and Carlos Vainer, *A cidade do pensamento único: Desmanchando consensos* (Petrópolis: Vozes, 2000), 78–80; emphasis added.

25. Ibid., 94.

26. Javier Mozas, "'Collage' metropolitano: Biblao, imperativos económicos y regeneración urbana," *Arquitectura Viva*, no. 55 (July 1997).

27. Beatriz Plaza, "Evaluating the Influence of a Large Cultural Artifact on Tourism: The Guggenheim Museum Bilbao Case," *Urban Affairs Review*, no. 36 (2000).

28. According to Joseba Zulaika, *Guggenheim Bilbao: crónica de una seducción* (Madrid: Nerea, 1997), 123–25.

29. Ibid., 35.

30. Ibid., 231.

31. Hal Foster, *Design and Crime (and Other Diatribes)* (London: Verso, 2002), 42.

32. Zulaika, Joseba, "'Plotach' arquitectónico: Guggenheim Bilbao, el precio de um símbolo," *Arquitectura Viva*, no. 55 (July 1997).

33. David Harvey, "The Art of Rent: Globalization, Monopoly and the Commodifiation of Culture," in *A produção capitalista do espaço* (São Paulo: Annablume, 2005).

34. Otília Arantes, "Os dois lados da arquitetura francesa pós-Beaubourg," in *O lugar da arquitetura depois dos modernos* (São Paulo: Edusp, 1993), 185–86.

35. Otília Arantes, "Os Novos Museus," in *O lugar da arquitetura depois dos modernos*, 239–41.

36. Ibid., 244.

37. Arantes, "Os dois lados da arquitetura francesa pós-Beaubourg," 190.

38. Ibid., 178.

39. Cited in Otília Arantes, "Cultura e transformação urbana," in Vera Pallamin, ed., *Cidade e Cultura: Esfera pública e transformação urbana* (São Paulo: Estação Liberdade, 2002), 69.

40. Ibid., 70.

41. Otília Arantes, "A 'virada cultural' do sistema das artes," *Margem esquerda*, no. 6 (2005): 64.

42. Ibid., 68.

43. Ibid., 69.

44. Ibid., 75.

45. Ibid.

46. Mike Davis, "Sand, Fear and Money in Dubai," in *Evil Paradises* (New York: New Press, 2007).

47. A "speculative" high, because it is a price that foresees a future scarcity and compares with other financial applications, having little to do with the production cost.

48. By 2018, the works of the Guggenheim Museum in Abu Dhabi had not yet begun, and only the landfill had been carried out on the sea. Artist and journalist Molly Crabapple managed to infiltrate and described the construction site of the Louvre unit and the earthworks for the Guggenheim (see "Slaves of Happiness Island," https://www.vice.com/en_us/article/gq889w / slaves-of -happiness-island-0000412-v21n8).

49. The term was coined by the media. See Donald McNeill, "McGuggenisation? National Identity and the Globalization in the Basque Country," *Political Geography,* no. 19 (2000).

50. George Ritzer, *The McDonaldization of Society: An Investigation into the Changing Character of Contemporary Social Life* (Thousand Oaks, Calif.: Pine Forge Press, 1995), chapter 1.

51. According to David Harvey, in "The Art of Rent," not only architecture, but also the whole cultural field, favors monopoly rents. Cultural commodities supposedly have a dynamic that differs from conventional commodities because of its language of exceptionality, originality, and authenticity being decisive for the establishment of the rents.

52. I use the term in reference to Marx's notion of "unproductive labor," that is, one that does not directly generate surplus value, and which relies, precisely, on its distribution and division.

53. Jacques Herzog, quoted in Luis Fernández-Galiano, "Diálogo e logo: Jacques Herzog piensa en voz alta," *Arquitectura Viva,* no. 91 (2003): 29.

54. As Manfredo Tafuri states, "architecture, at least according to the traditional concept, is a stable structure, gives form to permanent values, consolidates an urban morphology," in *Projecto e utopia* (Lisbon: Presença, 1985), 36.

55. Ibid., 26.

56. Naomi Klein, *No Logo: Taking Aim at the Brand Bullies* (Toronto: Canada Vintage, 2000), 22.

57. It is worth remembering, however, that this strategy does not stem exclusively from the current financial dominance of the accumulation regime. The possibility of diverting profit rate differentials basically goes back to the productive orbit itself. Today, rentier forms are actually exponentiating mechanisms of competition between capitals, especially when they manufacture imaginary differences to capture a greater share of total profit.

58. See Klein, *No Logo,* chapter 1; and Isleide Fontenelle, *O nome da marca* (São Paulo: Boitempo, 2004), 4.

59. Fontenelle, *O nome da marca.*

60. Harvey, "The Art of Rent."

61. Jorge Grespan, *O negativo do capital: o conceito de crise na crítica de Marx à economia poítica* (São Paulo: Hucitec, 1998), and Eleutério da Silva

Prado, *Desmedida do valor: crítica da pós-grande indústria* (São Paulo: Xamã, 2005). We will address disproportion in the architecture production in the next chapters.

62. François Chesnais, "A emergência de um regime de acumulação financeira," *Praga,* no. 3 (1997): 37.

63. According to information given by the architect Caio Faggin about the contracts of the Foster + Partners firm. Interview with the author.

64. Arantes, "A 'virada cultural' do sistema das artes," 71.

65. See Simone Schleifer, ed., *Spectacular Buildings* (Cologne: Evergreen Taschen, 2007), 75.

66. The expression is from the project description on the firm's Web site. Part of this show is the transport of cars still being assembled on high rails, from one building to another: http://www.zaha-hadid.com/architecture/bmw-cen tral-building/.

67. OMA/Koolhaas, *Projects for Prada—Part 1* (Milan: Fondazione Prada Edizioni, 2001).

68. Ibid.

69. See Rem Koolhaas, *The Harvard Design Guide to Shopping,* ed. Chuihua Judy Chung, Jeffery Inaba, Rem Koolhaas, and Sze Tsung Leong (Cologne: Taschen, 2002).

70. Gilles Lipovetsky and Elyette Roux, *O luxo eterno—da idade do sagrado ao tempo das marcas* (São Paulo: Companhia das Letras, 2005), 43.

71. Ibid., 48.

72. The great model of this system was Benetton, with design concentrated in Italy, printing in California, and the sewing of parts in East Asia. The fashionable Diesel brand, for example, produces its jeans sold for thousands of dollars at a factory in Ceará, Brazil.

73. According to information given by Martin Corullon and Caio Faggin, Brazilian architects who worked at Foster's firm between 2006 and 2009.

74. Cited in Eric Howeler, *Skyscrapers: Designs of the Recent Past and for the Near Future* (London: Thames & Hudson, 2003), 36.

75. The architect Caio Faggin comments that "Foster's high-tech is not always all that. When you are inside, seeing how the forms are born, you discover that there is a lot of makeup."

76. According to Caio Faggin, interview with the author.

77. Isleide Fontenelle, "Os caçadores do *cool,*" *Lua Nova,* no. 63 (2004).

78. Ibid.

79. Kevin M. Murphy, "The Economic Value of Investing in Architecture and Design" (2003), www.dqionline.com/downloads/MSallette_Ind_ Study.pdf; accessed February 2010.

80. Paul J. Davies, "Foster Clinches Gold after Olympic Triumph," *China-Fortune Capital* (September 3, 2008).

81. Research "Buyout Track," conducted by Lloyds TSB, and "Architect Foster Builds a Winning Business," *Sunday Times*, February 8, 2009.

82. Herzog cited in Fernandez-Galiano, "Diálogo y logo," 29.

83. Sanford Kwinter, *Far from Equilibrium: Essays on Technology and Design Culture* (New York: Actar, 2008), 132.

84. Cited in Fredric Jameson, "The Brick and the Balloon: Architecture, Idealism and Land Speculation," in *The Cultural Turn: Selected Writings on the Postmodern* (London and New York: Verso, 1998).

85. Wolfgang Fritz Haug, *Critique of Commodity Aesthetics: Appearance, Sexuality, and Advertising in Capitalist Society* (Cambridge: Polity Press 1986), 50.

86. Ibid.

87. Cited in Fernandez-Galiano, "Diálogo y logo," 26.

88. The Allianz Arena construction site is featured in the documentary by Su Turhan and Silvia Beutl, *Construindo o Superestádio*, Discovery Channel. The work was carried out by 1,500 workers from twenty different countries, in a regime of three shifts to meet the deadline of the inauguration required by FIFA.

89. Kai Strehlke, "El ornamiento digital: aproximaciones de um novo decoro," *Arquitectura Viva*, no. 124 (2009).

90. Adolf Loos, *Ornament and Crime: Selected Essays* (Riverside: California Ariadne Press, 1998).

91. A critique of Loos's text and the rationalism of modern architecture is made by Theodor Adorno in "Functionalism Today" (1967), *Gávea*, no. 15 (June 1997).

92. See Otília Arantes, "Arquitetura simulada," in *O lugar da arquitetura depois dos modernos*.

93. Sérgio Ferro, *Arquitetura e trabalho livre* (São Paulo: Cosac & Naify, 2006), 364.

94. Ibid.

95. Ibid.

96. Oliver Domeisen and Francesca Ferguson, presentation of the exhibition "Re-Sampling Ornament" (2008).

97. Ibid.

98. Interview with Hanno Rauterberg, *Talking Architecture, Interviews with Architects* (London: Prestel, 2008).

99. Cited in Branko Kolarevic, *Architecture in Digital Age: Design and Manufacturing* (New York: Taylor & Francis, 2003), 51.

100. Christian Schittich, *Building Skins: Concepts, Layers, Materials* (Basel, Switzerland: Birkhäuser, 2001), 25–26.

101. Pierre Lévy, Pierre, *Becoming Virtual: Reality in the Digital Age* (New York: Plenum Trade, 1998), 32.

102. Jeremy Rifkin, *The Age of Access: The New Culture of Hypercapitalism, Where All of Life Is a Paid-For Experience* (New York: TarcherPerigee, 2001), 137.

103. Walter Benjamin, "The Work of Art in the Age of Mechanical Reproduction," in *Illuminations: Essays and Reflections* (New York: Shocken Books, 2007), 239–41.

104. Jan Specht, "The Role of Architecture in the Tourism Destination Development and Branding," in Shaul Krakover and Natan Uriely, *Tourism Destination and Development Branding* (Eilat, Israel: Ben-Gurion University of the Negev, 2009), 99.

105. Ibid., 100.

106. Jean Baudrillard, *The System of Objects* (1968) (London: Verso, 1996).

107. Rifkin, *The Age of Access,* 150–51.

108. Kevin Meethan, "Imaginando a cidade para o turismo," *NOZ,* no. 2 (2008).

109. Rifkin, *The Age of Access,* 151.

110. Jacques Lang, quoted in Arantes, "Os dois lados da arquitetura francesa pós-Beaubourg," 160.

111. They represent, for example, 30 percent or more of the Employee Assistance Program of most North American urban centers, according to research by Richard Florida, *Cities and the Creative Class* (New York: Routledge, 2005).

112. Report produced by the city of Ontario, Canada, with the objective of becoming a top-notch cultural destination: *Ontario Cultural and Heritage Tourism Product Research Paper* (Toronto: Queen's Printer for Ontario, 2009), 12.

113. Ibid., 10.

114. Specht, "Architectural Tourism," 99.

115. Marc Augé defines nonplaces as spaces produced by supermodernity and which are characterized as nonidentitary, nonrelational, and nonhistorical. They are, in general, "facilities needed for the accelerated movement of people and goods," from transport infrastructure to large shopping centers (*Não-lugares: introdução a uma antropologia da supermodernidade* [São Paulo: Papirus, 2003], 36).

116. According to the presentation of the project on the firm's Web site.

117. Fuáo, "Papel do papel," 85.

118. Reproduced in Gentzane López, "The Guggenheim Effect: Positive Transformation for the City of Bilbao," in *Eurocultre 2006* (2006), www.euroculturemaster.org/pdf/lopez.pdf; accessed February 2010.

119. Interview given to Miguel Mora, from *El País*, reproduced at the *Folha de S. Paulo* (January 31, 2010).

120. "Forster asegura que la Ciudad de la Cultura es 'especial y única' y que el reto es atraer visitantes," http://www.elcorreogallego.es/santiago/ecg/forster-senala-reto-es-atraer-visitantes-estudiar-financiacion/idEdicion-2007–11–16/idNoticia-232986/ (November 15, 2007).

121. See Harvey, "The Art of Rent."

122. Plaza, "Evaluating the Influence of a Large Cultural Artifact on Tourism."

123. María Gómez and Sara Gonzáles, "A Reply to Beatriz Plaza's 'The Guggenheim-Bilbao Museum Effect,'" *International Journal of Urban and Regional Research* 25:4 (2001).

124. Peter Hall, "Los iconos arquitectónicos nos llevan a uma suma cero," *La Vanguardia*, June 15, 2009.

125. The Guggenheim, for example, absorbed 80 percent of the resources of the Basque department of culture. Galicia was indebted to more than 500 million euros to complete Peter Eisenman's cultural center.

126. In an interview with "Mais!"—cultural supplement of *Folha de S. Paulo*, January 31, 2010, 10.

127. Specht, "Architectural Tourism," 102.

128. According to Economic Impact Study presented in Gentzane López, "The Guggenheim Effect," 10.

129. According to Joseba Zulaika, "it is not surprising that Basque President José Antonio Ardanza (1985–1998) appeared on Wall Street to sign the Guggenheim deal, delivering a check for the $20 million down payment" (*Guggenheim Bilbao: crónica de una seducción* [Madrid: Nerea, 1997], 96).

130. Berk & Associates, *Seattle Central Library Economic Benefits Assessment: The Transformative Power of a Library to Redefine Learning, Community, and Economic Development* (2005), www.spl.org/pdfs/SPLCentral_Library_Economic_Impacts.pdf; accessed February 2010.

131. Ibid., 28.

132. Ibid., 38.

133. Ibid., 43.

134. "Moratória em Dubai assusta bolsas," *O Estado de S. Paulo*, November 27, 2009.

135. Arantes, "Os dois lados da arquitetura francesa pós-Beaubourg," 179.

136. In the case of Bilbao, the study by Beatriz Plaza shows that high-end hotels grew to 85 percent of the occupancy rate, while the rest stayed with only 46 percent ("The Guggenheim-Bilbao Museum Effect," 269).

137. See Beatriz Kara-José, *Políticas culturais e negócios urbanos* (São Paulo: Annablume, 2007).

138. Pedro Arantes, "Interesse público, poderes privados e práticas discursivas na política de renovação do Centro de São Paulo," in *Políticas públicas para o Centro: controle social do financiamento do BID à Prefeitura Municipal de São Paulo* (São Paulo: Instituto Pólis, 2008).

139. Interview with the author.

140. Interview with the author.

141. Project description.

142. Amount assessed by the Rio de Janeiro City Court of Auditors in 2012, after ten years of construction: http://www.jb.com.br/rio/noticias/2012/03/12/apos-10-anos-e-r-600-mi-cidade-das-artes-deve-abrir-em-2012/. Apparently, monuments to music often have very "dissonant" notes between the original budget and the work performed. The budget for Koolhaas's Casa da Música in Porto was also nearly quadrupled from the initial estimate of 34 million euros to 111 million, according to the Porto City Court of Auditors: https://www.publico.pt/2008/12/05/culturaipsilon/noticia/tribunal-de-con tas-confirma-derrapagem-de-dinheiros-e-prazos-da-casa-da-musica-1352185.

143. Debord, *Society of the Spectacle*, 14.

144. Ibid., 24.

145. Baudrillard cited in Foster, *Design and Crime (and Other Diatribes)*, 18.

146. Ibid., 21.

147. Ibid., 279.

148. Debord, *Society of the Spectacle*, 32–33.

149. Karl Marx, *Capital: A Critique of Political Economy*, vol. 1 (London: Penguin in association with *New Left Review*, 1990), 289.

150. Jameson, "The Brick and the Balloon."

151. The essay, dated 1976, was revised and published and republished in *Arquitetura e trabalho livre*.

152. Arantes, *O lugar da arquitetura depois dos modernos*, 65.

153. Cited in ibid., 51; translation retrieved from http://laurencefuller. squarespace.com/blog/2015/10/14/caro-fuller-saga-ii-the-interview.

154. Monopoly rent is based on the nonreproducibility of certain goods and commodities. In this sense, it is a rent whose gains come from factors opposed to the mass production of goods standardized by the commodity-producing system.

155. The financialization of public policies was the subject of my master's degree, *O ajuste urbano: as políticas do Banco Mundial e do BID para as cidades latino-americanas* (FAU-USP, 2004).

2. PROGRAMMED DESIGN

1. Francesco Dal Co and Kurt Forster, *Frank O. Gehry: Complete Works* (New York: Monacelli Press, 1998), 442.

2. Diane Ghirardo, *Architecture after Modernism* (London: Thames & Hudson, 1996). Diane reminds us that Gehry has already designed another fortress in Los Angeles, the Frances Goldwyn Library, in 1982–86. According to Mike Davis, it was the "most menacing library ever built" (Mike Davis, *City of Quartz* [London: Verso, 2006], 369).

3. Davis, *City of Quartz,* 37.

4. From *Sketches of Frank Gehry,* documentary by Sydney Pollack (2005).

5. Davis, *City of Quartz,* 368.

6. Sharon Zukin, "Learning from Disney World," in *The Cultures of Cities* (Cambridge: Blackwell, 1995), 55. See also Sharon Zukin, "Disneyworld: The Power of Facade, the Facade of Power," in *Landscapes of Power: From Detroit to Disney World* (Berkeley: University of California Press, 1993).

7. Mildred Friedman, *Gehry Talks: Architecture and Process* (New York: Universe, 2002), 15.

8. Jim Glymph, "Evolution of the Digital Design Process," in Branko Kolarevic, *Architecture in the Digital Age: Design and Manufacturing* (New York: Taylor & Francis, 2003), 105.

9. Ibid., 107.

10. To use the term employed by Fernando Haddad, *Em defesa do socialismo* (São Paulo: Vozes, 1998).

11. Kolarevic, *Architecture in the Digital Age.*

12. Dennis Shelden, "Tectonics, Economics and the Reconfiguration of Practice: The Case for Process Change by Digital Means," *Architectural Design* 76:4 (2006): 82–87.

13. Sérgio Ferro, *Arquitetura e trabalho livre* (São Paulo: Cosac & Naify, 2006), 151–200 and 330–78.

14. Ibid., 151–54.

15. Ibid., 153.

16. Giulio Carlo Argan, "O significado da cúpula," in *História da arte como história da cidade* (São Paulo: Companhia das Letras, 1992), 95.

17. Manfredo Tafuri, *Teorias e história da arquitectura* (Lisbon: Presença, 1979), 37.

18. Ferro, *Arquitetura e trabalho livre,* 130.

19. In the architectural firm, there is a command pyramid that starts with the chief architect (usually the "senior"), and then the full architect, followed by the junior architect, the designer, the designer-draftsman, the designer-assistant, the archivist, the model maker, and the intern. The firm also hires project and external consultants in various engineering specialties (electrical, hydraulics, structures, foundations, soil, etc.).

20. Ferro, *Arquitetura e trabalho livre,* 157.

21. Ibid., 130.

22. The following description is of the drawing method and its instruments from the 1980s and early 1990s, just before the introduction of digital design. Apart from my little experience with this type of design, I relied on the testimony of João Marcos Lopes and Renata Moreira.

23. "Consulate of representation" is a concept Sérgio Ferro uses to describe the tautological trend and self-referential meaning of architectural design: "architectural space will follow the norms of the representational space itself: it will become homogeneous, regulated, orthogonal, modulated, etc." and thus "the representation of itself"—even in the diplomatic sense, as ambassador of his interests (Ferro, *Arquitetura e trabalho livre,* 158–62). In this sense, it is possible to make a parallel with the ideas of Laymert Garcia dos Santos in "Informação após a virada cibernética [Information after the cybernetic turn]," in *Revolução Tecnológica, Internet e Socialismo* (São Paulo: Perseu Abramo, 2003).

24. Its first version was generated at MIT, after tests conducted at the U.S. Air Force, according to Marian Bozdoc, *The History of CAD* (2003), http://mbinfo.mbdesign.net/CAD-History.htm; accessed January 2010.

25. Kostas Terzidis, *Algorithmic Architecture* (Amsterdam and Boston: Architectural Press, 2006), 54.

26. According to Mahesh Senegala, "Deconstructing AutoCAD: Toward a Critical Theory of Software (in) Design," in *Proceedings of the 7th Iberoamerican Congress of Digital Graphics* (Rosario, Argentina: SIGraDi, 2003), http://cumincad.scix.net/cgi-bin/works/Show?sigradi2003_008; accessed January 2010.

27. Bozdoc, *The History of CAD.* At the time of writing, this was the most recent data available.

28. The following description of digital design is based on testimonies by the architects José Baravelli, Renata Moreira, and Guilherme Petrella.

29. Kolarevic, "Digital Production," in *Architecture in the Digital Age.*

30. See its use in some models at the 2009 São Paulo Architecture Biennial, notably the School of Architecture at Hong Kong University. Martin Corullon, who worked with Foster + Partners, says that his firm now possesses such machines.

31. Richard Sennett, *The Craftsman* (New Haven: Yale University Press, 2008), 40.

32. Ibid., 41.

33. This story has been investigated in great detail at the Dessin/Chantier Laboratory at the Grenoble School of Architecture, and summarized by Sérgio Ferro in "Comentários ao desenho e o canteiro," in *Arquitetura e trabalho livre*, 321.

34. Quoted in Kolarevic, *Architecture in the Digital Age*, 294.

35. Ibid.

36. German architect Bernhard Fraken states: "I am tired of software that is inadequate, so we started programming our own, out of necessity to get things done the way we want to have them done. We have to do it ourselves because the industry is not supplying the right software" (ibid., 295).

37. Ibid., 296.

38. Sennett, *The Craftsman*, 44.

39. The increase in the organic composition of capital and the reduction in the number of workers does not necessarily mean a drop in production of surplus value, because there is an increase in productivity, that is, relative surplus.

40. Marlies Ingeborg Mulder and John L. Heintz, "Offshore Outsourcing—Now Available for Architects," in H. A. J. de Ridder and J. W. F. Wamelink, eds., *World of Construction Project Management* (Delft, The Netherlands: TU-Delft, 2007).

41. Richard Antunes and Roy Braga, *Infoproletários: degradação real do trabalho virtual* (São Paulo: Boitempo, 2009).

42. As we can see in the discussion forum "Architect's wages and conditions," www.butterpaper.com.

43. Jennifer Sullivan, "It Hurts So Bad," www.salon.com/2000/02/29/rsi/.

44. Quoted in Kolarevic, *Architecture in the Digital Age*, 65.

45. The analogy was used by Haddad, *Em defesa do socialismo*.

46. Jon Peddie Research, *CAD Report*, 2008.

47. According to the report "Software Piracy in the CAD Industry," institutional material by SolidWorks, http://www.solidworkscommunity.com/feature_full.php?cpfeatureid=16515; accessed January 2010.

48. Former Autodesk director affirms that more than 50 percent of the machines run pirate AutoCAD (David Stone, *Software Piracy* [1999], http://www.ed.uiuc.edu/wp/crime/piracy.htm; accessed January 2010).

49. There are some incipient initiatives for the development of free CADs, such as the Archimedes, created at the IME-USP. Nonetheless, they do not have full resources for drawing and modeling. There are still other initiatives

that are further from the realm of architectural design, such as the Blendor (focused on generic modeling and animation).

50. According to Shelden, the chief technology officer of Gehry's Technologies, "Digital Surface Representation and the Constructibility of Gehry's Architecture," doctoral thesis, Cambridge, 2002, 28.

51. According to *Forbes* magazine and others: https://www.forbes.com/global/2004/0621/020.html#2ee91251557a; http://europe.autonews.com/article/20001106/ANE/11060864/dassault-systemes:catia-design; http://www.fundinguniverse.com/company-histories/dassault-syst%C3%A8mes-s-a-history/.

52. According to Glymph, Gehry's partner, in Kolarevic, *Architecture in the Digital Age*, 108.

53. Shelden," Tectonics, Economics and the Reconfiguration of Practice," 27.

54. Ibid., 28.

55. Ibid.

56. We will visit both these works' construction sites in the next chapter.

57. The design process of Gehry's firm is described in detail by Shelden in "Digital Surface Representation and the Constructibility of Gehry's Architecture."

58. Stephen Perrella in an interview with Mark Dippe, "Folding Architecture," *Architectural Design* (1993). The term "hyperreality," which I shall return to below, has been widely used by postmodernist theorists to designate this virtual universe of images, or simulacra of the real, which become more convincing than reality itself, increasingly unreal, or emptied of meaning. Umberto Eco, for example, begins his *Viagem na irrealidade cotidiana* (São Paulo: Nova Fronteira, 1984) using holography—at the time, "the latest technical miracle of laser rays"—to show that they were not restricted to mere playful or illusionistic effects, but were rather being studied and employed by NASA in space explorations (9).

59. Kolarevic, *Architecture in the Digital Age*, 8–10.

60. Wilson Flório, "O uso de ferramentas de modelagem vetorial na concepção de uma arquitetura de formas complexas," doctoral thesis, FAU-USP, 2005.

61. According to the account given by Shelden, a member of Gehry's team, in "Tectonics, Economics and the Reconfiguration of Practice."

62. Ibid., 55.

63. John Haymaker and Martin Fischer, "Challenges and Benefits of 4D Modeling on the Walt Disney Concert Hall Project," CIFE Working Paper #64 (January 2001), https://web.stanford.edu/class/cee214/Readings/Walt%20Disney%20Concer%20Hall%20Project.pdf.

64. Chris Luebkeman, "Performance-Based Design," in Kolarevic, *Architecture in the Digital Age,* 285.

65. Ibid.

66. Kolarevic, *Architecture in the Digital Age,* 59.

67. Jon Pittman, "Building Information Modeling: Current Challenges and Future Directions," in Kolarevic, *Architecture in the Digital Age,* 256.

68. BIMs are the current panacea of the software industry for construction, as stated in Steve Parnell's article in the English *Architect's Journal* of July 28, 2009, under the title "Building Information Modelling: The Golden Opportunity," *Architect's Journal Online,* http://www.architectsjournal.co.uk/building-information-modelling-the-golden- opportunity/5205851.article; accessed January 2010.

69. Pittman, "Building Information Modeling," 257.

70. Lynn Murray, "Building Information Modeling Takes Architectural Design to a New Dimension," *Design Cost Data* (2007), http://www.dcd.com/insights/insights_sepoct_2007.html; accessed January 2010.

71. National Institute of Building Sciences, *National Building Information Standard. Version 1—Part 1: Overview, Principles, Methodologies* (Washington, D.C.: NIBS, 2009), http://nbimsdoc.opengeospatial.org; accessed February 2010.

72. Vladimir Bazjanac, *Impact of the U.S. National Building Informational Model Standard on Building Energy Performance Simulation* (Berkeley: Lawrence Berkeley National Laboratory, 2008), http://www.escholarship.org/uc/item/3v95d7xpen; accessed January 2010.

73. According to Steve Parnell, "Building Information Modelling": "There are a couple of opportunities for architects: firstly, just as the 1990s CAD revolution brought a boom for bureaux specialising in visualisation, it is quite feasible that BIM will be outsourced to similar specialists. If UK architects are not interested in this as a business model, it can quite easily be sent to India or China. Companies such as Make already send their detail design to China and at least one large contractor, frustrated that architects are not willing to hand over their designs in 3D model format, is hiring people in India at its own expense to convert 2D drawings into 3D models in the knowledge that it will save money when it comes to construction."

74. Malcolm McCullough, *Abstracting Craft: The Practiced Digital Hand* (Cambridge: MIT Press, 1998), 17.

75. As Argan pointed out in his far-reaching text *Projeto e destino* (São Paulo: Ática, 2001).

76. Manfredo Tafuri, *Projecto e utopia* (Lisbon: Presença, 1985), 47.

77. Naomi Klein, *No Logo: Taking Aim at the Brand Bullies* (London: Flamingo, 2000).

78. Robert B. Reich, *The Work of Nations: Preparing Ourselves for 21st Century Capitalism* (New York: Vintage Books, 1992).

79. This formulation by Kolarevic in his book from 2003, *Architecture in the Digital Age*, is reinforced by several authors. We will come back to the ideology of the "digital master builder" in the next chapter.

80. Between 1986 and 2002, Sérgio Ferro coordinated the research lab Dessin/Chantier at the Grenoble School of Architecture. His aim was to "brush the history [of architecture] against the grain" (in Walter Benjamin's expression), that is, by the angle of the construction site, the relations of production, and evolution in the division of labor. The laboratory was closed with Ferro's retirement.

81. Information obtained on the Web site of the company Gehry Technologies, accessed in March 2008.

82. As Mildred Friedman notes in *Gehry Talks*: "How will Gehry adjust to the new process? His working method did not change because of the computer; what happened was that it became easier for his collaborators to make his more-than-unusual forms feasible" (17).

83. Pierre Lévy, *Becoming Virtual: Reality in the Digital Age* (New York: Plenum Trade, 1998), 108.

84. Ibid.

85. Ibid.

86. Peter Eisenman, *Written into the Void: Selected Writings, 1990–2004* (New Haven: Yale University Press, 2007), 124–25.

87. The connection between deconstructivist thought in philosophy and architecture occurred mainly through Eisenman and Bernard Tschumi, who belonged to the group of architects who were part of the famous 1988 exhibition "Deconstructivist Architecture," at MoMA, curated by Philip Johnson and Mark Wigley. Soon after, Andreas Papadakis published, with significant impact, the book *Deconstruction*, composed of critical essays by Derrida, Leonidov, and Charles Jencks and designs of those very architects who participated in the exhibition: Eisenman, Tschumi, Gehry, Koolhaas, Libeskind, Hadid, and Coop Himme(l)blau.

88. Otília Arantes, "Margens da arquitetura," from the catalog of the Eisenman exhibition at the MASP [Museu de arte de São Paulo], in 1993, reproduced in *O lugar da arquitetura depois dos modernos* (São Paulo: Edusp, 1993), 79.

89. Greg Lynn, *Folds, Bodies and Blobs : Collected Essays* (Brussels: La Lettre Volée, 1998).

90. Eisenman, *Written into the Void,* 122.

91. Luca Galofaro, *Digital Eisenman: An Office of the Electronic Era* (Basel, Switzerland: Birkhäuser, 1999), 42.

92. Arantes, "Margens da arquitetura," 70.

93. Terzidis, *Algorithmic Architecture,* 15.

94. Ibid., 57.

95. Lévy, *Becoming Virtual,* 185.

96. Edmond Couchot, "Da representação à simulação: evolução das técnicas e das artes de figuração," in André Parente, ed., *Imagem máquina: a era das tecnologias do virtual* (Rio de Janeiro: Editora 34, 1993), 42.

97. Ibid.

98. André Gorz, *O imaterial: conhecimento, valor, capital* (São Paulo: Annablume, 2004), 84.

99. Gilles Deleuze, *Conversações* (1977) (São Paulo: Editora 34, 2008), 194–202.

100. On the formal relation of Eisenman's works with forms generated by bioinformatics, see the text by Casey Alt and Timothy Lenoir, "Flow, Process, Fold: Intersections in Bioinformatics and Contemporary Architecture," in *Science, Metaphor, and Architecture* (Princeton, N.J.: Princeton University Press, 2002).

101. Edgar Morin, *Introduction to Complex Thinking* (Oxford: Oxford University Press, 2012).

102. Couchot, "Da representação à simulação," 42.

103. Cited in Flório, "O uso de ferramentas de modelagem vetorial na concepção de uma arquitetura de formas complexas."

104. According to Luca Galofaro, who worked in Eisenman's team on some of these projects *(Digital Eisenman).*

105. Ibid., 55.

106. Interview with Fredy Massad and Alícia Yeste, July 2005, originally published in Spanish in ABCDe las Artes y las Letras, Madrid, August 13, 2005, http://www.btbwarchitecture.com/2005/08/el-arquitecto-peter-eisenman .html.

107. Richard Buckminster Fuller realized, with his study of geodesic and mild forms through computers, that it was possible to do more with less: that is, more with less work, less energy, and fewer raw materials—what Fuller used to call the miniaturization of the structures. See Laymert Garcia dos Santos, *"Informação após a virada cibernética."* Eisenman's digital manipulation of form does not have the same concerns and remains in the formalism of the field.

108. Tafuri, *Teorias e história da arquitectura,* 103.

109. Ibid.

110. Guy Debord, *Society of the Spectacle* (New York: Zone Books, 1995).

111. Gorz, *O imaterial*, 83.

112. Ibid., 84.

113. Ibid., 85.

114. Here I am referring to the "symbolic" profitability of the entire operation in a manner comparable to that discussed in chapter 1, rather than to specific material gains, or to any material profits that accrue to specific architectural offices, which vary greatly because of many factors.

115. Sérgio Ferro talks about the anonymous Miesian paving stones as the archetype of the "zero-type" form. The indifference regarding its use continues the same, but now the demand is for the unique and nonanonymous form.

116. István Mézáros, *The Power of Ideology* (London: Zed Books, 2005), 441–42.

117. Ibid., 442–43.

118. Ibid.

119. See Karl Marx, *The Poverty of Philosophy* (Moscow: Progress Publishers, 1955) and *Grundrisse: Foundations of the Critique of Political Economy* (London: Penguin Classics, 1993).

120. See the documentary *Les LIP— L'Imagination au pouvoir* (2007), directed by Christian Rouaud, with testimonies by several workers who participated in this event, and an interview with Charles Piaget, one of its main characters. Bernard Ravenel, "Leçons d'autogestion" (April 5, 2007), http://www.mouvements.info/Lecons-d-autogestion.html.

3. ONE TO ONE

1. According to Sérgio Ferro, the value of labor condensed in the luxury building fulfills a function of "treasure": "Ostentation is basically the exhibition of unused but concentrated labor. The treasure in any of its forms has value determined by the average social labor hours put into it . . . The daring or elaborate forms with high expenditure of labor are therefore the most valuable." But, Ferro warned, the treasure is not only accumulation of concentrated labor; treasure "not only has a raw form, it also has an *aesthetic form*" (Sérgio Ferro, *Arquitetura e trabalho livre* [São Paulo: Cosac & Naify, 2006], 72–73).

2. Cited in ibid., 136.

3. Michael Ball, *Rebuilding Construction: Economic Change in the British Construction Industry* (London: Routledge, 1988), 24–25.

4. Ferro, *Arquitetura e trabalho livre*, 217.

5. This was not only the position of modern architects, but was also how the majority of authors who studied the construction industry in the 1970s and early 1980s referred to it.

6. In Marxist theory, the high organic composition of capital is a consequence of the progress of technology and the means of production. It occurs when the immobilization of part of the fixed capital in machines is high, increasing the volume (and mass of value) of production and consumption of raw material, associated with the relative decrease of the employed labor force. Technological progress is almost inevitable in nonmonopoly industries and thus entails a general tendency of industrial capital to increase its organic composition, reaching its limit in automation when, in reality, capital no longer "produces" surplus value, that is, profits. The increase of organic composition, with the relative decrease of the available labor force, results in the relative decrease in the surplus value produced and the tendency for the rate of profit to fall.

7. See Jorge Oseki, Paulo C. X. Pereira, Ermínia T. M. Maricato, and Yvonne M. M. Mautner, "Bibliografia sobre a Indústria da Construção: reflexão crítica," *Sinopses* (São Paulo: FAU-USP), no. 16 (1991): 41.

8. Such as the Brazilian Communist Party (PCB) and the Economic Commission for Latin America and the Caribbean (CEPAL).

9. Celso Furtado, "Subdesenvolvimento e dependência: conexões fundamentais," in *O mito do desenvolvimento* (Rio de Janeiro: Paz e Terra, 1974).

10. Sérgio Ferro, "O canteiro e o desenho," in *Arquitetura e trabalho livre*, 113. The 1979 book *O canteiro e o desenho* was revised and republished as a chapter in the 2006 complete collection of writings by Sérgio Ferro, *Arquitetura e trabalho livre*.

11. The main arguments are reproduced in Ermínia Maricato's thesis "Indústria da construção e política habitacional" (FAU-USP, 1984).

12. Unlike the high rate of organic composition, low composition implies relatively higher variable capital (employed labor force), lower mechanization, and consequently, a higher rate of profit per unit produced. That is why it is one of the barriers to the decline in the rate of profit arising from technological progress. The capitalist, who is well aware of this frighteningly decreasing tendency, maneuvers in various ways to stop it. Among the loopholes found, three are well known: monopolies, imperialism, and maintenance of retrograde production areas. Although they are closely associated, we are particularly interested in the third, which is the case of civil construction.

13. Ball, *Rebuilding Construction*, 27.

14. Jorge Oseki, "Arquitetura em construção," master's thesis (FAU-USP, 1983), 119.

15. Ferro, *Arquitetura e trabalho livre,* 139.

16. Ball, *Rebuilding Construction,* 32.

17. Benjamin Coriat, "Le procès de travail de type 'chantier' et sa rationalisation: remarques sur quelques tendances de la recherche actuelle," in *Plan Construction et Habitat. Le Travail en Chantiers: Actes du Colloque* (Paris: Ministère de l'Urbanisme, du Logement et des Transports. 1984), 90–98.

18. Ibid., 1.

19. Ibid., 2.

20. Myriam Campinos-Dubernet, "La rationalisation du travail dans le BTP: un exemple des limites du taylorisme orthodoxe," *Formation Emploi,* no. 6 (1984): 79–89.

21. Ibid., 7. In his thesis "Organização de trabalho e capital: um estudo da construção habitacional" (COPPE-UFRJ, 1979), engineer Nilton Vargas has studied the reasons of the incompatibility—and barriers—between Taylorism/Fordism and the construction-site production.

22. Coriat, "Le procès de travail de type 'chantier' et sa rationalisation," 11–12.

23. Helen Rainbird and Gerd Syben, eds., *Restructuring a Traditional Industry: Construction Employment and Skills in Europe* (New York: Berg, 1991), 8.

24. Ibid.

25. David Harvey has defined flexible accumulation paradigm by a direct confrontation with the rigidities of Fordism: "It rests on flexibility with respect to labour processes, labour markets, products, and patterns of consumption. It is characterized by the emergence of entirely new sectors of production, new ways of providing financial services, new markets, and, above all, greatly intensified rates of commercial, technological, and organizational innovation" (*The Condition of Postmodernity: An Enquiry into the Origins of Cultural Change* [Cambridge: Blackwell Publishers, 1990], 146–48).

26. Gerd Syben, "Strategies of Growth of Productivity in the Absence of Consumption Technological Change," in Rainbird and Syben, *Restructuring a Traditional Industry,* 103.

27. The mainstream reading of the theme proposes the adoption of chaos theory for managing the construction site, as we see in business self-help material produced by Neolabor Consulting Company, directed by Nilton Vargas, which provides services to many large Brazilian construction companies.

28. The book by Marc Silver, *Under Construction: Work and Alienation in the Building Trades* (New York: New York Press, 1986), analyzes the effects of outsourcing in relation to the alienation of work and its effects on trade unionism and labor rights.

29. Elisabeth Campagnac, "Computerisation Strategies in Large French Firms and Their Effect on Working Conditions," in Rainbird and Syben, *Restructuring a Traditional Industry,* 147.

30. In Robert Castel's expression in *From Manual Workers to Wage Laborers: Transformation of the Social Question* (Princeton, N.J.: Princeton University Press, 2002). See also Syben, "Strategies of Growth of Productivity in the Absence of Consumption Technological Change": "The focus on work organization changes," according to Syben, "expressed a surprising modernity" for the construction industry in the new accumulation system (91).

31. The book *Building Chaos: An International Comparison of Deregulation in the Construction Industry* (London: Routledge, 2003), edited by Gerherd Bosch and Peter Philips, provides a comparative picture of deregulation in the construction industries in several countries, and on systems of outsourcing and work precarization.

32. This term was introduced by Marta Farah in her book *Processo de trabalho na construção habitacional: tradição e mudança* (São Paulo: Annablume, 1996), 263.

33. André Gorz, *Misérias do presente, riqueza do possível* (São Paulo: Annablume, 2004), 63.

34. Ibid., 64.

35. François Chesnais, *The Globalization of Capital* (Paris: Éditions Syros, 1994) and *A mundialização financeira* (São Paulo: Xamã, 1998).

36. Harvey, *The Condition of Postmodernity,* 152.

37. Marcos Dantas, "Capitalismo na era das redes: trabalho, informação e valor no ciclo da comunicação produtiva," in Helena M. M. Lastres and Sarita Albagli, eds., *Informação e globalização na era do conhecimento* (Rio de Janeiro: Campus, 1999), 243.

38. Pierre Riboulet, "Éléments pour une critique de l'architecture," *Espaces et Sociétés,* no. 1 (November 1970).

39. Ulrich Beck, *The Brave New World of Work* (Oxford: Polity Press, 2000). See the comments by Paulo Arantes in "A fratura brasileira do mundo: visões do laboratório brasileiro da mundialização," in *Zero à esquerda* (São Paulo: Conrad, 2004).

40. Celso Furtado, *O mito do desenvolvimento.* (Rio de Janeiro: Paz e Terra, 1974) and *A construção interrompida* (Rio de Janeiro: Paz e Terra, 1992).

41. Arantes, "A fratura brasileira do mundo," 64.

42. Helena Hirata, ed., *Sobre o "modelo" japonês* (São Paulo: Edusp, 1993).

43. Many are the attempts to accelerate the productive process: the optimization in coordinating flows and teams, prefabrication, and overlapped execution of design and work, named "fast-track." Regarding this matter, see

David Gann, "New Management Strategies and the Fast-Track Phenomenon," in Rainbird and Syben, *Restructuring a Traditional Industry.*

44. Coriat, quoted in Antonio Cattani, *Trabalho e tecnologia: dicionário crítico* (Rio de Janeiro: Vozes, 1997), 209–10.

45. Hassan Fathy, *Architecture for the Poor: An Experiment in Rural Egypt* (Chicago: University of Chicago Press, 1973), 9–10.

46. Ferro, *Arquitetura e trabalho livre,* 148.

47. Frederick Winslow Taylor, *The Principles of Scientific Management* (New York and London: Harper & Brothers, 1911), 77–79.

48. Ruy Gama, *A tecnologia e o trabalho na história* (São Paulo: Studio Nobel, 1986), 4.

49. Tobias Bonwetsch, Fabio Gramazio, and Mathias Kohler, "The Informed Wall: Applying Additive Digital Fabrication Techniques on Architecture," in *Synthetic Landscapes* (annals of the 25th Annual Conference of the Association for Computer-Aided Design in Architecture), 489–95.

50. Ironically, I attended the lecture of Andreas Deplazes in the attic of Casa da Música, in the city of Porto, and saw a meteorite with a high-tech face, whose construction site was completely artisanal, however, as we will see.

51. Guilherme Aquino, "Pedreiro cibernético rouba a cena na Bienal de Arquitetura" (September 18, 2008), http://www.swissinfo.ch/por/Pedreiro_ciber netico_rouba_a_cena_na_Bienal_de_Arquitetura.html?cid=692269; accessed February 2010.

52. Similarly to the androids in *Blade Runner,* the only "humans" in the movie, who, moreover, were workers—designed to execute slave labors in spatial colonies.

53. "Robô pedreiro constrói muro artístico em Nova Iorque" (November 4, 2008), https://www.inovacaotecnologica.com.br/noticias/noticia.php?ar tigo=robo-pedreiro-constroi-muro-artistico-nova-iorque&id=010180091104.

54. Previous attempts that most advanced were the ROCCO (1994) and BRONCO (1996) projects, but the industry did not incorporate them.

55. Fabio Gramazio, Mathias Kohler, and Tobias Bonwetsch, "Digitally Fabricating Non-Standardized Brick Walls," in *ManuBuild—1st International Conference* (Rotterdam, 2007), 191–96.

56. Ibid., 193.

57. Ferro, *Arquitetura e trabalho livre,* 349.

58. Ibid., 402.

59. Kostas Terzidis, *Algorithmic Architecture* (Amsterdam and Boston: Architectural Press, 2006).

60. Dantas, "Capitalismo na era das redes," 253.

61. Ferro, *Arquitetura e trabalho livre,* 176.

62. The Technology Center of Sarah Networks, CTRS, is a factory of the Ministry of Health, coordinated by the architect Filgueiras Lima, in the city of Salvador. The Development Center for Urban and Community Equipment, CEDEC, existed during Luiza Erundina's administration (PT, Workers Party, 1989–92) in the city of São Paulo, and was coordinated by Mayumi Souza Lima, also assisted by Lelê.

63. Renato Dagnino, "Tecnologia social," in Antonio David Cattani, Jean-Louis Laville, Luiz Igácio Gaiger, and Pedro Hespanha, eds., *Dicionário internacional da outra economia* (Coimbra, Portugal: Almedina, 2009), 320.

64. Javier Cantalejo, in *Historia de un sueño: Guggenheim Bilbao Museoa, 1992–1997* (Barcelona: IDOM, 1997), 22.

65. Annette LeCuyer, "Building Bilbao," *Architectural Review: Museums,* no. 1210 (1997): 45.

66. Cattani, *Trabalho e tecnologia,* 171.

67. As Fernando Fraile narrates in *Historia de un sueño: Guggenheim Bilbao Museoa, 1992–1997* (Barcelona: IDOM, 1997), 18–19.

68. Kolarevic, *Architecture in the Digital Age,* 45.

69. Ibid.

70. Cantalejo, in *Historia de un sueño,* 22.

71. The Program Evaluation and Review Technique (PERT) is a project management system invented in the 1950s. PERT is a probabilistic system that calculates the weighted average of three possible scenarios of an activity (optimistic, realistic, and pessimistic). See Kolarevic, *Architecture in the Digital Age,* 58.

72. Ibid., 38, and LeCuyer, "Building Bilbao." At a certain stage of construction, the Guggenheim's work had eighteen CATIA stations being used simultaneously to locate parts, all of them hired from the aircraft industry next to Bilbao, according to LeCuyer.

73. LeCuyer, "Building Bilbao," 44.

74. See Branko Kolarevic, "Information Master-Builder," in Kolarevic, *Architecture in the Digital Age.*

75. Cited in Kolarevic, *Architecture in the Digital Age,* 58.

76. Michael Ball, *Rebuilding Construction: Economic Change in the British Construction Industry* (London: Routledge, 1988), 206.

77. Ibid.

78. Lord Esher and Lord Llewelyn-Davies, "The Architect in 1988," *RIBA Journal* 75 (October 1968): 450; quoted in Ball, *Rebuilding Construction,* 206.

79. Kolarevic, *Architecture in the Digital Age,* 57.

80. Chris Luebkeman, "Performance-Based Design," in ibid., 285. Luebkeman is a doctor of architecture from ETH Zurich.

81. See Bruce Lindsey, *Digital Gehry: Material Resistance, Digital Construction* (Basel, Switzerland: Birkhäuser, 2001).

82. Jim Glymph, quoted in Mildred Friedman, *Gehry Talks: Architecture and Process* (New York: Universe, 2002), 17.

83. Ibid.

84. Ball, *Rebuilding Construction,* 208–9.

85. Ibid., 209.

86. Gann, "New Management Strategies and the Fast-Tack Phenomenon," 120–21.

87. Ferro, *Arquitetura e trabalho livre,* 93.

88. Ibid., 193.

89. Stephen Kieran and James Timberlake, *Refabricating Architecture: How Manufacturing Methodologies Are Poised to Transform Building Construction* (New York: McGraw-Hill, 2004), 26–31.

90. Ferro, *Arquitetura e trabalho livre,* 116.

91. Such that many have already disappeared: the engraver, the plasterer, the wallpaper installer, the marble cutter, the brazier, the craftsman specialized in facades, the roofer, etc.

92. Cantalejo, in *Historia de un sueño,* 20.

93. David Jaggar and Ralph Morton, *Design and the Economics of Building* (London: Spon Press, 1995), 102–3.

94. Ball, *Rebuilding construction,* 215.

95. Quoted in Kolarevic, *Architecture in the Digital Age,* 69.

96. Dennis Shelden, "Digital Surface Representation and the Constructibility of Gehry's Architecture," doctoral thesis, Cambridge, 2002, 33.

97. Suzanne Goldenberg, "Gehry Sued over Leaky University Building," *The Guardian,* November 7, 2007, http://www.theguardian.com/world/2007/nov/07/internationaleducationnews.usa.

98. Glymph, quoted in Kolarevic, *Architecture in the Digital Age,* 108.

99. Shelden, "Digital Surface Representation and the Constructibility of Gehry's Architecture," 47.

100. According to Hugh Whitehead, director of the modeling team at Foster + Partners firm, "Laws of Form," in Kolarevic, *Architecture in the Digital Age*, 98.

101. Cantalejo, in *Historia de un sueño,* 16–19.

102. Ibid.

103. Ibid., 14.

104. Sarah Taylor, "Local Craftsmen Met Gehry's Challenge" (October 17, 2002), http://neogehry.org/art_local-craftsmen.php; accessed January 2010.

105. Danny Forster, Discovery Channel, *Build It Bigger: Mountain of Steel* (2007). I strongly recommend that all architecture students watch it. https://www.youtube.com/watch?v=bOB7wJ_0zf0.

106. Ibid.

107. Ibid.

108. "Reunião de obra," in a presentation by the Order of the Architects, southern regional section, October 6, 2005.

109. Statement of the author.

110. In the dozens of reports of the creation processes of the starchitects I have researched, no reference to this concern was found.

111. Jacques Herzog, in an interview with Suzanne Beyer and Ulrike Knöfel, "Only an Idiot Would Have Said No," *Der Spiegel Online* (July 30, 2008), http://www.spiegel.de/international/world/0,1518,569011,00.html; accessed January 2010.

112. Alex Marshall, "How to Make a Frank Gehry Building," *New York Times,* April 8, 2001.

113. Jay Merrick, "Angles from Heaven: Frank Gehry Takes on His Dream Project," *The Independent,* July 9, 2008, https://www.independent.co.uk/arts-entertainment/art/features/angles-from-heaven-frank-gehry-takes-on-his-dream-project-862877.html; accessed July 2008.

114. According to Thomas Campanella, "Mejoras capitales," *Arquitectura Viva,* no. 118–19 (2008): 42.

115. Discovery Channel, *Construindo o superestádio* (2005).

116. Discovery Channel, *Build It Bigger.*

117. Ferro, *Arquitetura e trabalho livre,* 424.

118. As one can see in the pictures of the construction work.

119. Lew Sichelman, "Homebuilders Say Immigrant's Work Is Vital—Houses Wouldn't Be Built on Time or on Budget without the Help of Foreign-Born Workers, Many of Whom Are Here Illegally," *San Francisco Chronicle,* May 28, 2006.

120. Ianna Andréadis, *Chantier ouvert au public: récit de la construction du Musée Quai Branly* (Paris: Éditions du Panama, 2006).

121. Discovery Channel, *Construindo o superestádio.*

122. Herzog, interview with Beyer and Knöfel.

123. Kathy Kieley, "Need for Immigrant Workers in Dispute," *USA Today,* June 24, 2007.

124. In England for example, a study commissioned by the Institution of Civil Engineers (ICE) concluded that of the 500,000 migrant workers in the country, 174,000 are in the field of construction, which accounts

for 20 percent of the total number of workers in this sector. Cited in "Immigrant Workers Lack Experience in Building," *Contract Journal,* September 5, 2007.

125. Tom Robbins, "Labor War in Chelsea" (May 9, 2006), http://www.swiftraid.org/media/articles/VillageVoice.pdf; accessed January 2010.

126. Dana Hedgpeth, "Builders Groups Decry Obama's Order on Projects," *Washington Post,* February 12, 2009, http://www.washingtonpost.com/wp-dyn/content/article/2009/02/11/AR2009021103953.html.

127. Michael Kuchta, "USA: Construction Workers Endure High Rates of Death, Injury," *Lakes and Plains Carpenters* (February 18, 2007), http://www.bwint.org/default.asp?index=641&Language=EN; accessed January 2010.

128. Ibid. Data from *National Census of Fatal Occupational Injuries,* Bureau of Labor Statistics, U.S. Department of Labor, 2005.

129. In seven years of the Iraq occupation, there were 4,374 casualties, or 610 per year. Data from the Ministry of Defense published in www.antiwar.com.

130. Natalia Siniavska, *Immigrant Workers in Construction* (Washington, D.C.: National Association of Home Builders, 2005), http://www.nahb.org/generic.aspx?genericContentID=49216%29; accessed January 2010.

131. Letter from AGC of America to Senator Mitch McConnell (December 23, 2009), http://newsmanager.commpartners.com/agcleg/downloads/091223%20Health%20Care%20-%20McConnell.pdf; accessed January 2010.

132. Hervé Dieux, "Eastern European Immigrants Exploited," *Le Monde diplomatique,* August 2002.

133. Bridget Anderson, Martin Rush, Sarah Spencer, and Ben Rogaly, *Migrants' Lives beyond the Workplace: The Experiences of Central and East Europeans in the UK* (May 29, 2007), http://www.jrf.org.uk/publications/experiences-central-and-east-european-migrants-uk; accessed January 2010.

134. http://Recruitment.globalchoices.co.uk/?id=37.

135. Anderson et al., *Migrants' Lives beyond the Workplace,* 48.

136. Human Rights Watch, *One Year of My Blood* 20:3 (2008), http://www.unhcr.org/refworld/docid/47d7fb772.html; accessed October 2009.

137. Ibid.

138. According to Ruth Aquino, "A arquitetura da nova China," *Época,* July 7, 2008.

139. Human Rights Watch, *One Year of My Blood,* 13.

140. Interview in Hanno Rauterberg, *Talking Architecture: Interviews with Architects* (London: Prestel, 2008), 100.

141. See Mike Davis, "Sand, Fear and Money in Dubai," in *Evil Paradises* (New York: New Press, 2007).

142. This data and the following are taken from reports by Human Rights Watch from 2006 and 2009, respectively: *Building Towers, Cheating Workers: Exploitation of Migrant Construction Workers in the United Arab Emirates* (2006); and "The Island of Happiness: Exploitation of Migrant Workers on Saadiyat Island, Abu Dhabi" (New York: HRW Report, 2009).

143. BBC, "Strike Halts Work at Dubai Tower" (March 23, 2006), http ://news.bbc.co.uk/2/hi/business/4836632.stm; accessed January 2010; accessed January 2010.

144. Human Rights Watch, "The Island of Happiness," 32.

145. Karl Marx, *Capital,* vol. 1, book 1, 184 and 203. Here, death in the strict sense of the word: according to Javier Montes, in the year 2004, Pakistan, India, and Bangladesh repatriated 880 corpses of construction workers ("Y en Arcadia, los egos: fábulas del arte para el Golfo," *Arquitectura Viva,* no. 111 [2006]: 36).

146. Davis, "Sand, Fear and Money in Dubai," 60.

147. A commission of Brazilian construction industry businessmen traveled to the United Arab Emirates in search of novelties for the organization of their construction sites, and there they found a true "paradise" of labor exploitation. Carlos Leal, from Sinduscon, the construction industry union, coming back from the trip, said that "there is no paternalism over there, which makes the relationship between employer and employee more transparent and correct." The euphoria of the entrepreneurs was described in "Dubai e os megaproyectos," *Construção Mercado,* no. 60 (July 2006): 21.

148. Human Rights Watch, "The Island of Happiness," 17.

149. Interview in Rauterberg, *Talking Architecture,* 98.

150. Otília Arantes, "Vendo cidades," *Veredas,* no. 38 (1998).

151. Pedro Arantes, "O ajuste urbano: as políticas do Banco Mundial e do BID para as cidades latino-americanas," master's thesis, FAU-USP, 2004.

152. Ruy Sardinha, *Informação, conhecimento e valor* (São Paulo: Radical Livros, 2008), 176.

153. In the sense of a "loss of reference of the valorization process in the value produced according to capitalist conditions," as Jorge Grespan explains in *O negativo do capital. O conceito de crise na crítica de Marx à economia política* (São Paulo: Hucitec, 1998), 138.

154. Karl Marx, *Grundrisse: Foundations of the Critique of Political Economy* (London: Penguin Classics, 1993), 705.

155. Grespan, *O negative do capital,* 145.

156. Ibid.

157. According to information of architect Jorge Carvalho, from the local firm that conducted the work.

158. "PSdeG y BNG piden un informe sobre las incompatibilidades de Péres Varela," *El País,* December 11, 2007.

159. Talita Figueiredo, "Câmara do Rio decide instaurar CPI da Cidade da Música," *O Estado de S. Paulo,* May 7, 2009.

160. Ibid.

161. "Una ponencia en Ciudad de la Cultura denuncia la 'voluntad premeditada'" (December 10, 2007), http://www.soitu.es/soitu/2007/12/10/info /1197312142_326263.htm; accessed February 2010.

162. Full report of the auditors: "Fiscal Council of Galicia. Inspection Report of the City of Culture of Galicia Foundation" (2004), http://www .consellodecontas.es/sites/consello_de_contas/files/contents/documents/2004/ FUNDACION_CIDADE_CULTURA_2004_C.pdf.

163. José Precedo and Sonia Vizoso, "Despilfarros em la Xunta de Fraga," *El País,* August 15, 2007.

164. Sonia Vizoso, "El alcalde de Ortigueira explota la cantera ilegal que surte a la Cidade da Cultura," *El País,* August 16, 2007, https://elpais.com/ diario/2007/08/16/galicia/1187259490_850215.html.

165. Sonia Vizoso, "La Xunta levanta la Cidade da Cultura con cuarcita de una cantera ilegal," *El País,* August 15, 2007, https://elpais.com/dia rio/2007/08/15/galicia/1187173089_850215.html.

166. Pablo Lopes, "Juez y Tribunal de Cuentas investigan el contrato de la cuarcita del Gaiás," *El País,* December 20, 2008, https://elpais.com/dia rio/2008/12/20/galicia/1229771893_850215.html.

167. Rafael Sierra, "Eisenman dice que la revolución de Bilbao con el Guggenheim es el modelo a seguir" [Eisenman claims that the revolution in Bilbao with the Guggenheim is the model to follow], *El Mundo,* April 14, 1999.

168. Andressa Fernandes, "CPI investiga irregularidades na Cidade da Música" (May 19, 2008), http://www.piniweb.com.br/construcao/arquitetura/ cpi-investiga-irregularidades-na-cidade-da-musica-89294–1.asp; accessed January 2010.

169. Alec Appelbaum, "Frank Gehry's Software Keeps Buildings on Budget," *New York Times,* February 10, 2009.

170. David Harvey, "The Art of Rent: Globalization, Monopoly and the Commodification of Culture," in *A produção capitalista do espaço* (São Paulo: Annablume, 2005).

171. The term "treasure-form" was coined by Sérgio Ferro, *Arquitetura e trabalho livre,* 67–75 and 127–29. In his definition, Ferro combines the notion of "hoarding," coined by Marx (*Capital,* vol 1, chapter 3, item 3a), with that of

"scarcity," by David Ricardo (chapter 1 of *On the Principles of Political Economy and Taxation* [London: John Murray, 1817]).

172. Ferro, *Arquitetura e trabalho livre*, 72.

173. Rem Koolhaas, in *Projects for Prada—Part 1* (Milan: Fondazione Prada Edizioni, 2001).

174. Otília Arantes, "Delírios de Rem Koolhaas," mimeo.

175. Gilles Lipovetsky and Elyette Roux, *O luxo eterno—da idade do sagrado ao tempo das marcas* (São Paulo: Companhia das Letras, 2005), 43–50.

176. Ibid., 20 and 34.

CONCLUSION

1. Author's interview with Caio Faggin in 2009.

2. Ibid.

3. Biographical notes, Announcement, Jury citation, and Foster's speech available on the Pritzker Prize Web site, https://www.pritzkerprize.com/laureates/1999.

4. Will Hurst, "Foster Set to Be Expelled from House of Lords" (April 24, 2008), http://www.bdonline.co.uk/news/foster-set-to-be-expelled-from-house-of-lords/3132908.article; accessed February 2010; "Foster under Pressure to Reveal Tax Status" (February 2, 2009), https://www.bdonline.co.uk/news/foster-under-pressure-to-reveal-tax-status/3111999.article; accessed February 2010.

5. Polly Curtis, "House of Lords Peers Who Resigned for Tax Reasons Will Keep Titles," *The Guardian*, July 7, 2010, https://www.theguardian.com/politics/2010/jul/07/house-of-lords-peers-titles; accessed December 2010. Jonathan Glancey, "Norman Foster in the Lords: What Might Have Been," *The Guardian*, July 12, 2010, https://www.theguardian.com/artanddesign/2010/jul/12/norman-foster-house-of-lords; accessed December 2010.

6. Hurst, "Foster Set to Be Expelled from House of Lords."

7. Interview with Corullon. Martin Corullon is a Brazilian architect and director of the well-known architecture office METRO. He worked at Foster + Partners from 2008 to 2009.

8. Speeches available on the Pritzker Prize Web site. Ada Louise Huxtable essay, https://www.pritzkerprize.com/sites/default/files/inline-files/1989_essay.pdf.

9. Gehry's speech, https://www.pritzkerprize.com/sites/default/files/inline-files/Frank_Gehry_Acceptance_Speech_1989.pdf.

10. https://www.pritzkerprize.com/sites/default/files/inline-files/2001_Acceptance_Speech.pdf.

11. Interview with the author in 2008.

12. Mike Davis, *Planet of Slums* (London: Verso, 2006).

13. Speeches available on the Pritzker Prize Web site. Koolhaas's speech, https://www.pritzkerprize.com/sites/default/files/inline-files/Rem_Koolhaas_Acceptance_Speech_2000.pdf.

14. Fredric Jameson, "The Brick and the Balloon: Architecture, Idealism, and Land Speculation," in *The Cultural Turn: Selected Writings on the Postmodern* (London and New York: Verso, 1998).

15. Gabriel Palma, "The Revenge of the Market on the Rentiers," unpublished article, presented at a conference at the FGV School of Economics in São Paulo in 2008.

16. Martine Bulard, "Uma nova geografia dos capitais," *Le Monde diplomatique Brasil,* November 2008.

17. Mariana Fix, "Financeirização e transformações recentes no circuito imobiliário no Brasil," doctoral thesis, Institute of Economics, Unicamp, 2011.

18. Some examples include Russia Tower (Norman Foster), Minerva Building London (Nicholas Grimshaw), Chicago Spire (Santiago Calatrava), and Dubai Towers (TVSDesign).

19. David Teather, "Recession and Debt Dissolve Dubai's Mirage in the Desert," *The Guardian,* November 29, 2009, https://www.theguardian.com/business/2009/nov/29/dubai-financial-crisis; "Dubai Government to Inject US$9.5 Billion to Reduce Dubai World and Nakheel Debt," *Asia News,* March 25, 2010, http://www.asianews.it/news-en/Dubai-govt-to-inject-US$-9.5-billion-to-reduce-Dubai-World-and-Nakheel-debt-17982.html.

20. Interview with Miguel Mora, *El País,* republished in *Folha de S. Paulo,* January 31, 2010.

21. Article published in *O Estado de S. Paulo,* November 8, 2009.

22. Jonathan Glancey, "Review of the Decade: Jonathan Glancey on Architecture," *The Guardian,* December 7, 2009.

23. Interview with Miguel Mora, *El País,* republished in *Folha de S. Paulo,* January 31, 2010.

24. This expression is the title of the book by Johan van Lengen, a bestseller in Brazil on sustainable architecture, *Manual do arquiteto descalço* (São Paulo: B4 editores, 2014).

25. See a repertoire of these practices in Jorge Oseki and Paulo Pelegrino, "Sociedade e ambiente," in Arlindo Philippi Jr., Marcello Andrade Romero, and Gilda Bruna, eds., *Curso de gestão ambiental* (São Paulo: Manole, 2004).

26. This was one of the research themes of my dissertation adviser, Professor Jorge Oseki, at the time he passed away in 2008. He was studying policies for renaturation of urban rivers: environmental interventions that mobilize different social forces, but whose agendas and political presuppositions were

different, which resulted in significant conflicts in the effective conduct of its implementation.

27. On the subject, see David Harvey, "Valuing Nature," in *Justice, Nature and the Geography of Difference* (New York: Wiley-Blackwell, 1996).

28. Jean-Marie Harribey, "Marxismo ecológico ou ecologia política marxista," in Jaque Bidet and Eustache Kouvélakis, eds., Jorge Hajime Oseki and Inês Oseki, trans., *Dictionnaire Marx contemporain* (Paris: Presses Universitaires de France, 2001).

29. This "contamination market," explains Michael Löwy, allows "richer countries to continue to contaminate the world, but based on the possibility of buying from poor countries the right to contaminate what they are not using" ("Ecología y socialismo," *La Haine* [January 25, 2007], http://www.lahaine .org/index.php?p=20019; accessed February 2010).

30. Quoted by Otília Arantes, "Xangai 2010," in *Chai-na* (São Paulo, Edusp, 2012).

31. According to Martin Corullon, interview with the author.

32. Interview with Hanno Rauterberg, *Talking Architecture: Interviews with Architects* (London: Prestel, 2008), 50. The schedule of the construction of the works of the city has already been postponed to 2025–30.

33. Other sustainable cities, as artificial social microcosms on a smaller scale and associated with university centers, have already been implemented in other countries, notably Japan, but have not yet achieved zero emissions rates and energy autonomy as proposed in Masdar.

34. Interview with Hanno Rauterberg, *Talking Architecture,* 50.

35. See Vandana Shiva, *Biopirataria—a pilhagem da natureza e do conhecimento* (Petrópolis, Brazil: Vozes, 2001).

36. When asked about the fact that the innovative city is being constructed by a nondemocratic regime, Foster replies, "Why shouldn't I do it? Undreamed-of possibilities open up there, the thinking is radical and so are the decisions. Decisions that take ten years here take ten months at most there" (interview with Hanno Rauterberg, *Talking Architecture,* 57).

37. Suzanne Goldenberg, "Masdar's Zero-Carbon Dream Could Become World's First Green Ghost Town," *The Guardian* (February 16, 2016), https:// www.theguardian.com/environment/2016/feb/16/masdars-zero-carbon-dream -could-become-worlds-first-green-ghost-town.

38. https://www.pritzkerprize.com/laureates/2016; emphasis added.

39. "What really sets Aravena apart is his commitment to social housing" (ibid.).

40. This was the subject of my master's degree thesis, "The Urban Adjustment: World Bank and IDB Policies for Cities in Latin America" (2004). A summary was published in the United States: Pedro Arantes, "Urban Adjustment:

World Bank and IDB Policies for Cities," in Márcio Moraes Valença, Fernanda Cravidão, and José Alberto Rio Fernandes, eds., *Urban Developments in Brazil and Portugal* (New York: Nova Science Publishers, 2012).

41. https://www.pritzkerprize.com/laureates/2016.

42. A merciless analysis of Aravena is carried out by the Argentinian critic Freddy Massad, "The Stardom of Demagogy: Another Wrong Move" (http://www.transfer-arch.com/stardom-demagogy/), and, more complete, in Spanish, "Aravena, la autoconstrucción de una infâmia" (http://abcblogs.abc.es/fredy-massad/2016/02/04/aravena-la-autoconstruccion-de-una-infamia/).

43. Guilherme Wisnik, "Arquitetura expansiva," http://www1.folha.uol.com.br/colunas/guilherme-wisnik/2016/01/1733084-arquitetura-expansiva.shtml.

44. The assumptions and methodologies behind Aravena's designs, exemplified in concrete cases, are presented in Alejandro Aravena, *Elemental: Incremental Housing and Participatory Design Manual* (Berlin: Hatje-Cantz Verlag, 2012).

45. João Marcos Lopes, "Três tempos e uma dissonância: notas sobre o problema da produção da moradia na cidade neoliberal," presented at the Contested Cities conference, Madrid, 2016.

46. This is the expression adopted by João Marcos Lopes (ibid.).

47. Alfredo Rodríguez and Ana Sugranyes, eds., *Los con techo: un desafío para la política de vivienda social Santiago de Chile* (Santiago: Ediciones SUR, 2005).

48. See the material available on the Web site (http://www.fucvam.org.uy/) and the book by Gustavo Gonzales, *Una historia de FUCVAM* (Montevideo, Uruguay: Trilce, 2013), http://www.hic-al.org/documentos.cfm?id_categoria=3.

49. See the material available on the Web site (http://moi.org.ar) and the book by María Carla Rodríguez, *Autogestión, políticas de hábitat y transformación social* (Buenos Aires: Espacio Editorial, 2009).

50. The bibliography in Portuguese is broad. In Portuguese, see Habitação Nabil Bonduki, *Mutirão e autogestão: a experiência da administração Luiza Erundina em São Paulo* (São Paulo: Studio Nobel, 1997). In English, see Pedro Fiori Arantes, "Reinventing the Building Site," in *Brazil's Modern Architecture,* ed. Elisabetta Andreoli and Adrian Forty (London: Phaidon Press, 2004). See the site of the Usina collective for information on projects by one of the main Brazilian groups, http://www.usina-ctah.org.br/.

51. See https://produccionsocialhabitat.wordpress.com/galeria-de-casos/pioneros-kaika-shi.

BIBLIOGRAPHY

Adorno, Theodor. "Functionalism Today." *Gávea,* no. 15 (June 1997): 655–79. Rio de Janeiro: Arara Azul Comunicação.

AGC of America. Letter to Senator Mitch McConnell (December 23, 2009), http://newsmanager.commpartners.com/agcleg/downloads/091223%20Health%20Care%20-%20McConnell.pdf; accessed January 2010.

Alliez, Éric. "Carta a André Parente: Entre Imagem e Pensamento." In André Parente, *Imagem máquina: a era das tecnologias do virtual.* São Paulo: Editora 34, 1993.

Alt, Casey, and Timothy Lenoir. "Flow, Process, Fold: Intersections in Bioinformatics and Contemporary Architecture." In *Science, Metaphor, and Architecture.* Princeton, N.J.: Princeton University Press, 2002.

Anderson, Bridget, Martin Rush, Sarah Spencer, and Ben Rogaly. *Migrants' Lives beyond the Workplace: The Experiences of Central and East European Migrants in the UK* (May 29, 2007), http://www.jrf.org.uk/publications/experiences-central-and-east-european-migrants-uk; accessed January 2010.

Anderson, Perry. *The Origins of Postmodernity.* London: Verso, 1998.

Andréadis, Ianna. *Chantier ouvert au public: récit de la construction du Musée Quai Branly.* Paris: Éditions du Panama, 2006.

Antunes, Bianca. "Luiz Fernández-Galiano. Entrevista." *aU—Arquitetura e Urbanismo,* no. 181 (April 2009). São Paulo: PINI Ltda.

Antunes, Ricardo, and Ruy Braga. *Infoproletários: degradação real do trabalho virtual.* São Paulo: Boitempo, 2009.

Appelbaum, Alec. "Frank Gehry's Software Keeps Buildings on Budget." *New York Times,* February 10, 2009.

Aquino, Guilherme. "Pedreiro cibernético rouba a cena na Bienal de Arquitetura" (September 18, 2008), http://www.swissinfo.ch/por/Pedreiro_ciber netico_rouba_a_cena_na_Bienal_de_Arquitetura.html?cid=692269; accessed February 2010.

Aquino, Ruth. "Arquitetura da nova China." *Época* (July 7, 2008).

Arantes, Otília. "Alta cultura." N.d., mimeo.

————. "A 'virada cultural' do sistema das artes." *Margem Esquerda,* no. 6 (2005).

————. "Cultura e transformação urbana." In Vera Pallamin, ed., *Cidade e Cultura: Esfera pública e transformação urbana.* São Paulo: Estação Liberdade, 2002.

————. "Delírios de Rem Koolhaas." N.d., mimeo.

————. *O lugar da arquitetura depois dos modernos.* São Paulo: Edusp, 1993.

————. *Urbanismo em fim de linha.* São Paulo: Edusp, 1999.

————. "Vendo cidades." *Veredas,* no. 36 (1998).

————. "Xangai 2010." In *Chai-na.* São Paulo: Edusp, 2011.

Arantes, Otília, Erminia Maricato, and Carlos Vainer. *A cidade do pensamento único: Desmanchando consensos.* Petrópolis, Brazil: Vozes, 2000.

Arantes, Paulo. "A fratura brasileira do mundo: visões do laboratório brasileiro da mundialização." In *Zero à esquerda.* São Paulo: Conrad, 2004.

Arantes, Pedro. "Interesse público, poderes privados e práticas discursivas na política de renovação do Centro de São Paulo." In *Políticas públicas para o Centro: controle social do financiamento do BID à Prefeitura Municipal de São Paulo.* São Paulo: Instituto Pólis, 2008.

————. "O ajuste urbano: as políticas do Banco Mundial e do BID para as cidades latino-americanas." Master's thesis, FAU-USP, 2004.

————. "Urban Adjustment: World Bank and IDB Policies for Cities." In Márcio Moraes Valença, Fernanda Cravidão, and José Alberto Rio Fernandes, eds., *Urban Developments in Brazil and Portugal.* New York: Nova Science Publishers, 2012.

Aravena, Alejandro. *Elemental: Incremental Housing and Participatory Design Manual.* Berlin: Hatje-Cantz Verlag, 2012.

"Architect Foster Builds a Winning Business." *Sunday Times,* February 8, 2009.

Argan, Giulio Carlo. *História da arte como história da cidade.* São Paulo: Cia das Letras, 1992.

————. *Projeto e destino.* São Paulo: Ática, 2001.

Augé, Marc. *Não-lugares: Uma introdução a uma antropologia da supermodernidade.* São Paulo: Papirus, 2003.

Ball, Michael. *Rebuilding Construction: Economic Change in the British Construction Industry.* London: Routledge, 1988.

Barbosa, Antônio Agenor. "Entrevista de Alfredo Sirkis." January 4, 2003, http://www.vitruvius.com.br/entrevista/sirkis/sirkis.asp; accessed February 2010.

Baudrillard, Jean. *The Consumer Society.* London: Sage Publications, 1998.
_____. *The System of Objects* (1968). London: Verso, 1996.

Bauman, Zygmunt. *Liquid Modernity.* Cambridge: Polity Press, 2000.

Bazjanac, Vladimir. "Impact of the U.S. National Building Information Model Standard (NBIMS) on Building Energy Performance Simulation." Berkeley: Lawrence Berkeley National Laboratory (2008), http://www.escholarship.org/uc/item/3v95d7xp; accessed January 2010.

BBC. "Strike Halts Work at Dubai Tower" (March 23, 2006), http://news.bbc.co.uk/2/hi/business/4836632.stm; accessed January 2010.

Beck, Ulrich. *The Brave New World of Work.* Oxford: Polity Press, 2000.

Benevolo, Leonardo. *The Architecture of the New Millennium.* New York: Phaidon Press, 2009.

Benjamin, Andrew, Catherine Cooke, and Andreas Papadakis. *Deconstruction.* London: Academy Editions, 1989.

Benjamin, Walter. "The Work of Art in the Age of Mechanical Reproduction." In *Illuminations: Essays and Reflections.* New York: Shocken Books, 2007.

Berk & Associates. *Seattle Central Library Economic Benefits Assessment: The Transformative Power of a Library to Redefine Learning, Community, and Economic Development* (2005), www.spl.org/pdfs/SPLCentral_Library_Economic_Impacts.pdf; accessed February 2010.

Beyer, Susanne, and Ulrike Knöfel. "Only an Idiot Would Have Said No." Interview with Jacques Herzog. *Der Spiegel Online* (July 30, 2008), http://www.spiegel.de/international/world/0,1518,569011,00.html; accessed January 2010.

Boal, Iain, T. J. Clark, Joseph Matthews, and Michael Watts. *Afflicted Powers: Capital and Spectacle, in a New Age of War.* London: Verso, 2005.

Bonduki, Nabil. *Habitação, mutirão e autogestão: a experiência da administração Luiza Erundina em São Paulo.* São Paulo: Studio Nobel, 1997.

Bonwetsch, Tobias, Fabio Gramazio, and Mathias Kohler. "The Informed Wall: Applying Additive Digital Fabrication Techniques on Architecture." In *Synthetic Landscapes.* Annals of the 25th Annual Conference of the Association for Computer-Aided Design in Architecture, 489–95.

Bosch, Gerhard, and Peter Philips, eds. *Building Chaos: An International Comparison of Deregulation in the Construction Industry.* London: Routledge, 2003.

Bourdieu, Pierre. *Razões práticas: sobre a teoria da ação.* São Paulo: Papirus, 2008.

Bozdoc, Marian. *The History of Cad* (2003), http://mbinfo.mbdesign.net/CAD -History.htm; accessed January 2010.

Building Towers, Cheating Workers (2006), http://www.unhcr.org/refworld/ docid/45dadd9b2.html; accessed October 2009.

Bulard, Martine. "Uma nova geografia dos capitais." *Le Monde diplomatique Brasil,* November 2008.

Butterpaper. "Architect's Conditions and Wages" (2005), http://www.butter paper.com/vanilla/comments.php?DiscussionID=294&page=1; accessed January 2010.

Caicoya, César. "Acuerdos formales: el museo Guggenheim, del proyecto a la construcción." *Arquitectura Viva,* no. 55 (July 1997).

Campanella, Thomas. "Mejoras capitales." *Arquitectura Viva,* no. 118–19 (November 2008): 36–47.

Campinos-Dubernet, Myriam. "La rationalisation du travail dans le BTP: un exemple des limites du taylorisme orthodoxe." *Formation Emploi,* no. 6 (1984): 79–89.

Canal, José Luiz. "Projeto em construção." In *Fundação Iberê Camargo.* São Paulo: Cosac & Naify, 2008.

Castel, Robert. *From Manual Workers to Wage Laborers: Transformation of the Social Question.* Princeton, N.J.: Princeton University Press, 2002.

Cattani, Antonio. *Trabalho e tecnologia: dicionário crítico.* Rio de Janeiro: Vozes, 1997.

Chesnais, François. "A emergência de um regime de acumulação financeira." *Praga,* no. 3 (1997): 37.

———. *A mundialização financeira.* São Paulo: Xamã, 1998.

———. *The Globalization of Capital.* Paris: Éditions Syros, 1994.

Coehlo, Eliomar. "Por fora, bela viola . . ." *O Globo,* June 24, 2003.

Contract Journal. "Immigrant Workers Lack Experience in Building" (September 5, 2007), http://www.contractjournal.com/Articles/2007/09/05/56143/ immigrant-workers-lack-experience-in-building.html; accessed February 2010.

Coriat, Benjamin. "Le procès de travail de type 'chantier' et la rationalisation: remarques sur quelques tendances de la recherche actuelle." In *Plan Construction et Habitat. Le Travail en Chantiers: Actes du Colloque.* Paris: Ministère de l'Urbanisme, du Logement et des Transports, 1984.

Costa, Eduardo, and Sonia Gouveia. "Nelson Kon, uma fotografia de arquitetura brasileira." *Revista da Pós,* no. 24 (December 2008): 16.

Couchot, Edmond. "Da representação à simulação: evolução das técnicas e das artes da figuração." In André Parente, ed., *Imagem máquina: a era das tecnologias do virtual,* 37–48. Rio de Janeiro: Editora 34, 1993.

Crema, Adriana, Maristela Gava, and Hugo Segawa. *Revistas de arquitetura, urbanismo, paisagismo e design: a divergência de perspectivas (Ci. Inf.* [online] 32: 3 [2003]): 120–27, http://www.scielo.br/scielo.php?pid=S0100-196520 03000300014&script=sci_abstract&tlng=pt; accessed February 2010.

Curtis, Polly "House of Lords Peers Who Resigned for Tax Reasons Will Keep Titles." *The Guardian* (July 7, 2010), https://www.theguardian.com/poli tics/2010/jul/07/house-of-lords-peers-titles; accessed December 2010.

Dagnino, Renato, "Tecnologia social." In Antonio David Cattani, Jean-Louis Laville, Luiz Inácio Gaiger, and Pedro Hespanha, eds., *Dicionário internacional da outra economia.* Coimbra, Portugal: Almedina, 2009.

Dal Co, Francesco, and Kurt Foster. *Frank O. Gehry: Complete Works.* New York: Monacelli Press, 1998.

Dantas, Marcos. "Capitalismo na era das redes: trabalho, informação e valor no ciclo da comunicação produtiva." In Helena M. M. Lastres and Sarita Albagli, eds., *Informação e globalização na era do conhecimento.* Rio de Janeiro: Campus, 1999.

Davies, Paul. "Foster Clinches Gold after Olympic Triumph." *China-Fortune Capital,* September 3, 2008.

Davis, Mike. *City of Quartz.* London: Verso, 2006.

———. *Planet of Slums.* London: Verso, 2006.

———. "Sand, Fear and Money in Dubai." In *Evil Paradises.* New York: New Press, 2007.

Debord, Guy. *Society of the Spectacle.* New York: Zone Books, 1995.

Deleuze, Gilles. *Conversações.* São Paulo: Editora 34, 2008.

Dieux, Hervé. "Eastern European Immigrants Exploited." *Le Monde diplomatique,* August 2002.

Domeisen, Oliver, and Francesca Ferguson. "Press Release: Re-Sampling Ornament" (2008), www.sam-basel.org/uploads/File/SAM_Ornament_Presstext _e.pdf; accessed February 2010.

"Dubai Government to Inject US$9.5 Billion to Reduce Dubai World and Nakheel Debt." *Asia News,* March 25, 2010, http://www.asianews.it/news-en/ Dubai-govt-to-inject-US$-9.5-billion-to-reduce-Dubai-World-and-Nakheel -debt-17982.html.

Dunlap, David. "Guggenheim Drops Plans for East River Museum." *New York Times,* December 31, 2002.

Eco, Umberto. *Viagem na irrealidade cotidiana.* São Paulo: Nova Fronteira, 1984.

Eisenman, Peter. *Written into the Void: Selected Writings, 1990–2004.* New Haven: Yale University Press, 2007.

Elwall, Robert. *Building with Light: An International History of Architectural Photography.* London: Merrel, 2004.

Farah, Marta. *Processo de trabalho na construção habitacional: tradição e mudança.* São Paulo: Annablume, 1996.

Fathy, Hassan. *Architecture for the Poor: An Experiment in Rural Egypt.* Chicago: University of Chicago Press, 1973.

Feiden, Douglas. "Why Is Ground Zero Rebuilding Taking So Long?" *Daily News,* August 4, 2009.

Fernandes, Andressa. "CPI investiga irregularidades na Cidade da Música" (May 19, 2008), http://www.piniweb.com.br/construcao/arquitetura/cpi-investiga -irregularidades-na-cidade-da-musica-89294–1.asp; accessed January 2010.

Fernandez-Galiano, Luiz. "Diálogo y logo: Jacques Herzog piensa en voz alta." *Arquitectura Viva,* no. 91 (2003): 29.

———. "Papel fotográfico: imagens que constroem a arquitetura." *Projeto.* July 1994, 81.

Ferro, Sérgio. *Arquitetura e trabalho livre.* São Paulo: Cosac & Naify, 2006.

Figueira, Jorge. "Mundo Coral." In *Fundação Iberê Camargo.* São Paulo: Cosac & Naify, 2008.

Figueiredo, Talita. "Câmara do Rio decide instaurar CPI da Cidade da Música." *O Estado de S. Paulo,* May 7, 2009.

Fix, Mariana. "Como o governo Lula pretende resolver o problema da habitação." *Correio da Cidadania* (2009).

———. "Financeirização e transformações recentes no circuito imobiliário no Brasil." Doctoral thesis, Institute of Economics, Unicamp, 2011.

Florida, Richard. *Cities and the Creative Class.* New York: Routledge, 2004.

Flório, Wilson. "O uso de ferramentas de modelagem vetorial na concepção de uma arquitetura de formas complexas." Doctoral thesis, FAU-USP, 2005.

Fontenelle, Isleide. *O nome da marca.* São Paulo: Boitempo, 2004.

———. "Os caçadores do *cool.*" *Lua Nova,* no. 63 (2004).

Foster, Hal. *Design and Crime (and Other Diatribes).* London: Verso, 2002.

Fracalanza, Paulo Sérgio, and Lício da Costa Raimundo. "Gestão da riqueza e transformações do mundo do trabalho: a crise do trabalho no regime de acumulação liderado pela finança." *Economia e Sociedade,* 2008.

Frampton, Kenneth. *Labour, Work and Architecture.* London: Phaidon, 2002.

———. *Studies in Tectonic Culture.* Cambridge: MIT Press, 2001.

Friedman, Mildred. *Gehry Talks: Architecture and Process.* New York: Universe, 2002.

Fuão, Fernando Freitas. "Papel do papel: as folhas da arquitetura e a arquitetura mesma." *Projeto* (July 1994): 84–85.

Furtado, Celso. *A construção interrompida.* Rio de Janeiro: Paz e Terra, 1992.

———. *O mito do desenvolvimento.* Rio de Janeiro: Paz e Terra, 1974.

Galofaro, Luca. *Digital Eisenman: An Office of the Electronic Era.* Basel, Switzerland: Birkhäuser, 1999.

Gama, Ruy. *A tecnologia e o trabalho na história.* São Paulo: Studio Nobel, 1986.

Gann, David. "New Management Strategies and the Fast-Track Phenomenon." In Helen Rainbird and Gerd Syben, eds., *Restructuring a Traditional Industry: Construction Employment and Skills in Europe.* New York: Berg, 1991.

Garcia dos Santos, Laymert. "Informação após a virada cibernética [Information after the cybernetic turn]." In *Revolução Tecnológica, Internet e Socialismo.* São Paulo: Perseu Abramo, 2003.

————. *Politizar as novas tecnologias: o impacto sócio-técnico da informação digital e genética.* São Paulo: Editora 34, 2003.

Gazolla, Ana. *Espaço e imagem.* Rio de Janeiro: UFRJ, 1994.

Germano, Wagner, and João Marcos Lopes. "Jorge, professor de todos nós." Interview with Jorge Oseki. *Revista da Pós,* no. 25 (2009): 10–12.

Ghirardo, Diane. *Architecture after Modernism.* London: Thames & Hudson, 1996.

Glancey, Jonathan. "A era da ostentação chegou ao fim?" *O Estado de S.Paulo,* Caderno 2, December 26, 2009, D5.

————. "Norman Foster in the Lords: What Might Have Been." *The Guardian,* July 12, 2010, https://www.theguardian.com/artanddesign/2010/jul/12/norman-foster-house-of-lords.

————. "Review of the Decade: Jonathan Glancey on Architecture," *The Guardian,* December 7, 2009.

Glymph, Jim. "Evolution in the Digital Design Process." In Branko Kolarevich, *Architecture in the Digital Age: Design and Manufacturing.* New York: Taylor & Francis, 2003.

————. *Gehry Talks: Architecture and Process.* New York: Universe, 2002.

Goldenberg, Suzanne. "Gehry Sued over Leaky University Building." *The Guardian,* November 7, 2007, http://www.theguardian.com/world/2007/nov/07/internationaleducationnews.usa.

————. "Masdar's Zero-Carbon Dream Could Become World's First Green Ghost Town." *The Guardian,* February 16, 2016, https://www.theguardian.com/environment/2016/feb/16/masdars-zero-carbon-dream-could-become-worlds-first-green-ghost-town.

Gómez, María, and Sara Gonzáles, "A Reply to Beatriz Plaza's 'The Guggenheim-Bilbao Museum Effect.'" *International Journal of Urban and Regional Research* 25:4 (2001): 898–900.

Gonzales, Gustavo. *Una historia de FUCVAM.* Montevideo, Uruguay: Trilce, 2013, http://www.hic-al.org/documentos.cfm?id_categoria=3.

Gorz, André. *Misérias do presente, riqueza do possível.* São Paulo: Annablume, 2004.

————. *O imaterial. Conhecimento, valor, capital.* São Paulo: Annablume, 2005.

Gramazio, Fabio, Masthias Kohler, and Tobias Bonwetsch. "Digitally Fabricating Non-Standardised Brick Walls." In *ManuBuild—1st International Conference.* Rotterdam, 2007, 191–96.

Grespan, Jorge. "A crise de sobreacumulação." *Crítica Marxista,* no. 29 (2009).

————. *O negativo do capital: O conceito de crise na crítica de Marx à economia política.* São Paulo: Hucitec, 1998.

"Guggenheim irá a Guadalajara." *Folha de S. Paulo,* October 18, 2005.

Haddad, Fernando. *Em defesa do socialismo.* São Paulo: Vozes, 1998.

Hall, Peter. "Los iconos arquitectónicos nos llevan a uma suma cero." *La Vanguardia,* June 15, 2009.

Harribey, Jean-Marie. "Marxismo ecológico ou ecologia política marxista." In Jaque Bidet and Eustache Kouvélakis, eds., Jorge Hajime Oseki and Inês Oseki, trans., *Dictionnaire Marx contemporain.* Paris: Presses Universitaires de France, 2001.

Harvey, David. "The Art of Rent: Globalization, Monopoly and the Commodification of Culture." In *A produção capitalista do espaço.* São Paulo: Annablume, 2005.

————. *The Condition of Postmodernity: An Enquiry into the Origins of Cultural Change.* Cambridge: Blackwell Publishers, 1990.

————. *Justice, Nature and the Geography of Difference.* New York: Wiley-Blackwell, 1996.

————. *Limits to Capital.* Brooklyn: Verso, 1999.

Haug, Wolfgang Fritz. *Critique of Commodity Aesthetics: Appearance, Sexuality, and Advertising in Capitalist Society.* Cambridge: Polity Press, 1986.

Haymaker, John, and Martin Fischer. "Challenges and Benefits of 4D Modeling on the Walt Disney Concert Hall Project." CIFE Working Paper #64 (January 2001), https://web.stanford.edu/class/cee214/Readings/Walt%20 Disney%20Concer%20Hall%20Project.pdf; accessed December 2010.

Hedgpeth, Dana. "Builders Groups Decry Obama's Order on Projects." *Washington Post,* February 12, 2009, http://www.washingtonpost.com/wp-dyn/content/article/2009/02/11/AR2009021103953.html; accessed December 2010.

Hirata, Helena, ed. *Sobre o "modelo" japonês.* São Paulo: Edusp, 1993.

História de un sueño: Guggenheim Bilbao Museoa. Barcelona: IDOM, 1997.

Howeler, Eric. *Skyscraper: Designs of the Recent Past and for the Near Future.* London: Thames & Hudson, 2003.

Human Rights Watch. *Building Towers, Cheating Workers: Exploitation of Migrant Construction Workers in the United Arab Emirates* (2006), https://

www.hrw.org/report/2006/11/11/building-towers-cheating-workers/ex
ploitation-migrant-construction-workers-united; accessed October 2009.

———. "The Island of Happiness: Exploitation of Migrant Workers on Saadiyat Island, Abu Dhabi." New York: HRW Report, 2009.

———. *One Year of My Blood* 20:3 (2008), http://www.unhcr.org/refworld/
docid/47d7fb772.html; accessed October 2009.

Hurst, Will. "Foster Set to Be Expelled from House of Lords" (February 2,
2009), http://www.bdonline.co.uk/news/foster-set-to-be-expelled-from-house
-of-lords/3132908.article; accessed February 2010.

———. "Foster under Pressure to Reveal Tax Status" (February 2, 2009),
https://www.bdonline.co.uk/news/foster-under-pressure-to-reveal-tax-sta
tus/3111999.article; accessed February 2010.

———. "Norman Foster's Tax Status Questioned in Parliament" (April 24,
2008), http://www.bdonline.co.uk/story.asp?storycode=3112065; accessed
February 2010.

Inovação Tecnoógica. "Robô-pedreiro constrói muro artístico em Nova Iorque
(November 4, 2008), http://www.inovacaotecnologica.com.br/noticias/no
ticia.php?artigo=robo-pedreiro-constroi-muro-artistico-nova-iorque&id=;
accessed February 2010.

"Interesse público, poderes privados e práticas discursivas na política de renovação do Centro de São Paulo" (2007), http://www.centrovivo.org/node/970;
accessed February 2010.

Jaggar, David, and Ralph Morton. *Design and the Economics of Building*. London: Spon Press, 1995.

Jameson, Fredric. "The Brick and the Balloon: Architecture, Idealism and
Land Speculation." In *The Cultural Turn: Selected Writings on the Postmodern*. London and New York: Verso, 1998.

———. "Os limites do pós-modernismo." In *Espaço e imagem*. Rio de Janeiro:
UFRJ, 1994.

———. *Postmodernism, or, the Cultural Logic of Late Capitalism*. Durham,
N.C.: Duke University Press, 1991.

Jon Peddie Research. "The 2008 CAD Report" (2008), http://www.jonpeddie
.com/publications/cad_report/; accessed January 2010.

Kara-José, Beatriz. *Políticas culturais e negócios urbanos*. São Paulo: Annablume,
2007.

Keeley, Graham. "Guggenheim Architect Frank Gehry to Create City of Wine
Complex for Marques de Risca." *Daily Mail*, January 20, 2010.

Kiely, Kathy. "Need for Immigrant Workers in Dispute." *USA Today*, June 24,
2007.

Kieran, Stephen, and James Timberlake. *Refabricating Architecture: How Manufacturing Methodologies Are Poised to Transform Building Construction.* New York: McGraw-Hill, 2004.

Klein, Naomi. *No Logo: Taking Aim at the Brand Bullies.* London: Flamingo, 2000.

Klingmann, Anna. *Brandscapes: Architecture in the Experience Economy.* Cambridge: MIT Press, 2007.

Kolarevic, Branko, ed. *Architecture in the Digital Age: Design and Manufacturing.* New York: Taylor & Francis, 2003.

Koolhaas, Rem. *Delirious New York: A Retroactive Manifesto for Manhattan.* New York: Thames & Hudson, 1978.

_____. *The Harvard Design Guide to Shopping.* Ed. Chuihua Judy Chung, Jeffery Inaba, Rem Koolhaas, and Sze Tsung Leong. Cologne: Taschen, 2002.

———. *Projects for Prada—Part 1.* Milan: Fondazione Prada Edizioni, 2001.

———. *S M L XL.* New York: Monacelli Press, 1995.

Kuchta, Michael. "USA: Construction Workers Endure High Rates of Death, Injury." *Lakes and Plains Carpenter* (February 18, 2007), http://www.bwint.org/default.asp?index=641&Language=EN; accessed January 2010.

Kwinter, Sanford. *Far from Equilibrium: Essays on Technology and Design Culture.* New York: Actar, 2008.

Leal, Carlos. "Dubai e os megaprojetos." *Construção Mercado,* no. 60 (July 2006).

Lecuyer, Annette. "Building Bilbao." *Architectural Review: Museums,* no. 1210 (1997): 43–45.

Lévy, Pierre. *Becoming Virtual: Reality in the Digital Age.* New York: Plenum Trade, 1998.

Libeskind, Daniel. "Architect's Statement for the Proposed Plans for the New York World Trade Center" (February 24, 2008), http://architecture.about.com/library/bl-libeskind-statement.htm; accessed January 2010.

Lindsey, Bruce. *Digital Gehry: Material Resistance, Digital Construction.* Basel, Switzerland, Birkhäuser, 2001.

Lipovetsky, Gilles. *A era do vazio.* Barueri, Brazil: Manole, 2005.

Lipovetsky, Gilles, and Elyette Roux. *O luxo eterno—da idade do sagrado ao tempo das marcas.* São Paulo: Companhia das Letras, 2005.

Loos, Adolf. *Ornament and Crime: Selected Essays.* Riverside: California Ariadne Press, 1998.

Lopes, João Marcos. "Três tempos e uma dissonância: notas sobre o problema da produção da moradia na cidade neoliberal." Presented at the Contested Cities conference, Madrid, 2016.

Lopes, Pablo. "Juez y Tribunal de Cuentas investigan el contrato de la cuarcita del Gaiás," *El País* (December 20, 2008), https://elpais.com/diario/2008/12/20/galicia/1229771893_850215.html.

Lopes, Ruy Sardinha. *Informação, conhecimento e valor.* São Paulo: Radical Livros, 2008.

López, Gentzane. "The Guggenheim Effect: Positive Transformations for the City of Bilbao" (2006), www.euroculturemaster.org/pdf/lopez.pdf; accessed February 2010.

Löwy, Michael. "Ecología y socialismo." *La Haine* (January 25, 2007), http://www.lahaine.org/index.php?p=20019; accessed February 2010.

Luebkeman, Chris. "Performance-Based Design." In Branko Kolarevic, ed., *Architecture in the Digital Age: Design and Manufacturing.* New York: Taylor & Francis, 2003.

Lynn, Greg. *Folds, Bodies and Blobs: Collected Essays.* Brussels: La Lettre Volée, 1998.

Mageste, Paula. "A defesa da cria." *Época,* 2003.

Marcuse, Peter. "The Ground Zero Architectural Competition: Designing without a Plan." In *Progressive Planning Reader 2004.* Ithaca, N.Y.: Planners Network, 2004.

Maricato, Ermínia. "Indústria da construção e política habitacional." Doctoral thesis, FAU-USP, 1984.

Marshall, Alex. "How to Make a Frank Gehry Building." *New York Times,* April 8, 2001.

Marx, Karl. *Capital: A Critique of Political Economy.* London: Penguin in association with *New Left Review,* 1990.

————. *Grundrisse: Foundations of the Critique of Political Economy.* London: Penguin Classics, 1993.

————. *The Poverty of Philosophy.* Moscow: Progress Publishers, 1955.

Massad, Fredy. "Aravena, la autoconstrucción de una infamia." *La viga en el ojo blog* (February 4, 2016), http://abcblogs.abc.es/fredy-massad/2016/02/04/aravena-la-autoconstruccion-de-una-infamia/; accessed April 2016.

————. "The Stardom of Demagogy: Another Wrong Move," http://www.transfer-arch.com/stardom-demagogy/; accessed February 2010.

Massad, Fredy, and Alicia Yeste. "Arquiteto Peter Einsenman" (interview with Peter Eisenman) (July 2005), http://www.vitruvius.com.br/entrevista/eisenman/eisenman.asp; accessed February 2010.

McCullough, Malcolm. *Abstracting Craft: The Practiced Digital Hand.* Cambridge: MIT Press, 1998.

McNeill, Donald. "McGuggenisation? National Identity and Globalisation in the Basque Country." *Political Geography,* no. 19 (2000): 473–94.

Meethan, Kevin. "Imaginando a cidade para o turismo." *NOZ*, no. 2 (2008).

Merrick, Jay. "Angles from Heaven: Frank Gehry Takes on His Dream Project." *The Independent*, July 9, 2008.

Mészáros, István. *The Power of Ideology*. London: Zed Books, 2005.

Montes, Javier. "Y en Arcadia, los egos: fábulas del arte para el Golfo." *Arquitectura Viva*, no. 111 (2006): 36.

Mora, Miguel. "Entrevista a Miguel Mora" (Frank Gehry is interviewed). *El País*, reproduced in *Folha de S.Paulo*, January 31, 2010.

"Moratória em Dubai assusta bolsas." *O Estado de S. Paulo*, November 27, 2009.

Moreau, Denis. "La petite fabrique d'effets spéciaux: artefactory au générique." *L'Architecture d'Aujourd'hui*, no. 354 (2004): 72–79.

Morin, Edgar. *Introduction to Complex Thinking*. Oxford: Oxford University Press, 2012.

Mozas, Javier. "'Collage' metropolitano: Bilbao, imperativos económicos y regeneración urbana." *Arquitectura Viva*, no. 55 (July 1997).

Mulder, Marlies Ingeborg, and John L. Heintz. "Offshore Outsourcing—Now Available for Architects." In H. A. J. de Ridder and J. W. F. Wamelink, eds., *World of Construction Project Management*. Delft, The Netherlands: TU-Delft, 2007.

Murphy, Kevin M. "The Economic Value of Investing in Architecture and Design" (2003), www.dqionline.com/downloads/MSallette_Ind_Study.pdf; accessed February 2010.

Murray, Lynn. "Building Information Modeling Takes Architectural Design to a New Dimension." *Design Cost Data* (2007), http://www.dcd.com/insights/insights_sepoct_2007.html; accessed January 2010.

National Institute of Building Sciences. *National Building Information Standard. Version 1—Part 1: Overview, Principles, Methodologies*. Washington, D.C.: NIBS, 2009, http://nbimsdoc.opengeospatial.org; accessed February 2010.

Nesbit, Kate, ed. *Theorizing a New Agenda for Architecture: An Anthology of Architectural Theory 1965–1995*. Princeton, N.J.: Princeton Architectural Press, 1996.

Nobre, Lígia. "Guggenheim-Rio é visão estereotipada do brasil" (2007), http://forumpermanente.incubadora.fapesp.br/portal/.rede/numero/rev-numero2/ligia-nobre; accessed February 2010.

Nogueira, Ítalo. "Projeto espanhol dá início à revitalização do porto do Rio." *Folha de S. Paulo*, February 26, 2010, C8.

Nouvel, Jean. "Editorial" (September 2009), http://larchitecturedaujourdhui.fr/en/edito.htm; accessed February 2010.

Oliveira, Francisco de. *O ornitorrinco*. São Paulo: Boitempo, 2004.

Ontario Municipality. *Ontario Cultural and Heritage Tourism Product Research Paper.* Toronto: Queen's Printer for Ontario, 2009.

Oseki, Jorge, and Paulo Pelegrino. "Sociedade e ambiente." In Arlindo Philippi Jr., Marcello Andrade Romero, and Gilda Bruna, eds., *Curso de gestão ambiental.* São Paulo: Manole, 2004.

Oseki, Jorge Hajime. "Arquitetura em construção." Master's thesis, FAU-USP, 1983.

Oseki, Jorge, Paulo C. X. Pereira, Ermínia T. M. Maricato, and Yvonne M. M. Mautner, "Bibliografia sobre a Indústria da Construção: reflexão crítica." *Sinopses* (São Paulo: FAU-USP), no. 16 (1991).

Ouroussoff, Nicolai. "O fim melancólico de uma época." *O Estado de S. Paulo,* November 8, 2009.

Palma, Gabriel. "The Revenge of the Market on the Rentiers." Unpublished article, presented at a conference at FGV in São Paulo in 2008.

Parente, André. *Imagem máquina: a era das tecnologias do virtual.* São Paulo: Editora 34, 1993.

Parnell, Steve. "Building Information Modelling: The Golden Opportunity" (July 28, 2009), http://www.architectsjournal.co.uk/building-information -modelling-the-golden-opportunity/5205851.article; accessed January 2010.

Perrela, Stephen. "Folding in Architecture" (interview conducted by Mark Dippe). *Architectural Design.* Seattle: Academy Press, 1993.

Philippi Jr., Arlindo, Marcello de Andrade Romero, and Gilda Bruna, eds. *Curso de Gestão ambiental.* São Paulo: Manole, 2004.

Pimenta, Ângela. "A festa que pode levar um museu para o Rio de Janeiro." *Veja,* November 22, 2000.

Pittman, Jon. "Building Information Modeling: Current Challenges and Future Directions." In Branko Kolarevic, ed., *Architecture in the Digital Age: Design and Manufacturing.* New York: Taylor & Francis, 2003.

Plaza, Beatriz. "Evaluating the Influence of a Large Cultural Artifact in the Attraction of Tourism: The Guggenheim Museum Bilbao Case." *Urban Affairs Review,* no. 36 (2000): 264–74.

———. "The Guggenheim-Bilbao Museum Effect: A Reply to María V. Gómez's 'Reflective Images: The Case of Urban Regeneration in Glasgow and Bilbao.'" *International Journal of Urban and Regional Research,* no. 23 (1999): 589–92.

Podestá, Sylvio. "Por que publicar? Como publicar? Quem publicar?" http://www.podesta.arq.br/index.php?option=com_content&view=article&id= 57:texto-porque-publicar&catid=30:entrevista&Itemid=43; accessed February 2010.

Prado, Eleutério da Silva. *Desmedida do valor: crítica da pós-grande indústria*. São Paulo: Xamã, 2005.

Precedo, José, and Sonia Vizoso. "Despilfarros en la Xunta de Fraga." *El País*, August 15, 2007.

Rainbird, Helen, and Gerd Syben, eds. *Restructuring a Traditional Industry: Construction Employment and Skills in Europe*. New York: Berg, 1991.

Rauterberg, Hanno. *Talking Architecture: Interviews with Architects*. London: Prestel, 2008.

Ravenel, Bernard. "Leçons d'autogestion" (April 5, 2007), http://www.mouve ments.info/Lecons-d-autogestion.html; accessed February 2010.

Reich, Robert B. *The Work of Nations: Preparing Ourselves for 21st Century Capitalism*. New York: Vintage Books, 1992.

Reiser & Umemoto. *Atlas of Novel Tectonics*. New York: Princeton Architectural Press, 2006.

Riboulet, Pierre. "Éléments pour une critique de l'architecture." *Espaces et Sociétés*, no. 1 (November 1970).

Ricardo, David. *On the Principles of Political Economy and Taxation*. London: John Murray, 1817.

Rifkin, Jeremy. *The Age of Access: The New Culture of Hypercapitalism, Where All of Life Is a Paid-For Experience*. New York: TarcherPerigee, 2001.

Ritzer, George. *The McDonaldization of Society: An Investigation into the Changing Character of Contemporary Social Life*. Thousand Oaks, Calif.: Pine Forge Press, 1995.

Robbins, Tom. "Labor War in Chelsea." (May 9, 2006), http://www.swiftraid .org/media/articles/VillageVoice.pdf; accessed January 2010.

Rodríguez, Alfredo, and Ana Sugranyes, eds. *Los con techo: un desafío para la política de vivienda social Santiago de Chile*. Santiago: Ediciones SUR, 2005.

Rodríguez, María Carla. *Autogestión, políticas de hábitat y transformación social*. Buenos Aires: Espacio Editorial, 2009.

Sardinha, Ruy. *Informação, conhecimento e valor*. São Paulo: Radical Livros, 2008.

Sardinha, Ruy, and David Sperling. "Deslocamentos da experiência espacial: de *earthwork* à arquitetura líquida." *SIGraDi 2007* (2007), http://cumin cades.scix.net/data/works/att/sigradi2007_af93.content.pdf; accessed February 2010.

Saunders, William. *Judging Architectural Value: A Harvard Design Magazine Reader*. Minneapolis: University of Minnesota Press, 2007.

Schittich, Christian. *Building Skins: Concepts, Layers, Materials*. Basel, Switzerland: Birkhäuser, 2001.

Schleifer, Simone, ed. *Spectacular Buildings*. Cologne: Evergreen Taschen, 2007.

Schumacher, Patrik. *Digital Hadid: Landscapes in Motion*. Basel, Switzerland: Birkhäuser, 1994.

Sebestyen, Gyula. *Construction: Craft to Industry*. London: Taylor & Francis, 1998.

Senagala, Mahesh. "Deconstructing AutoCAD: Toward a Critical Theory of Software (in) Design." In *Proceedings of the 7th Iberoamerican Congress of Digital Graphics* (Rosario, Argentina: SIGraDi, 2003), http://cumincad.scix.net/cgi-bin/works/Show?sigradi2003_008; accessed January 2010.

Sennett, Richard. *The Craftsman*. New Haven: Yale University Press, 2009.

———. *The Fall of Public Man*. New York: W. W. Norton, 1992.

Shelden, Dennis. "Digital Surface Representation and the Constructibility of Gehry's Architecture." Doctoral thesis, Cambridge, 2002.

———. "Tectonics, Economics and the Reconfiguration of Practice: The Case for Process Change by Digital Means." *Architectural Design* 76:4 (2006): 82–87.

Shiva, Vandana. *Biopirataria—a pilhagem da natureza e do conhecimento*. Petrópolis, Brazil: Vozes, 2001.

Shulman, Julius. *Photographing Architecture and Interiors*. New York: Whitney Library of Design, 1962.

Sichelman, Lew. "Homebuilders Say Immigrants' Work Is Vital—Houses Wouldn't Be Built on Time or on Budget without the Help of Foreign-Born Workers, Many of Whom Are Here Illegally." *San Francisco Chronicle,* May 28, 2006.

Sierra, Rafael. "Eisenman dice que la revolución de Bilbao con el Guggenheim es el modelo a seguir." *El Mundo,* April 14, 1999.

Silver, Marc. *Under Construction: Work and Alienation in the Building Trades*. New York: New York Press, 1986.

Siniavska, Natalia. *Immigrant Workers in Construction*. Washington, D.C.: National Association of Home Builders, 2005, http://www.nahb.org/generic.aspx?genericContentID=49216%29; accessed January 2010.

SolidWorks. "Software Piracy in the CAD Industry," http://www.solidworks community.com/feature_full.php?cpfeatureid=16515; accessed January 2010.

Specht, Jan. "Architectural Tourism: Building for Urban Travel Destinations." In Shaul Krakover and Natan Uriely, *Tourism Destination and Development Branding*. Eilat, Israel: Ben-Gurion University of the Negev, 2009.

Spencer, Sarah, Martin Ruhs, Bridget Anderson, and Ben Rogaly. "Migrants' Lives beyond the Workplace: The Experiences of Central and East Europeans in the UK." Joseph Rowntree Foundation (May 29, 2007), http://www.jrf.org.uk/publications/experiences-central-and-east-european-migrants-uk, 60; accessed January 2010.

Stevens, Garry. *O círculo privilegiado: fundamentos sociais da distinção arquitetônica.* Brasília: UnB, 2003.

Stone, David. *Software Piracy* (1999), http://www.ed.uiuc.edu/wp/crime/piracy.htm; accessed January 2010.

Strehlke, Kai. "El ornamiento digital: aproximaciones de um novo decoro." *Arquitectura Viva,* no. 124 (2009): 26.

Sullivan, Jennifer. "It Hurts So Bad" (February 29, 2000), http://www.salon 1999.com/tech/feature/2000/02/29/rsi/index.html; accessed January 2010.

Syben, Gerd. "Strategies of Growth of Productivity in the Absence of Consumption Technological Change." In Helen Rainbird and Gerd Syben, eds., *Restructuring a Traditional Industry: Construction Employment and Skills in Europe.* New York: Berg, 1991.

Tafuri, Manfredo. *Projecto e utopia.* Lisbon: Presença, 1985.

———. *Teorias e história da arquitectura.* Lisbon: Presença, 1979.

Taylor, Frederick Winslow. *The Principles of Scientific Management.* New York and London: Harper & Brothers, 1911.

Taylor, Sarah. "Local Craftsmen Met Gehry's Challenge" (October 17, 2002), http://neogehry.org/art_local-craftsmen.php; accessed January 2010.

Teather, David. "Recession and Debt Dissolve Dubai's Mirage in the Desert." *The Guardian,* November 29, 2009, https://www.theguardian.com/business/2009/nov/29/dubai-financial-crisis.

Terra. "Forster asegura que la Ciudad de la Cultura es 'especial y única' y que el reto es atraer visitantes" (November 15, 2007), http://terranoticias.terra.es/articulo/html/av22017387.htm.

Terzidis, Kostas. *Algorithmic Architecture.* Amsterdam and Boston: Architectural Press, 2006.

Turner, John F. C. *Housing by People: Towards Autonomy in Building Environments.* New York: Pantheon Books, 1976.

"Una ponencia en Ciudad de la Cultura denuncia la 'voluntad premeditada'" (December 10, 2007), http://www.elselectordenoticias.es/soitu/2007/12/10/info/1197312142_326263.html; accessed February 2010.

USINA. http://www.usina-ctah.org.br/; accessed February 2010.

Vargas, Nilton. "Organização do trabalho e capital: um estudo da construção habitacional." Master's thesis, COPPE-UFRJ, 1979.

Venturi, Robert, Denise Scott Brown, and Steven Izenour. *Aprendiendo de Las Vegas.* Madrid: Gustavo Gili, 1998.

Vizoso, Sonia. "El alcalde de Ortigueira explota la cantera ilegal que surte a la Cidade da Cultura." *El País,* August 16, 2007, https://elpais.com/diario/2007/08/16/galicia/1187259490_850215.html.

―――. "La Xunta levanta la Cidade da Cultura con cuarcita de una cantera ilegal." *El País,* August 15, 2007, https://elpais.com/diario/2007/08/15/gali cia/1187173089_850215.html.

Wheatley, Catherine. "Buyout Track." *Sunday Times,* February 8, 2009.

Zukin, Sharon. *The Cultures of Cities.* Cambridge: Blackwell, 1995.

―――. *Landscapes of Power: From Detroit to Disney World.* Berkeley: University of California Press, 1993.

―――. "Our World Trade Center." In Michael Sorkin and Sharon Zukin, eds., *After the World Trade Center: Rethinking New York City.* New York: Routledge, 2002.

Zulaika, Joseba. *Guggenheim Bilbao: crónica de una seducción.* Madrid: Nerea, 1997.

―――. "'Plotach' arquitectónico: Guggenheim Bilbao, el precio de um símbolo." *Arquitectura Viva,* no. 55 (July 1997).

FILMS

Copans, Richard. *Collection Architectures.* France, 2003, 5 vols.

Discovery Channel. *Build It Bigger: Mountain of Steel.* USA, 2007, 45 min.

Discovery Channel. *Construindo o Superestádio.* USA, 2005, 45 min.

Pollack, Sydney. *Sketches of Frank Gehry.* USA, 2005, 83 min.

Rouaud, Christian. *LIP—L'Imagination au pouvoir.* France, 2007, 118 min.

INDEX

Aaron, Peter, 100
abstractions, 12, 74, 84, 118, 121
Abu Dhabi, 26, 27, 190, 216, 217;
    green building in, 214
Abu Dhabi Energy Company, 217
Abu Dhabi International Airport,
    216
accumulation, 29, 79, 134, 185; cap-
    ital, 2, 15, 28, 84, 91, 121, 128,
    129, 130, 133, 208; flexible, 127,
    135; primitive, 131
Adorno, Theodor, 240n91
advertising, 2, 12–13, 65, 75;
    starchitecture, 14 (fig.)
Aegis Hyposurface, 54; photo of, 55
aesthetics, 10, 23, 58, 128, 129, 148,
    199, 211
Agbar tower, 53
Age of Access, The (Rifkin), 57
AIA. See American Institute of
    Architects
Alexander, Christopher, 222
All-China Federation of Trade
    Union, 186

Allen, Paul, 12
Allen, Woody, 13
Allianz Arena, 44, 180, 182,
    240n88; photo of, 45, 46
Alliez, Éric, 15
Alternative Method of Management
    (AMM), 165, 166
Alvorada Palace, 30
American Institute of Architects
    (AIA), 107, 163, 167, 202
Ando, Tadao, 34, 191, 202, 230
Andréadis, Ianna, 181
Apple, 41
Arab World Institute, 53
Arantes, Otília, 23, 33, 69, 75, 114
Arantes, Paulo, 138
Arantes, Pedro Fiori, ix, xi, 23
Aravena, Alejandro, 206, 223, 230,
    231, 264n39, 265n42; collabora-
    tive practice and, 218; designs of,
    265n44; rise of, 227; social
    dimension and, 207
Arc de Triomphe, 71
ArchiCAD, 107

architect-programmers, 108, 110
architects: barefoot, 211; as conductors, 117; as coolhunters, 41; high-tech, 39, 216–17; influential, 201, 233; labor power of, 99
Architecttours, 65
Architectural Design, 103
architectural firms, 40, 65, 81, 90, 93, 98, 195, 245n19; digital platforms of, 105, 108; sterilization of, 92
Architectural Record, 219; designs published in, 220 (table); location of works/projects published in, 221 (table)
architecture: as art form, 202, 204; Brazilian, 6, 30; commercial, 10, 48; corporate real estate, 108; dematerialization of, 55; English, 201–2; green, 211; iconic, 62, 75–76, 78, 224; industrial production of, 128, 129; operative mode of, 119; random structures of, 197; social dimensions of, 29; spectacular, 30, 78, 81; terminal stage in, 4; unfeasable work of, 80–83; visual dramatization and, 11
Architecture and Digital Fabrication, 145
architecture magazines, 10, 13, 219
Ardanza, José Antonio, 242n129
Argan, Giulio Carlo, 84, 108, 248n75
Armani, 34
Arquitectura Viva, 219; designs published in, 220 (table); location of works/projects published in, 221 (table)

Arquitetura na era digital-financeira: desenho, canteiro e renda da forma (Arantes), ix
Arquitetura Nova, x
art, 60, 113, 116; commodification of, 27–28
Artefactory, 15
Artigas, João Batista Vilanova, x
artisan-architects, 165
artists, 224; as sculptor of the virtual, 115
Arup Associates, 106
Associated General Contractors of America (AGC), 183
Asymptote, 27
Audi, 13
Augé, Marc, 62, 241n115
aura, tourism of, 55, 57–71
AutoCAD, 93, 100
Autodesk, 93, 100, 107, 246n48
automation, 83, 99, 127, 136, 140, 173; digital, 152; of form, 113–19
automotive industry, 33, 36, 133, 139
Avatar (Cameron), 103

Baan, Iwan, 10; photo by, 187, 188
Ball, Michael, 129, 130, 131, 132, 163; AMM and, 165; skill crisis and, 169
balloon effect, 46, 68, 208
Ban, Shigeru, 27, 206, 231
banking, 20, 99, 203
Baravelli, José, 245n28
Barcelona, 19, 53, 101, 102
Barra da Tijuca, 70, 71
Baudrillard, Jean, 60, 72
Bauman, Zygmunt, 43
Bearth, Valentin, 146

Beatriz Plaza, 64, 243n136
Beaubourg Effect, 24, 61
Beck, Ulrich, 138
Beekman Tower, 170, 197, 211;
    photo of, 172
Beijing, 30, 44, 62, 184, 185, 186
Beijing National Aquatics Center,
    44
Beijing National Stadium, 54, 180
Beijing Olympics, 44, 53, 186
Belaúnde, Fernando, 222
Benetton, 239n72
Benjamin, Walter, 58, 72, 249n80
Bentley, 107
Berlin, 34, 52, 71, 156
Berlin Wall, 80
Big Ben, 60
Bilbao, 20–21, 24, 62, 125, 153,
    173, 250; attractions in, 70;
    finances of, 21
Bilbao Effect, 16–17, 19–21, 23–28,
    61
Bilbao Metrópoli 30, 19
Bilbao Ría-2000, 20
BIM. See Building Information
    Modeling
Binet, Hélène, 10
Biological Research Center, 118
Bird's Nest, 30, 54, 180; photo of,
    187
Blade Runner, 255
blueprints, 86, 88, 90, 94
Blur Building, 54
BMW, 34, 36, 193
BMW Welt and Museum, 34; photo
    of, 36
Bofill, 48
Bonwetsch, Tobias, 145
Borja, Jordi, 20
Bosch, Gerhard, 254n31

Bourdieu, Pierre, 193
brand architecture, 19, 28–34,
    36–41, 57, 79, 148, 150, 216
Brandenburg Gate, 71
brands, 49, 59, 73, 203, 211;
    identity of, 37, 38; logic of, 17;
    transcendental value of, 193; valu-
    ation of, 193
Brave New World of Work, 138
Brazilian Communist Party (PCB),
    252n8
bricklaying, 140, 142, 143, 150,
    184
British Museum, 156, 190
BRONCO, 255n54
Brooklyn Bridge, 26, 170
Brunelleschi, Filippo, 3, 58, 83, 84,
    110, 167
Bryant, Richard, 10
budgets, 11; economical/balanced,
    204
builders, 151; anonymous, 211;
    designers and, 108
Building Department, 182
Building Information Modeling
    (BIM), 106–7, 108, 110, 112,
    153, 154, 160, 164, 248n68,
    248n73
building process, 152, 163, 164
buildings: architecture and, 90, 128;
    conventional, 180; corporate, 110;
    cultural, 63, 69; erecting, 120,
    170–71; glass, 42–43; green, 214;
    industrial, 28, 129; monumental,
    60, 69, 71; postmodern, 13;
    prefabricated, 152; sports, 63;
    university, 180
Build It Bigger (Forster), 176
Bulard, Martine, 209
Burj Dubai, 210

Cache, Bernard, 99
CAD. *See* computer-assisted design
CAD-monkeys, 99, 110
Café Condé, 156
Calatrava, Santiago, 20, 62
Caldeira, Marta, xi
Cameron, James, 103
Campinos-Dubernet, Myriam, 133, 136
Campo, Antonio, 196
Camps of Pioneers, 232
Cantalejo, Javier, 152–53
capital, 16, 17, 122, 124, 127; command of, 84; concentration of, 209; construction industry and, 136; cultural bait for, 24–25; economic, 76; fictitious, 32, 64, 73, 209; finance, 73, 121; fixed, 98, 111, 129, 153; flows, 23, 191; immobilization of, 131; interest-bearing, 73, 76; labor and, 73, 137, 169, 185; overaccumulated, 208; surplus, 194, 200, 209; symbolic, xi, 31, 65, 67, 122, 193; tourism and, 68; variable, 98
Capital (Marx), 137, 235n2
capitalism, 16, 25, 48, 110, 121, 131, 190, 233; advanced, 72, 80–83; complexity and, 122; global, 80, 181; green, 212; periphery of, 124; post-Fordist, 136; production/domination and, 84; sustainability and, 213; technological innovation in, 151
carbon credits, 212
Carroll, Lewis, 133
Carvalho, Jorge, 177, 261n157
Casa da Música, 52–53, 177, 181, 182, 195, 243n142, 255n50; construction of, 179 (fig.)

Castel, Robert, 254n30
Castro, Fidel, 222
CATIA. *See* Computer Aided Three-Dimensional Interactive Application
CCTV Tower, 180, 186; photo of, 187, 188
Center for Integrated Facility Engineering (Stanford University), 106
Central Library, 66, 67
Centre Georges Pompidou, 24
ceramics, 42, 143–44, 145, 146, 232
Cerrutti, 13
Chantier ouvert au public (Andréadis), 181
chaos theory, 120, 253n27
Château de Vincy, 202
Chesa Futura (Home of the Future), 173; photo of, 174, 175
Chesnais, François, 137
Church of the Year 2000, 118
CIAM, 221
Cidade das Artes, 195
"cities for sale" strategies, 2, 19
City of Culture, 64, 118, 176, 195, 196; photo of, 177
City of Music, 70, 71
class struggle, 48, 131
"clean-tech" city, 217–18
CNCs. *See* computer numerical control machines
co-branding, 21, 36–37
commodities, 194, 198; cultural, 32, 238n51; enchantment of, 73; manufactured, 135; mobile, 135; monopoly rent by, 32
commodity-house, 229
Communist Party, 186
competition, 31, 60, 64, 106, 238n57

complex forms, 42, 128; ideology/ economics of, 119–25

complexity, 120, 125, 135, 175, 216; capitalism and, 122; environmental, 225; fetishized, 122, 123; legal, 225; theory, 92

components, 148, 162; serialized, 153; standardization of, 129

Computer Aided Three-Dimensional Interactive Application (CATIA), 100, 102, 104, 153, 156, 162, 180, 256n72; BIM of, 112; commercial version of, 101

computer-assisted design (CAD), 85, 94, 99–100, 103, 108, 154; conventional, 92–93, 105; drawing, 97, 99; introduction of, 98; representation, 106

computer numerical control machines (CNCs), 101, 154, 155, 156, 169, 170; using, 171, 173, 180

computers, 44, 81, 91, 114, 121; designing on, 75, 96; performance of, 101

Consello de Contas, 196

construction, 15, 36, 104, 110, 111, 120, 128, 194, 198, 213; civil, 82, 138, 217, 252n12; complexity of, 163; development of, 170; military, 82; modernization of, 129; political economy of, 131; process of, 128, 167; supervision of, 163; surplus value of, 131

construction companies, 77, 101, 103, 105, 165, 168, 194, 197; financial imbalances and, 195; health insurance and, 183; safety and, 182

construction costs, 66, 194, 196

construction industry, 42, 81, 132, 133, 164, 169, 181, 182; BIM and, 106–7; capital and, 136; exploitation by, 184, 185, 191, 193; health-care reform and, 183; migrant labor and, 183, 189; restructuring of, 135; technology and, 152

construction processes, 106, 107, 150, 176, 195, 197; mimicking, 148

construction site-form, currentness of, 128–39

construction sites, 27, 74, 83, 104, 122, 127, 141, 144, 151, 156, 160, 162, 163, 165, 194; analysis of, 185; archaic, 128, 130; automated, 175; design and, 168; digital automation of, 152; displacement of, 138; drawing and, 167; experimentation at, 134; freedom of motion at, 147; hard production at, 138; hybrid, 168–71, 173, 175–78; production/ domination on, 139; productive rationality of, 130; reproduction at, 150; underdevelopment on, 131; working conditions at, 178, 185

"Construction-Site Type Work Process and Its Rationalization" (Coriat), 133

construction work, 12, 98, 129–30, 168, 196; deaths/accidents and, 182

construction workers, 71, 129; criticism of, 184; death of, 182; pay of, 169; photo of, 187, 188, 192

consumption, 16, 29, 33, 139, 199, 213; circulation and, 72; patterns of, 253n25
continuous flow, 152–56, 160, 162
Coop Himmelb(l)au, 34, 36, 249n87
Copan, 30
Coriat, Benjamin, 130, 133, 135, 140; construction site-form and, 134; variability regime and, 136
Corullon, Martin, 13, 203, 239n73, 245n30, 262n7
Couchot, Edmond, 115
Crabapple, Molly, 238n48
craftsmanship, 48, 147, 173
craftsmen, 90, 97, 98, 119, 151, 167, 171, 173, 178, 257n91; new economy and, 111; physical models and, 112
creation, 83, 118, 119; art/architecture and, 113
creativity, 25, 61, 67, 110
Credit Suisse, 217
cultural appropriation, politics of, 23
cultural entertainment, 4, 23, 24, 37
cultural heritage, 24, 106
culture, 60, 74, 204; autonomous realm of, 25; brand, 49; construction, 217; economy and, 25, 73; electronic, 114; entertainment, 110; high, 25, 205; Japanese, 139; marketing and, 25; material, 110; strange, 61
culture industry, x, 32, 58, 59, 76
cybernetics, 93, 113, 119, 121

Dance Hall, 205
Dancing House, 171
Dantas, Marcos, 150

da Silva Matos, Valdeci (Lelê), 140, 143, 144, 151, 256n62
data, 108; bidirectional, 115; design, 153; packets, 107; processing, 92, 104
David Rockefeller Center, 225
Davis, Mike, 26, 189, 190, 232; on eutopic logic, 80; on Gehry, 80–81; planet of slums and, xi
Debord, Guy, 15, 16, 72, 73–74
Deconstruction (Papadakis), 249n87
"Deconstructivist Architecture" (exhibition), 249n87
Deleuze, Gilles, 116
Delungan and Meissl (architects), 36
de Meuron, Pierre, 205
de Moraes, Vinicius: poem by, 148, 150
de Moura, Eduardo Souto, 231
Department of Architecture, 49, 145
Department of Culture, 20
Department of Economics (University of Chicago), 41
Department of Political and Social Order (DOPS), 70
Deplazes, Andreas, 146, 255n50
de Riscal, Marqués, 193
Derrida, Jacques, 114, 249n87
design, 15, 17, 90–91, 104, 156; act of, 117–18; artisanal nature of, 91; building and, 165; construction sites and, 168; development of, 13, 170; digital, 21, 48, 79, 80, 96, 98, 103, 113, 127, 152, 153, 154, 164, 167; economics of, 99; execution and, 166; as ideation, 98; innovative, 218, 224; ornamental, 49, 52; production and, 112, 153, 166; self-referential meaning of, 245n23; separate, 84,

91; standardization of, 129; three-dimensional, 155
design/construction site (*dessin/ chantier*), 112
designer-builders, 167
designers, 105, 167, 245n19; builders and, 108
de Soto, Hernando, 229
Dessault Systèmes, 100, 101, 112
Dessin/Chantier Laboratory, 129, 246n33, 249n80
development, 13, 63, 111, 170, 201; capitalist, 130; economic, 67; real-estate, 24, 77, 78, 80, 91, 129, 131, 197; software, 97; sustainable, 212; technological, 151; urban, 20, 214
Development Center for Urban and Community Equipment (CEDEC), 256n62
d-fab-arch, 145, 146, 148
DG Bank, 156, 173, 193
Diesel brand, 239n72
Dieux, Hervé, 183
Digbeth district, urban renewal in, 47
digital age, 3, 17, 32, 49, 78, 110, 164
digital master builders, 82, 162–68, 249n79
Digital Materiality in Architecture, 145
digital platforms, boosting, 105
Digital Project, 112, 154
digital rehabilitation, 49, 52
digital tools, 107, 119, 151, 166
Diller & Scofidio, 54
Dippe, Mark, 103, 247n58
Disney Concert Hall, 80, 105, 112, 155
Disney Imagineering, 106

Division of Construction Inspections, 182
Domeisen, Oliver, 49
Downtown Seattle Association, 67
draftsmen, 86, 87, 92, 93–94, 97, 151
drawing: algorithmic, 114; artisanal execution of, 91; CAD, 97, 99; cleaning, 93–94; computers and, 91; construction, 81, 167; digital, 85, 93; drafting, 107; freehand, 89; orthogonal, 89; pencil, 88; scale change in, 89; 3-D, 89; 2-D, 248n73
drawing boards, digital, 91–100
drawing site, 83–91
Dreiner, Dominik, 52
Drupsteen, Jaap, 52
Dubai, 68, 191, 203; photo of, 192
Dubai Opera, 53
Dubai World, 68
Dutch embassy (Berlin), 52

Eberswalde Library, 52
Eco, Umberto, 247n58
Economic Commission for Latin America and the Caribbean (CEPAL), 252n8
economic crisis (2008), 27, 41, 65, 183, 200, 202, 206, 210, 211, 217–18, 224, 226, 230, 233; effects of, 203; economic gains, 57, 67, 121, 194
economic impact, 17, 65, 66, 110
Economics Department (University of Chicago), 190
economy, 81, 166; culture and, 25, 73; digital-financial, 29, 208; knowledge, 61, 76; luxury, 128; symbolic, 200

education, 27, 71, 209, 225, 232
Eiffel Tower, 60, 71
Eisenman, Peter, 64, 83, 112, 116, 117, 122, 127, 168, 180, 197, 249n87; on Bilbao, 113; bioinformatics and, 250n100; on creation, 118; cultural center of, 242n125; deconstructionists and, 114; digital manipulation and, 250n107; methodology of, 140; signature/authorship and, 119; work of, 176, 177, 196
Elemental Company, social frontier and, 218–19, 221–33
EMP. See Experience Music Project
Employee Assistance Program, 241n111
Engels, Friedrich, 184
engineering, 65, 74, 104, 107, 141, 164
entertainment industry, 29, 34, 57, 82
entrepreneurship, 19, 25, 76, 229, 260n147; trade unions and, 231
environmental issues, 36, 39, 101, 106, 212, 219
Erundina, Luiza, 256n62
Esher, Lord, 163
Espacio de las Artes, 52
ETA, 19, 63, 68
Euclidean geometry, 1, 91, 93, 103, 118
Ewall, Robert, 10
excess, times of, 208–11
Existenzminimum, 221
experience, 33, 44, 58, 73; authentic/memorable, 57; cultural, 37, 59, 62; social, 11, 62, 205
Experience Music Project (EMP), 111 (fig.), 155, 173

exploitation, labor, 27, 73, 137, 184, 185, 191, 193, 260n147
Expo, 214

facades, 33, 34, 36, 41, 42, 47, 52, 145, 146, 156, 170, 173, 223; fake, 48
factories, 127, 134, 162; Ford, 128, 129, 130
Faculty of Architecture and Urbanism, x
Faggin, Caio, 201, 239n63, 239n73, 239n75, 239n76
Farah, Marta, 254n32
Fathy, Hassan, 140, 141
favelas, 71, 207, 224, 225, 228
Federation of Housing Cooperatives for Mutual Assistance (FUCVAM), 231, 232
Fehn, Sverre, 205
Ferguson, Francesca, 49
Fernández-Galiano, Luis, 7
Ferro, Sérgio, 12, 48, 84, 86, 130, 132, 140, 151, 167, 185, 198, 245n23, 249n80, 251n115, 252n10, 261n171; Arantes and, x; concentrated labor and, 251n1; on construction sites, 141; on design, 85; fetish and, 74; interpretation by, 131; on masonry, 148; separate design and, 83
fetish, rent/interest and, 72–78
FGV School of Economics, 263n15
Filgueiras Lima, Joaquim (Lelê), 151, 256n62
financial dominance, 3, 137, 208, 238n57
financial economy, 25, 69, 74
financialization, 72, 218
Fink, Michael, 181

Finotti, Leonardo, 6–7, 235n4
"Fish" (sculpture), 101
Fleming, Ulrich, 98
Fontenelle, Isleide, 32
Fordism, 42, 127, 128, 129, 130,
133, 134, 135, 139, 153; legacy
of, 160; rigidities of, 253n25
form, 2, 3, 23, 77, 191; automation
of, 113–19; complex, 92, 123,
180; difficult, 193–200; exclusivity effect of, 122; fluidization of,
122; generation of, 112–13;
manipulation of, 116, 250n107;
organic, 46, 147; symbolic wealth
of, 24–25
formalism, 13, 24, 69, 75, 84, 113,
250n107
Forster, Danny, 176
Forster, Kurt, 63–64
Foster, Hal, 21, 72
Foster, John Bellamy, 212
Foster, Norman, 13, 20, 38, 40, 62,
78, 156, 173, 190, 207, 216, 217,
230, 264n36; biography of, 201,
202; green building and, 214;
high tech and, 239n75; HSBC
building and, 124; medals for,
203; projects by, 39; visualization
team and, 236n16
Foster + Partners, 13, 40, 156, 175,
239n63, 245n30, 262n7; brand
of, 41, 203; global crisis and, 202;
local techniques and, 217; Pritzker
Prize and, 41; project of, 214
(fig.); studio of, 95 (fig.)
Fourier, Charles, 221
Fraken, Bernhard, 246n36
Frankenstein, Dr., 145
French Communist Party, 132, 133
French Museums Agency, 191

Friedman, Mildred, 249n82
Friedman, Thomas, 214
Fuão, Fernando, 7, 9, 63
Fujimori, Alberto, 229
Fuksas, Massimiliano, 27, 62
Fuller, Richard Buckminster, 119,
250n107
funds, public/private, 76, 225, 227
Furtado, Celso, 130
Future Systems Group, 46

Gadanho, Pedro, 224
GA Document, 219; designs published in, 220 (table); location of
works/projects published in, 221
(table)
Galeries Lafayette, 34
Galicia City of Culture, 63–64
Galofaro, Luca, 250n104
Gama, Ruy, 145
Gann, David, 166
Gates, Bill, 12
Gehry, Frank, 22, 27, 33, 62, 74, 75,
78, 98, 100, 103, 105, 106, 154,
156, 162, 164–65, 168, 169, 172,
176, 190, 191, 196, 203; adjustment by, 249n82; advertising for,
14 (fig.); BIM and, 107; budgets
by, 197; CATIA and, 101; construction sites of, 127; deconstructionists and, 114; design by, 111
(fig.), 112, 247n57; digital design
and, 152, 211; on excess, 210;
formalism and, 113; Guggenheim
Museum Bilbao and, 17, 18, 21,
26, 63; medals for, 202; Music
Experience and, 12; Neuer Zollhoft and, 157, 158, 160; New
York by Gehry and, 170; prefabrication and, 155; promotional

building of, 24; sculptures by, 122; sketches by, 82 (fig.), 102 (fig.), 109 (fig.); skins and, 52; software and, 112; waste age and, 65; work of, 21, 23, 80–81, 81–82, 83, 104, 171, 173, 180

Gehry Partners, 82, 83; studio of, 96 (fig.)

Gehry Talks (Friedman), 249n82

Gehry Technologies, 83, 98, 112, 249n81

geometry, 112, 116, 118, 151; complex, 34, 101

Ghirardo, Diane, 80, 244n2

Gilbreth, Frank, 140, 142, 143

Giscard d'Estaing, Valéry, 124

Giuliani, Rudolph, 26

Glancey, Jonathan, 210

global crisis (2008), 27, 41, 65, 183, 200, 202, 206, 210, 211, 217–18, 224, 226, 230, 233; effects of, 203

globalization, 29, 137

Global North, 219, 222, 230

Global South, 181, 219, 221, 222, 227, 232; BIM operators for, 108; housing conditions in, 224; legal/environmental/social complexity in, 225; neoliberal policies for, 223; urbanization in, 230

Gluckman, Richard, 27

Glymph, Jim, 101, 165, 166, 169; on Czech labor rates, 171, 173

Goldberg, Jeff, 10

Goldberger, Paul, 39

Golden Lion, 5, 231

Gómez, María, 64

Gorz, André, 116, 121, 136

Goulthorpe, Mark, 54

Gramazio, Fabio, 145, 146

Gran Misión Vivienda (Great Housing Mission), 232

graphics, 15, 53, 86, 88, 93, 94

Graphisoft, 107

Graz Music Theater, 52

Great Art, architecture as, 204, 205

Greater London Authority, 39

Great Projects, 24, 61, 69

green frontier, 211–14, 216–18

Gregotti, Vittorio, 27

Grenoble School of Architecture, 112, 246n33, 249n80

Grespan, Jorge, 195

Grundrisse (Marx), 195

Guardian, 210

Guerra, Fernando, 5, 10

Guevarra, Che, 222

Guggenheim Foundation, Gehry and, 26

Guggenheim Museum Abu Dhabi, 27, 64, 190, 238n48

Guggenheim Museum Bilbao, 17, 19, 20, 21, 70, 105, 124–25, 195; change and, 113; construction of, 152, 155, 156, 157 (fig.), 165, 168; digital model of, 109 (fig.); ideology of place and, 23; images of, 12–13; inauguration of, 101; model of, 33; as money machine, 63; opening of, 26; photo of, 18, 22; resources for, 242n125; success of, 24, 64, 101

Guggenheim Museum New York, 21, 26, 36, 64

Guggenheim Museum SoHo, 26, 27

Gursky, Andreas, 10

Hadid, Zaha, 27, 34, 62, 190, 204, 249n87

Halbe, Roland, 10

half-house, 223, 233
Hall, Peter, 24, 64
Hal 9000, 164
Harribey, Jean-Marie, 212
Harvard Graduate School of Design, 226, 227
Harvey, David, 23, 137, 198, 235n2
Haug, Wolfgang Fritz, 43
health, 36, 71, 136, 209
health care, 183, 185, 189
Hegel, Friedrich, 167
Hermès, Piano and, 33
Herzog, Jacques, 29–30, 44, 78, 182, 205; on construction site organization, 178; labor abuse and, 186; materiality of architecture and, 42
Herzog & de Meuron, 44, 45, 46, 70, 75, 180, 186, 228, 231; ornamentation by, 52, 53; Prada and, 33–34
Holl, Steven, 213
Hollein, Hans, 27
House of Lords, 202
housing, 71; building, 199; collective, 219; complexes, 221; evolutionary, 206; higher-density, 227; improving, 224, 230; market, 77; policy, 209, 223, 227; production of, 232, 233; projects, 221, 223, 229; proletarian, 129; provision of, 163, 221, 223, 229; public, 4; social, 69, 218, 219, 222, 229, 264n39
housing bubble, 183, 224
housing rights, 228–29
"How to Make a Frank Gehry Building" (Marshall), 178
HSBC building, 39, 124

human rights, 190, 229
Human Rights Watch (HRW), 191, 260n142; construction sites and, 185, 186; migrant labor and, 185, 186, 189, 190
Huxtable, Ada Louise, 203
hyperreality, 12, 103, 108, 247n58

Iacobelli, Andrés, 226
Iberê Camargo Foundation, 8
Iberê Camargo Museum, 4
Ibirapuera Park, 30
IBM, 101, 112
iconic works, 62, 64, 75–76, 78, 110, 211, 224
identity: brand, 37, 38; civic, 80; corporate, 30; urban, 81; visual, 30
ideology, 3, 225; Brazilian, 206; dominant, 212; luxury, 199; sphere of, 31
images, 9, 31, 60, 120–21; advertising, 75; architectural, 6, 13, 16; autonomous, 15, 72; brand, 32; building, 39–40; circulation of, 57, 59; dissemination of, 13, 16, 17; global hunters of, 7; high-quality, 6; photogenic, 12, 59; profitable, 119; promotion of, 20; reality and, 16; social relationships and, 16; spectacular, 9, 38; tourist, 59
IMF, 223, 229
incremental house, 218, 227, 228
industrial capital, 1, 28, 29, 252n6
industrialization, 139, 152, 223, 227; Fordist, 128; peripheral, 130
industry, 29, 74, 84, 128, 133
info-proletarians, 99, 111

information, 14, 16, 97, 107, 108, 117; accuracy of, 92; concentration of, 110, 164; control of, 167; flow of, 139, 153; mobilizing, 113; parametric, 154; sequence of, 124; three-dimensional, 105–6
innovation, 110, 153, 166, 178; agents, 82; architectural, 164; technological, 108, 122, 151, 166
Institut de Recherche et Coordination Acoustique/Musique (IRCAM), 180–81
Institute of Sound and Vision, 52
Institution of Civil Engineers (ICE), 258n124
intellectual work, 84, 108, 167
Inter-American Development Bank (IDB), 225
interest, 91, 189; rent/fetish and, 72–78
International Arts Center, 197
International Olympic Committee, labor abuse and, 186
International Renewable Energy Agency (IRENA), 217
International Union of Architects, 222
investments, 19, 41, 62, 65, 69, 78; private, 20; public, 20, 67
investors, 2, 65, 68, 77
Isosaki, Arata, 26
Itamaraty Palace, 30
Ito, Toyo, 54, 56, 206

Jahn, Helmut, 62
Jameson, Fredric, 13, 43, 74, 208
Jencks, Charles, 43, 249n87
Jerez de La Frontera, 53
Johnson, Philip, 249n87
Joncas, Kate, 67

Kieran, Stephen, 167
Klein, Naomi, 31, 32, 212
knowledge, 25, 61, 76, 99; constructive, 217; craft, 206; externalization of, 83–84; partial, 110; popular, 222; valorization of, 216–17
Kohler, Matthias, 145, 146
Kolarevic, Branko, 153, 162, 164, 166, 249n79
Kon, Nelson, 5, 6, 7, 9, 10–11, 235n1
Koolhaas, Rem, 13, 26, 27, 62, 66, 75, 78, 177, 180, 186, 207; on architecture/shopping, 37; Casa de Música and, 243n142; on Dubai, 191; marketing by, 199–200; medals for, 202; ornamental effects by, 52; Prada and, 36–37, 199; work of, 49, 52
Krens, Thomas, 21, 26, 27, 33
Krier, Léon, 47
Kubrick, Stanley, 164
Kyoto Protocol, 213

labor, 99, 133, 136, 151, 194, 200, 212; abstract, 101; accumulated, 199; capital and, 73, 137, 169, 185; collective, 84, 85, 123, 124, 125, 131, 135; concentrated, 198; costs, 181; division of, 84, 85, 90, 131; forced, 190; intellectual, 90, 167; living, 191, 208; manual, 90, 111, 152, 167, 183; migrant, 3, 183–84, 185, 189–90; production and, 76; skilled, 140, 148, 150, 170; slave, 210, 255n52; socially necessary, 32, 194, 208; unproductive, 132, 238n52; volume of, 198; wage, 29

labor camps, 27, 189–90
labor market, 132–33, 171, 182,
    183, 253n25; construction, 181;
    dualization of, 138
labor value, 68, 194, 208
La Défense, 24
land: appreciation, 78; price of, 77;
    real-estate development and, 131;
    urbanized, 132; value of, 76
landowners, 129, 132, 184
landscapes, 9, 58, 61, 85, 211, 223
language, 120; algorithmic, 114,
    115; architectural, 49; post-
    modern fragmentation of, 97;
    universal, 116
La Salve Bridge, 155, 176; photo of,
    18
Latin America Memorial Park, 30
La Tourette, 129, 178
Leal, Carlos, 260n147
Learning from Las Vegas, 48
Le Corbusier, 128, 129, 130, 178
Leewood Real Estate Group, 181
Lefebvre, Henri, ix
Leibniz, 116
Lelê, 140, 143, 144, 151, 256n62
Le Monde diplomatique, 183
Lenin, Vladimir, 128
Lepik, Andres, 224
Lévy, Pierre, 57, 113, 115
Lewis, Peter, 26
Libeskind, Daniel, 27, 249n87
lighting, 9, 19, 43, 44, 46, 53, 54,
    147, 178
Linked-Hybrid project, 213
LIP factory, 123, 124
Lipovetsky, Gilles, 24, 38, 199, 200
Llewelyn-Davies, Lord, 163
Logo-Design, 44
logomuseum, 33

logotectures, 1
London, 37, 60, 202
Loos, Adolf, 47, 48, 49, 240n91
Lopes, João Marcos, 245n22
Louvre Abu Dhabi Museum, 53,
    190
Louvre Museum, 24, 238n48
Löwy, Michael, 212, 264n29
Luebkeman, Chris, 106, 164
Lynn, Greg, 114

machines, 98, 131, 139; program-
    mable, 154, 166, 170; screening,
    162; stereolithography, 96. See also
    computer numerical control
    machines
machinofacture, 173
Maison Hermès, photo of, 35
Malagamba, Duccio, 5, 10
management, 62, 139, 166; brand,
    32, 37, 216; business, 111; con-
    struction, 2, 135, 165; produc-
    tion, 138, 165; risk, 136, 168–69
manufacturing, 95, 131, 133, 134,
    135, 164, 165; digital, 145, 148
Marias district, revitalization of, 24
Maritime Museum, 191
marketing, 10, 23, 31, 60, 216, 218;
    city, 19; culture and, 25
Marshall, Alex, 178
Marx, Karl, 1, 123, 131, 137, 190,
    195, 235n2; hoarding and,
    261n171; unproductive labor and,
    238n52
Marxism, 152, 212, 252n6
Masdar City, 217, 218, 264n33;
    design for, 214; location of, 216;
    photo of, 214, 215
Masdar Institute of Science and
    Technology, opening of, 217

Masdar Program, 211–14, 216–18
masons, 140, 141, 148, 151, 180,
    228
Massachusetts Institute of Technol-
    ogy (MIT), 100, 171, 217,
    245n24
materiality, 19, 42, 68, 97
materials, 106, 129, 171; gathering,
    141–42; raw, 153, 252n6
Mathesis Universalis, 116
McCormick Campus Center, 52
McDonaldization, 27, 28
mechanical systems, optimization of,
    106
medals, distribution of, 201–7
media, 13, 219; architecture, 6, 196;
    aura of, 59; coverage by, 67; social,
    16; surfaces, 55
Meethan, Kevin, 61, 62
Meier, Richard, 202
Memorial da Resistência, 70
Mendes da Rocha, Paulo, 205, 206,
    231
Mercedes-Benz, 34; museum for, 36
Merrill Lynch, 21
Mészáros, István, 122, 123
METRO, 262n7
Michelangelo, 58
Microsoft, 12
Midas, 74
Mies van der Rohe, Ludwig, 42,
    202, 210
migrations, violations and, 178,
    180–86, 189–91, 193
Mikimoto, 33
Mingongs, 186
Ministry of Defense, data from,
    259n129
Ministry of Health, 256n62
Mitchell, William, 97

models, 107, 110, 171; business
    management, 111; complex, 103,
    106; design, 127, 139; digital,
    121, 153, 165, 167, 178; ele-
    mental, 228; generic, 247n49;
    handling, 120; handmade, 103;
    multidimensional, 154; open-
    platform, 228; physical, 95, 112;
    production of, 96; 3-D, 101, 104,
    106, 248n73; volumetric, 116–17;
    wooden, 89–90
modern architecture, 9, 17, 28, 29,
    128, 199, 226; glass in, 42; ratio-
    nalism of, 240n91; simplistic/
    authoritarian, 120
modernism, 23, 25, 74, 83; light/
    liquid, 43; postmodernity and, 72
Moët Hennessy Louis Vuitton SE
    (LVMH), 34
MoMA. See Museum of Modern Art
Moneo, Rafael, 20, 202
money, 210; spectacle of, 73–74
Monge, Gaspard, 83
monopoly, 3, 16, 27, 31, 65, 77,
    243n154, 252n12; rent, 21, 29,
    32, 58, 64, 76, 99, 122, 132, 208,
    238n51
Montes, Javier, 260n145
monuments, 62, 69, 71, 81
Moore, Jacob, xi
Moreira, Renata, 245n22, 245n28
morphogenesis, 83, 92, 116, 117,
    119
Morris, William, 48
motor memory, 108, 151
Movimiento de Ocupantes y Inquili-
    nos (Occupiers and Tenants
    Movement), 232
Munich, 44, 46, 182; photo of, 36,
    45

Murphy, Kevin, 41
Museum of Fine Arts, 70
Museum of Modern Art (MoMA), 223–24, 249n87
Museum of the Portuguese Language, 70
museums, 23, 25, 61, 70, 210, 223–24
Music Experience, 12

National Building Information Modeling Standard, 107
National Congress, 30
Nationale Nederlanden, 101
National Housing Law, 231
National Institute of Building Sciences, 107
nature, 115; society and, 217; work and, 212
Nenê, 143
Neolabor Consulting Company, 253n27
neoliberalism, 19, 124, 190, 209, 218, 223, 229
Nervion River, 20, 70; photo of, 18
Neuer Zollhoft Tower, 156; construction of, 160 (fig.), 161 (fig.); prefabrication for, 158 (fig.), 159 (fig.)
Neutelings and Riedijk (architects), 52
New York by Gehry, 170; photo of, 172
New York City, 37, 60, 147
New York Times, 178, 210
Niemeyer, Oscar, 30, 31
Nike, 38
Nishizawa, Ryūe, 204
Non-Uniform Rational Basis Splines (NURBS), 104

Norten, Enrique, 27
Nouvel, Jean, 27, 34, 62, 181, 190, 191, 207
Novais, Fernando, 236n20
"Nova Luz" (New Light), 70

O canteiro e o desenho (Jameson), 74, 130
Occupy Movement, 231
"O concreto como arma" (Ferro), 148
Odyssey, 164
Office of Metropolitan Architecture (OMA), 177, 179, 187, 188
Olympic Village, 101
"O operário em construção" (de Moraes), 150
Opera House, 60, 70, 197
Order of Architects, 177
organization, 163, 254n30; industrial, 137; multilateral, 223; post-Fordist, 139; productive, 132
original, 58; copy and, 57
"Ornament and Crime" (Adolf Loos), 47
ornaments, 49, 52, 53; digital, 19, 47, 55
Oseki, Jorge, 132, 263n26
otherness, 115, 150
Otto, Frei, 206
Ouroussoff, Nicolai, 210
outsourcing, 136, 138, 254n31
Ove Arup Associates, 164
Owen, Robert, 221

Palace of the Congress, 70
Palma, Cristobal, 10
Pampulha Park, 30
Papadakis, Andreas, 249n87
Paracelsus, 145

Paris, 53, 60, 71
Parliamentary Commission of
    Inquiry, 195
Pei, I. M., 20, 202
Pelli, Cesar, 20
performance, 170, 213; certification,
    107; computer, 101; high, 171;
    professional, 218
Performing Arts Center, 190
Permasteelisa, 101
Perrella, Stephen, 247n58
Persian Gulf, 26
PERT, 160
Petrella, Guilherme, 245n28
Philips, Peter, 254n31
photographers, 6, 7, 16; architec-
    tural, 11; as cool hunters, 10
photography, xi, 7; architectural, 9,
    63, 236n12; color, 9, 10; reduc-
    tion and, 11–12; twilight, 9
physics, 117, 119, 171
Piaget, Charles, 251n120
Piano, Renzo, 62, 180, 202, 231;
    Hermès and, 33
Pinacoteca do Estado museum, 70
Pittman, Jon, 107
Planalto Palace, 30
"Planet of Slums," xi, 206, 232, 233
planning, 25; city, 17; environmen-
    tal, 211, 216; strategic, 19, 20, 77;
    urban, 24, 76, 163
political economy, 55, 76, 131
Pollack, Sydney, 244n4
pollution permits, 213
Pontes, Ana Paula, 71
Pop movement, 48
Popular Party (PP), 196
Porsche, 34, 36
Porto, 52, 177, 181, 195, 243n142,
    255n50; photo of, 179

Porto Alegre, 6
Porto City Court of Auditors,
    243n142
Portoghesi, Paolo, 47
Portuguese revolution (1974), 124
Portzamparc, Christian de, 34, 62,
    70, 71, 195, 197
postindustrialism, x, 138
postmodernism, 3, 47, 48, 72, 74,
    247n58
poststructuralism, 114
poverty, 224, 231, 233
power: economic, 190; labor, 148;
    political, 190; social, 200; sym-
    bolic, 17, 62; technology of, 124
Prada, 26, 33–34, 36–37, 199
prefabrication, 129, 139, 152, 153,
    162, 175, 178, 194, 213; CNC,
    170; Fordist, 140; nonstandard-
    ized, 155; partial, 128; photo of,
    158, 159; state-of-the-art, 173
PREVI, 222, 231
printers, 3-D, 90, 96
Pritzker Prize, 30, 41, 65, 70, 201,
    202, 204, 211, 218, 219, 223,
    225, 226, 227, 230, 233; award-
    ing, 203, 205, 206
privatization, 16, 205, 229
production, 10, 19, 48, 74, 76–77,
    132, 137, 168, 169, 182, 195;
    architectural, 2, 11, 16, 81, 104,
    124, 151, 162; commodity, 15,
    73, 229, 243n154; decentraliza-
    tion of, 136; design and, 112,
    153, 166; economic, 181; existing
    relations of, 93; exporting, 138;
    factory-based mode of, 130–31;
    hegemonic method of, 128; indus-
    trial, 129, 153; labor and, 76;
    large-scale, 170; lean, 135; mass,

17, 29, 90, 199; means of, 152, 252n6; naturalization of, 229–30; post-Fordist, 79; process of, 98, 167, 171; relations of, 93, 132; restructuring, 123; schedules, 198; self-managing, 232; stages of, 128–29; techniques/methods of, 84, 131; transformations in, 127, 152
profitability, 24, 32, 64, 91, 122, 137, 251n114
Program Evaluation and Review Technique (PERT), 256n71
programs, 46, 110, 115, 118; CAD, 100; computer, 49, 120
Projecto, 6
Prometheus, 74
property, 233; autonomization of, 73; value of, 69
property rights, 229
Pro-Viaggi Architettura, 65
PTW, 44
public funds, 2, 17, 68, 205
public policy, 204, 211, 223, 225, 232, 244n155
public services, 185, 194, 229
publishing market, 7, 65, 76, 121
Pyramids, 199

Quai Branly Museum, 181
Quinta Monroy, 227, 228

Rabanne, Paco, 13
Rainbird, Helen, 134
rationalism, 28, 47, 84, 116, 240n91
rationality, 134; Cartesian, 119; economic, 166; productive, 130; social, 24
real-estate market, 77–78, 181, 193, 208, 210, 219, 226, 230; software in, 197

reality, 15; image and, 16; social, 121; virtual, 105, 111–16
Rebuilding Construction (Ball), 131
Rêgo, Paula, 206
relationships, 175; commercial, 136; producer–receiver, 58; space–time, 113, 118; subject–object, 113; symbiotic, 57; tautological, 16
Renaissance, 3, 83, 113, 164
Renault, 124
rent: art of, 198; boosting, 68, 79; capturing, 65; democratization of, 57; distribution-concentration of, 55, 69, 71; future, 67–68; green, 213; interest/fetish and, 72–78; knowledge, 99; land, 1, 77, 131, 235n2; magnets, 23; as Marxian idiom, xi; maximum, 59, 208; monopoly, 21, 29, 32, 58, 64, 76, 99, 122, 132, 208, 238n51; production of space and, 76; profit and, 32; social, 221, 229; value and, 19, 77
rentier economy, 61, 74, 185, 191
rentiers, 195, 208, 210; gains of, 27, 68, 91, 99
rent of art, 198
rent of form, xi, 3, 12, 15, 17, 75, 76, 78, 91, 122, 152, 162, 195, 200, 212, 213, 219; exchange value and, 16; gains through, 170; novelty and, 154; symbolic capital and, 31
Renzo Piano Building Workshop (RPBW), 35
Reporting from the Front, 230
representation, 2, 73, 85, 128; abstract, 74; consulate of, 91; conventional, 153; hypertrophy of, 16; techniques, 91; 3-D, 105; 2-D, 11

reproduction, 117; capital, 49, 92, 164; financial forms of, 16; symbolic forms of, 16

"Re-Sampling Ornament" (exhibition), 49

Research Institute, 217

Revit, 107

RIBA. *See* Royal Institute of British Architecture

Riboulet, Pierre, 138

Ricola box factory, 52

Rifkin, Jeremy, 57, 60, 61

Rio de Janeiro, 60, 70, 195, 197, 207; music palace in, 34

Rio de Janeiro City Court of Auditors, 243n142

Ritzer, George, 27

Rô, 142, 151

R-O-B, 49, 140, 145, 146, 147, 148, 152, 168, 170; photo of, 50, 149; wall by, 51 (fig.)

robot-mason, 127, 140–48, 150–52

robots, 49, 139, 145, 147, 148, 151, 166, 170, 173

ROCCO, 255n54

Rogers, Richard, 62, 207, 230

roofs, green, 213

Rouaud, Christian, 251n120

Royal Institute of British Architecture (RIBA), 163–64, 202

Saadiyat, migrant workers at, 190

safety, 106, 136, 182, 185

Sala São Paulo, 70

SANAA, 206, 231

Santiago de Compostela, 118, 176, 195; photo of, 177

São Paulo, 30, 70, 205, 206, 232, 256n62

São Paulo Architecture Biennial, 245n30

Sayad, João, 70, 205

Schlaich, Jorg, 156

School of Architecture (Hong Kong University), 245n30

sculpture, 75, 101, 113, 122, 175

Seagram Building, 42

Sejima, Kazuyo, 204

self-construction, 28, 143, 227

self-management, 123, 124, 125, 167

Selfridges shopping center, 46

Sennett, Richard, 96, 97, 98, 111

separatism, 19, 20, 23

serialization, 28, 29, 42, 139, 152, 153, 199

service, 19, 71, 137

Shanghai Airport, expansion of, 62–63

Sheikh Zayed Museum, 190

Shelden, Dennis, 106, 154, 169, 247n50, 247n61

Shelley, Mary, 145

shingles, 173; photo of, 174, 175

shipbuilding industry, 104, 156, 169, 173

shopping, cultural experience of, 37, 71

Shulman, Julius, 6, 9

Siedlungs, 221

Siemens, 217

Simple Minds, 13

Single Calculus, 116

Siza, Álvaro, 5, 6, 75, 202, 205, 207

Skidmore, Owings & Merrill (SOM), 112

skins, 19, 104, 105; tattooed, 42–44, 46–49, 52–55

"Small Scale, Big Change" (exhibition), 224
Smashing Pumpkins, 13
social architecture, 211, 226
social concerns, 79, 218, 219
social frontier, 218–19, 221–33
socialism, 23, 151
social policies, 68, 69, 223
social production, 78, 204, 231
social protection, 23, 37, 71, 124, 136
social reproduction, 123, 181, 185, 219
social security, 209, 229
social wealth, 61, 77, 209
social welfare, 124, 204, 229
Society of Jesus, 225
software, 3, 11, 82, 93, 101, 105, 110, 169, 198, 213; architecture, 92; CAD, 99–100; construction, 92; design, 85, 98, 112, 146; high-precision industry, 168; image-editing, 10; modeling, 145; real-estate, 197; using, 103, 108
SolidWorks, 100
Souto de Moura, Eduardo, 205
Souza Lima, Mayuma, 256n62
space: alloplastic, 54; autoplastic, 54; display, 33; information, 113; Leibnizian, 117; non-Cartesian concept of, 116; production of, 76, 204; public, 20, 204
spatiotemporal relations, 84, 114, 206
Specht, Jan, 59–60, 62, 65
spectacle, 74; term, 72
standardization, 25, 42, 107, 135, 139, 152, 153, 199
starchitects, 2, 29, 30, 33, 42, 105, 122, 162, 168, 210, 211, 214, 218, 258n124; stimulation by, 225; term, x; work of, 91, 127, 200
starchitecture, 17, 38, 55, 57, 152, 185, 197, 219, 226; in digital-financial age, 78, 79; global photographers of, 6; monuments of, 81; works of, 193
Stata Center, 171
steel flowers, 100–101, 103–8, 110–13
Steingard, Jordan, xi
Stirling, James, 20, 222
Strada Novissima, 47
strikes, 123, 124; prohibition of, 190
structures, 33, 85, 103, 105, 204, 228; complex, 120; conflicting, 216; miniaturization of, 250n107; mixed-use, 232
Study of American Architecture, xi
subcontractors, 125, 136, 139, 163, 165, 168
Sugar Loaf, 60
surfaces, 33; fluid, 42–44, 46–49
surplus value, 57, 123, 131, 185, 191, 198; allocation of, 29; distribution, 132; rent and, 77; social, 65, 122
sustainability, 213, 217
Swiss Federal Institute of Technology (ETH), 145
Swiss Pavilion, 147
Swiss RE Building, 13, 39; photo of, 40
Syben, Gerd, 134
symbolism, 24, 47, 53, 210

Tafuri, Manfredo, 84, 108, 120
Tate Modern, 30
Taylor, Frederick Winslow, 140, 142
Taylorism, 130, 133, 134, 135, 253n21

technological progress, 92, 152, 168, 170, 214, 252n6, 252n12; impact of, 212; linear, 130; paraphernalia of, 217

technology, 40, 44, 49, 110, 119, 136, 153, 169, 170, 206, 214; clean, 217; communication, 57; construction industry and, 152; digital, 3, 10, 17, 80, 93, 112, 113, 128, 164, 211; fetishized view of, 130; green, 218; high, 152; information, 65, 80; low-cost, 231; modeling, 111; mystical reason and, 115; structural coherence in, 48; 3-D, 114; using, 39, 98

Technology Center of Sarah Networks (CTRS), 256n62

Terminator 2 (Cameron), 103

Terzidis, Kostas, 114, 150

Thames Bank, 202

Thames River, 39, 201

Therme Vals, 64

Third World, 61, 125, 216, 222

Thom, René, 116

3i investment fund, 41

Tiffany Company, advertising for, 14 (fig.)

Timberlake, James, 167

Tod's, 33

Tomorrow Never Dies, 13

tourism, 2, 27, 57, 59, 77, 199; capital and, 68; cultural, 20, 60, 61; increase in, 62, 63; rent in, 64

tourism industry, 65, 68, 69, 76, 122; defeat imposed by, 60–61

Tower of Winds, 54; photo of, 56

Toyo Ito and Associates, 56

transformation, 37; cognitive, 113; digital, 169; urban, 69–70

transparency, 42, 53, 95, 117

treasure-form, 198, 199, 200, 208, 261n171

Turner, John F. C., 222, 223

2001: A Space Odyssey (Kubrick), 164

underdevelopment, 130, 131, 132, 138

unemployment, 19, 230, 231, 233

"Uneven Growth: Tactical Urbanisms for Expanding Megacities" (exhibition), 224

União dos Movimentos de Moradia (Union of Housing Movements), 232

unions, 99, 137, 190, 253n28; construction, 182, 260n147; entrepreneurship and, 231; migrant labor and, 185, 186, 190

United Arab Emirates, 26, 190, 210; construction sites in, 27; contemporary architecture in, 189; novelties for, 259n147

United Nations, awards from, 225

UnitéLip, 124

UN Studio, 36, 52

urban fabric, 129, 151, 231

urbanism, 19, 24, 213, 224, 231

urbanization, 213, 216, 224, 230, 233

urban problems, 110, 129, 204, 227

Urban Reform, 222

urban renewal, 20, 47

Uruguayan Cooperative Center (CCU), 231

Uruguayan Federation of Housing for Mutual Assistance (FUCAVAN), 222

Uruguayan National Housing Law, 222

Vainer, Carlos, 19
valorization, 212, 216–17; capital, 208; financial, 195; patrimonial, 24; rentier, 195
value, 25, 69, 195; auratic, 199; cultural, 110; dominant, 233; extrinsic, 121; immaterial, 33, 205; labor, 128; law of, 197; monumental, 204; object and, 31; price and, 198; production of, 101, 128; real-estate, 229; rent and, 19; symbolic, 204
Van Eyck, Aldo, 222
Van Lengen, Johan, 263n24
Vargas, Nilton, 253n21, 253n27
variability regime, 133, 134, 135, 136
VectorWorks, 107
Venice Biennale of Architecture, 5, 47, 147, 219, 225–26, 230, 233
Versace, 34
vertical groups, 38, 213
Viagem na irrealidade cotidiana (Eco), 247n58
Viñoly, Rafael, 62, 191
violations, migrations and, 178, 180–86, 189–91, 193
violence, 84, 85; deindustrial, 23; symbolic, 48; urban, 60
Virilio, Paul, 15
visualization, 13, 113, 120, 216, 236n16
Volkswagen, 13

wall, concrete fabricated, 51 (photograph)
Wall Street, 21, 26, 66
Walt Disney Concert Hall, 80, 100, 103, 203; design of, 81; sketch of, 82

Walt Disney Corporation, 80, 81
Wang, Wilfried: photograph by, 157
Wang Shu, 231
Water Cube, 44
Weber, Max, 27, 47
Weintraub, Alan, 10
welfare, 4, 17, 79, 123, 125, 209
welfare state, 25, 228
Wigley, Mark, 249n87
Wilford, Michael, 20
Wilson, Frank R., 99
Windows, 12, 100
Wisnik, Guilherme, 226
workers, 175; alienation of, 131; collective of, 152; fragmentation/ dispersion of, 110; heteronomy of, 131; submission of, 181
Workers Party (PT), 256n62
workers' rights, 190, 204
worker trafficking companies, 189
working class, 123, 125, 221
working conditions, 128, 150, 168, 178, 180, 185
World Bank, 194, 213, 223, 229
World Cup, 44
World Expo, 213
Wright, Frank Lloyd, 26, 36

Young, Nigel, 95

Zapatero, Carlos, 196
zero degree, 3, 55
Zukin, Sharon, 81
Zulaika, Joseba, 20, 21, 66
Zumthor, Peter, 64, 75, 205, 206, 211, 231
Zurich Institute of Technology (ETH Zurich), 49; photo of, 149